Creating Life on Stage

Alvina Krause, the renowned acting teacher from Northwestern University, whose vision of a living theater inspired the author to create the Circle Repertory Company. Photograph by Glen Edwards, Eagles Mere Playhouse, 1961.

Creating Life on Stage

A Director's Approach to Working with Actors

MARSHALL W. MASON

HEINEMANN
Portsmouth, NH

Heinemann
A division of Reed Elsevier Inc.
361 Hanover Street
Portsmouth, NH 03801–3912
www.heinemanndrama.com

Offices and agents throughout the world

Library of Congress Cataloging-in-Publication Data
Mason, Marshall W.
  Creating life on stage : a director's approach to working with actors / Marshall W. Mason.
    p. cm.
  Includes bibliographical references and index.
  ISBN-13: 978-0-325-00919-3
  ISBN-10: 0-325-00919-8
  1. Theater—Production and direction. I. Title.

PN2053.M373 2007
792.02'33—dc22   2006020008

Editor: Lisa A. Barnett
Production coordinator: Elizabeth Valway
Production service: Matrix Productions Inc.
Typesetter: SPi Publisher Services
Cover design: Jenny Jensen Greenleaf
Manufacturing: Steve Bernier

Printed in the United States of America on acid-free paper
11 10 09 08 07 VP 1 2 3 4 5

For Danny,
Mi compañero de por vida

Contents

Foreword

WILLIAM HURT

An actor can investigate life's unfolding surprise as responsibly as a physicist or chemist or biologist and without diminishing the return, without quelling inspiration, passion, or enthusiasm. Indeed, quite the opposite: in becoming more grounded and methodical, the character becomes exponentially more vivid while remaining appropriate.

But it isn't easy to learn the craft of acting in our culture. We do not have a collective commitment to keep alive a body of knowledge in the theatrical arts; our culture does not admit the importance of the history of theater. The effort that goes into the making of what is generally distributed as entertainment is not meant to satisfy "what we really want" or certainly not, "what we need." Our tastes as a public are not refined, because our education, upon which a discerning appreciation would be based, is not, relatively speaking, thorough.

This is not said in arrogance. Neither is it arch, pompous, careless, or cruel to say it. It's a statement of the truth, and it is made by a caring (and responsibly tax-paying) citizen of our country, a country that has the greatest industrial and temporal power on earth and therefore the greatest resources for educating and supporting its people. Nor does making a critical remark like this mean I am not amazed and humbly inspired by many of the people I meet and observe, in every walk of life, every day. But I also know that the education I was lucky enough to have bestowed on me is not conferred on many and that this is unjust.

Theatrical art is by its essence participative, actively so, and as such is a realization in and of itself. The artist meditates on his or her own personal existence as an example of the human state. As Stanislavski said, "Breathing the ethic into the play is the actor's job." (Although who does not do this? Who does not pretend and imagine being somewhere else, someone else, in order to second-guess a worrisome scenario or examine an important question?)

It's my conviction that theater is a serious venue for a serious intellect. And although a serious intellect does not necessarily need a staid, conservative education, it must have a sincere openness, eager to be refreshed and rejuvenated, rekindled and renewed. It must wish for knowledge of itself, of others, of the past and present, and must wish to discern the future, too. The mandate of life is to live, and we must therefore cast our eye forward with wit. Aware of the limits of mortality, we are fated to try to subvert it, and to do that, we must know ourselves for what we are and imagine ourselves as what we might be.

I have been an actor for forty years. It took me almost thirteen years to feel for the first time that I had acted well, had based my performance on a specific, conscious, crafted process. For purposes of dependability and integrity, in the theater in all its forms, it all comes down to that word *craft*. It is a term wantonly bandied about and woefully abused (as are the terms *collaboration* and *ensemble*). But if you can craft a flute, you can craft a flautist.

Many wonderful teachers taught me many necessary things: the elocution and movement classes, the scene work, all become part of the craft. But I have met only two people who, I felt, grasped the concept of a natural, developmental process through which an actor can explore the questions and structure of a play, a process that is complete and at the same time simple and utterly reliable. Both these theatrical artists studied with a drama professor I personally never met. Both identified her as an essential figure in their artistic nurturing. Her name was Alvina Krause, and the two students of hers who in turn left her indelible mark on me are Gerald Freedman, a teacher, and Marshall W. Mason, the greatest director of actors I have known in my life. Gerry directed me in one production at The Julliard School; Marshall directed me in many productions at the Circle Repertory Company.

Gerry was the first person to introduce me to "playing an action" in a real way, and it was a completely revelatory experience. It's a simple idea but not easy to accomplish. After years of work, of feeling very, very alone (a seemingly endless period in which I doubted that I or any actors were effectively being taught the concepts that would allow us to approach our work with confidence instead of anxiety and insecurity), it was Marshall who corroborated my lonely convictions about how these concepts actually worked.

When I finally got to Circle Rep and experienced the atmosphere of genuine exploration and support there, I felt I had found my artistic home. Marshall really understood the principles and their application to acting and made the concepts tangible. And as the members of the company followed the steps of this system, ensembles come into being. It was a great relief. Marshall was able to articulate these goals and, beyond that, fulfill them, reliably and regularly. Here was someone who could provide a rehearsal structure in which the actors could suck the play inside themselves and render it back with all its potential intact (or in some cases with all its flaws on display). The rehearsal process and the resulting performances were geared to discovering—through the actors—the potential and truth of the play, no matter the style or period.

Marshall is first and foremost an actor's director. I happen to agree with him that this is a good thing to be, no matter how devalued an actor's worth may have come to be in our time. Marshall understands the process of discovery of both character and circumstance, and he follows the process carefully and lucidly so that the actors—together—can find the deep questions of the play within themselves and the play can find itself in their creativity. With Marshall's guidance, I finally understood what the Method was, and there was no madness in it at all. It was beautiful and simple and reliable if an actor wanted to put in the work. As Marshall quotes, "Ninety percent of talent is sweat."

His system is quite simple, as many sophisticated systems end up appearing: give the actors permission to use their curiosity, skill, mind, and heart to seek out the dramatic experience of the play and express it in its most truthful rendering. Simple, yes, but not at all simplistic or facile, most definitely not a shortcut.

This book encapsulates the best modern understanding of solid acting craft. It is utterly invaluable.

Acknowledgments

Writing a book on any subject calls into question the essence of one's self. A person is the sum of his experiences: the choices he's made as a consequence of his beliefs. Beliefs are based on values, which he's learned from his influences. Let me begin, then, with a catalogue of my influences.

The source of my first inspiration was the director Elia Kazan. Seeing his film *Pinky* when I was nine years old made me aware of the existence of directors. In his subsequent films (particularly *East of Eden* and *A Streetcar Named Desire*), Kazan proved a hero worthy of emulation. The most remarkable aspect of Kazan's work was the extraordinary performances he evoked from James Dean and Marlon Brando, among others. From the beginning, I understood that the key to a director's success was an ability to elicit honest performances.

Later at Northwestern University, a magnetic teacher of acting, the great Alvina Krause challenged her students to work tirelessly and without compromise. It's to Miss Krause that I owe my belief in the power of the theater, the standards of truth to which my work aspires, and the practical approach I employ in working with actors. "Talent," Miss Krause would declare, "is 90 percent sweat."

In terms of excellence, the actor John Gielgud was a paradigm of inspiration, giving me a glimpse of the heights theatrical artistry can attain. One of the thrills of my life was meeting him backstage at the 1961 Broadway production of *The School for Scandal*, where he graciously, generously, and patiently allowed me to pick his brains. I hungered to cannibalize his talent.

In New York, my work with Harold Clurman and Lee Strasberg in the Director's Unit of the Actors Studio helped me to transfer the ideals of my education into the sometimes bizarre realities of the professional theater. These two visionary men demanded the highest standards and a disciplined approach to work.

I've had the good fortune for much of my professional life to work with Lanford Wilson, a great playwright who's also a very wise person. Lanford expanded my horizons by insisting on the importance to our times of contemporary plays, urging me to apply my exalted standards of production (developed at Northwestern for bringing to life the plays of Chekhov, Ibsen, Euripides, and Shakespeare) to the work of living playwrights.

My all-too-brief collaboration with Tennessee Williams taught me that ideals must not be fragile. It takes a tough, muscular sensitivity to endure the slings and arrows of a hostile world, and to survive with grace and dignity.

My partnership with Rob Thirkield, who cofounded the Circle Repertory Company, gave me the courage to aim high, and the financial means to accomplish my lofty goals in a four-dimensional form.

Almost everybody in the contemporary theater has been influenced by the writings of Constantine Stanislavski. He was the first to suggest a systematic approach to the artistic process, developing techniques to induce an actor's creativity, even when a state of inspiration is absent. It was my intention to pay homage to his monumental breakthrough by calling my book, which proposes a systematic approach for directing actors, *A Director Prepares*. Obviously, Anne Bogart beat me to the finish line with her book pre-empting that title. Still, because Stanislavski's system set the goal of actors living their roles onstage, my present title *Creating Life on Stage* is no less an homage to him.

Three great books inspired me as a young director. Robert Edmond Jones' *The Dramatic Imagination* speculated about the origins of the theater in Stone Age storytelling and the challenges theater would face in the future. Peter Brook's *The Empty Space* revealed the basic elements needed to produce theater: a stage, an actor, and imagination. Most of all, Harold Clurman's seminal book *On Directing* provided a summary of the phases a production goes through to achieve artistic results.

The person who bears the responsibility for my discovery that I might be a director is Dr. James Gousseff, Professor Emeritus of Eastern Michigan University. At the end of my sophomore year at Northwestern, I had realized my artistry as an actor would never equal that of a Gielgud, so I had decided to transfer from theater to prelaw. Jim, who was a graduate assistant to Miss Krause, deterred me by stressing how much the theater needed people who believed in it as I did. He suggested that if I couldn't become a great actor, perhaps I should try my hand at directing. Although I had never considered it as a vocation, I admitted there was one play I longed to direct, because there were no roles in the script I was suited to perform. Jim convinced me to stay on for Northwestern's summer repertory season, and try directing in the fall.

That summer I played in *Oedipus Rex, A Midsummer Night's Dream, St. Joan,* and the choice role of Faulkland in *The Rivals*. It was a delight each morning to discover from the repertory schedule who I was to be that night. The experience of playing rotating rep convinced me of its value as a model for producing artistic theater.

Then, as Jim had suggested, in the fall of 1959, I directed my first production: *Cat on a Hot Tin Roof*. Its success swayed me to believe that I might continue to serve the theater in another capacity, with a new challenge for attaining artistic excellence.

Miss Krause had famously declared, "I am training you for a theater that does not exist." She was referring to the kind of artistic theater that was exemplified by the Moscow Art Theater and, in our country, by The Group Theater. Ten years later, with the help of my colleagues, I founded Circle Repertory Company in New York with those models in mind, and for years, we included a season of rotating rep as part of our subscription program. I owe a debt of deep gratitude to all the members of Circle Rep for helping me bring that vision of an artistic theater into existence. I'm also grateful to the incomparable expert William Esper, Professor Emeritus of Rutgers University, for introducing me to the Meisner techniques.

After I had been directing in the professional theater for thirty-six years, Dr. Lin Wright persuaded me to become a teacher of acting and directing at Arizona State University. She assured me my new duties would not prevent me from continuing to direct professionally in theaters throughout the country, so the academic opportunity seemed a good one. At A.S.U., my acting students benefited from the guidance of *An Actor Prepares*, but I soon discovered there was no equivalent guide for student directors.

During my own college days at Northwestern, people always were urging Miss Krause to document her approach to acting, but she demurred, saying the dynamics of teaching were nearly impossible to capture in writing. Once I became a teacher myself, I began to feel I had an obligation at least to try. My classroom experience of exploring the techniques I had developed to collaborate with actors contributed substantially to this present effort.

Of course, my mentor Harold Clurman wrote many books and weekly critiques in *The Nation*. His example of expressing his ideals through his writing encouraged me to accept a job as a drama critic at *New Times*, a weekly newspaper in Phoenix, Arizona. There I encountered Anne de Corey, an editor whose vigilance forced me to express ideas simply, making it possible to write, rewrite, and finally, finish this book.

If you have quarrels with what follows, the blame is mine, not theirs. If anything expands your understanding of the theater, it's to these masters I owe acknowledgment. Their gift of enlightenment obligates me to pass on their wisdom, refracted through my own experience. I hope my employment of their values will guide your own exploration of the mysterious process of the director's art.

Special thanks must be given to Jeffrey Sweet, who steered me to my editor Lisa Barnett, and to William Hurt for his eloquent preface. Their enthusiasm and encouragement guided the final realization of a longtime project, turning the effort of many years into a manual for sustaining the future of a living theater.

Lisa Barnett died only a few months before our publication date. I hope that she would be proud of this, one of her final editorial achievements. I honor her invaluable contribution, and I miss her wisdom and grace.

Introduction

What distinguishes theater from other art forms is its life.

When we go to a movie theater to see *Star Wars*, we're captivated by George Lucas' imaginative saga. But when Anakin decapitates Count Dooku, taking one step closer in his transformation into Darth Vader, we never worry that the actor Christopher Lee is at that moment actually losing his life, along with his head. It's something we can see again and again, and it will always happen the same way. We know perfectly well that we're not seeing human beings, or even genuine androids, but only images of them captured in a can of film that's now being projected onto a screen, for us to watch passively while passing the popcorn.

But when we go to a theater to see a play, we are in the presence of living human beings, who share with us a singular condition: both actors and audience are alive in the present moment. The audience is challenged to engage with the actors on a journey of shared belief. The drama, comedy, or saga we see onstage is fictional, to be sure, but when live theater is at its best, it's impossible to detect what is fictional from what is actual.

On a subconscious level, we never lose awareness that the characters we see before us are breathing as we breathe. We see unconscious behavior in the performers that keeps us constantly in tune with our shared humanity. Their eyes blink, they perspire, they fidget or tremble, they swallow, they think, they feel. These unconscious behaviors signal to us that they are truly alive, and not merely images. We recognize them as if they were intimate acquaintances, seen across a threshold of recognition. They are just as subject to the unexpected as we are.

When an actor is successful at convincing us of the truth of his fictional circumstances, we are enraptured by the reality of it. He doesn't seem to be acting, but actually *living* the events of the story. So when he feels sadness or anguish or love, we feel along with him; and when he dies, we find tears in our eyes at the loss of the person we've come to know. While consciously we understand the actor hasn't actually died, our rational perceptions are overwhelmed by our belief in the fictional truth.

It's like the difference between hearing *A New York Minute* on the radio and seeing Don Henley live in concert; we are *there* at the instant he is singing and playing. It's thrilling.

Think of the moments you've experienced in the theater, when your belief superseded your conscious awareness of the artifice.

I remember such a moment when The Old Vic visited New York in 1962 with Franco Zeffirelli's staging of *Romeo and Juliet*, starring a young Judi Dench and John Stride. Late in the play, Romeo is desperate to reunite with his bride, when the friar suggests that he should accept the impossibility of their union, and find another girl to love. Stunned by the insensitivity of Friar Lawrence, Romeo cried out, "Oh, you're old!" I was shocked. You can't make up words in Shakespeare! But this teenager's lament sprang spontaneously from the depths of his soul, and I, little more than a teenager myself, felt the full force of his pain. After the performance, I looked up the scene in Shakespeare's play, to see exactly where the actor had uttered his brilliant improvisation. There in the text were Shakespeare's words: "O, you are old!"

I've always enjoyed the comedy and performances of Billy Crystal, as host of the Academy Awards on television or in the film *The Princess Bride*, but nothing prepared me for the power of his presence in *700 Sundays*, his recent Broadway show. Everyone in the audience emerged from that performance as his friend. We knew him to the core of his being. At the curtain call, he didn't want to let us go, because we were all having such a good time together.

Of course, actors don't always achieve a sense of truth that makes them appear to be living in the circumstances of the play. Even though we still can appreciate an actor's flashy technique, the visual spectacle of the designers, and the intellectual joys of a playwright's art, we're left with a hollow feeling. We know the actors have only pretended, which is a kind of lie. That's when the theater seems old-fashioned, irrelevant, or just plain tedious.

When a company of actors brings the script to spontaneous life, we experience the play directly. Our contact with the living characters is palpable. Sometimes, only one performer in a production achieves this remarkable authenticity, while other characters are conventionally predictable. But when a whole company conspires together to create life onstage, the living play strikes an audience deeply and unforgettably.

I had such an experience with John Crowley's recent Broadway production of Martin McDonagh's *Pillowman*: the cast uniformly blended into the horrific, yet funny story, so it became impossible to guess what might happen next. It was as if *they* didn't know either.

On such an occasion, when we experience the play directly from the living actors, there is an invisible creativity that lies beyond our immediate experience. That unseen hand is the contribution of the director, who has seamlessly inspired his actors and designers to subsume their individual contributions to the collective creation of the world of the play. The script springs to life onstage.

This book is an attempt to suggest how a director can stimulate an ensemble to achieve such a goal.

Since Constantine Stanislavski's revolutionary documentation of a creative approach to acting, actors have been trained to explore how his method can be used to attain the goal of "living the role." They have done this with the help of teachers in acting studios and workshops; but afterwards when they've attempted to apply what they've learned to professional work, they've been condemned to labor by themselves in trying to achieve their sense of truth.

With the exception of a handful of directors, like Harold Clurman and Elia Kazan, who trained as actors in Stanislavski's system, few directors have shown any inclination to integrate the actor's work into a production process. Even Lee Strasberg admitted that it was very difficult to apply the techniques he'd taught members of the Actors Studio to the pragmatic, result-oriented demands of professional production.

The director has been seen as a no-nonsense disciplinarian who could corral unbridled actors into safe and practical performance. So, directors concentrate on rounding up talented actors, preferably stars, and then herding them into mechanical blocking that will keep the traffic flowing smoothly. Their main concerns are the external aspects of production: stage pictures, pace, and volume. Their work with actors remains determinedly exterior, demanding only the *results* that they, the producers, and the playwrights would like to see in the actor's performance.

In most cases, the actor's process is so ignored that she's not even required to learn her lines until the director has worked out every other detail of production. Instead, a director's communication with his actors is usually limited to intellectual concepts, generalized attitudes, abstract imagery, and physical results, such as line readings, demonstrated gestures, and a quick tempo. Exploration is considered a waste of valuable time.

It's my hope that the techniques I suggest here can offer guidance in how a director can make use of the acting techniques devised by Stanislavski and Sanford Meisner, and incorporate the exploration they offer into his own method of work.

When producer/director Mark Ramont read the manuscript, he suggested I should mention whether the techniques I describe work equally well for all types of theater, that is, whether this approach would work with a musical or a Shakespearean classic, as well as realism.

My answer is that no matter what the style, an audience expects the actors to deliver believable performances and to behave truthfully within the world of the play. What is offered here is one director's approach to working with actors to achieve that sense of truth.

While the process I describe works especially well for realism, the techniques should work equally well for other kinds of plays. I've used it in directing 185 productions, twelve of them on Broadway, many more off-Broadway, and in regional theaters throughout the country. Four of them were musicals; three were Shakespearean plays; others were in various styles, ranging from *The Trojan Women* to Pirandello's *Enrico IV*, and from Molière's *A Doctor in Spite of Himself* to Noël Coward's *Private Lives.*

Of course when directing a musical, a director must allot time in the schedule for the choreographer and the music director to make their contributions to the dancing and singing, but the approach described here is the best way I know to elicit good acting work from performers. Seasoned musical stars like Donna McKechnie or classically trained actors like Irene Worth and Jonathan Pryce have delighted in the freedom of exploration this approach affords.

It should be apparent that when a director is staging an enormous cast, such as in *Cyrano de Bergerac,* not every move can arise from the instincts of each actor. In this case, a director must envision a stage picture that conveys the action of the play, and yet be true to the impulses of the living actors. Even a large cast, once arranged in "pictorial groups," can be trusted to believe in the circumstances of the play, and therefore to produce impulses that can fill out the life of a crowded scene. And of course, all such spectacles have intervals in which there are fewer characters onstage, wherein these exploratory techniques should work splendidly.

My goal in sharing my approach with other directors (as well as actors, designers, producers, and all lovers of the living theater) is to suggest how a director can support and inspire the work of actors to achieve genuine, seemingly spontaneous life onstage. Living performances will keep the art of the theater vibrant and alive, even as our contemporary world becomes increasingly impersonalized by technology. Truthful behavior onstage can transport us to a world where we can laugh, cry, and celebrate life together, when the action of the play becomes the *experience* of the audience.

Chapter One

The Challenge

It's hard to describe the art of directing for the stage. A director has many roles to play, and everyone needs him to be something different. A playwright prays for a partner who understands the play and, if possible, appreciates both how and why it was written.

Actors dream of a parental figure that will provide honest, compassionate guidance that still allows them the freedom to discover for themselves.

Designers hope for a trailblazer who will foresee potential problems on the sometimes-rocky terrain of production, but can be both flexible and decisive about which adventurous path to follow.

A producer yearns for a captain who will chart a safe course through a choppy sea of conflicting pressures, while keeping a steady eye on the budget.

Everyone expects a director to be a sorcerer who can turn leaden obstacles to golden opportunities, and who will conjure a success by the opening night.

The Craft of Directing

Such a complicated craft defies simple definition, but we can consider some of the miracles a director is expected to perform.

First, with the help of actors and designers, a director must transform the words of an author's script into a living, three-dimensional experience to be shared with an audience. This means he must stimulate the creativity of everyone he works with, implement and coordinate their contributions, and blend all this creativity into a single organic vision.

A director is a sculptor of motion, who choreographs human behavior into a spatial narrative that conveys a story. He helps actors discover behavior based on impulses that arise from a belief in the given circumstances of the play. He edits and designs that behavior so an audience can understand the characters and action, both visually and viscerally.

His vision of the play is the source of the imagery an audience will see, and his ear orchestrates the tempo and rhythm of what an audience will hear. Essentially, a director guides all the choices for everything an audience will experience, except for the words themselves.

In fact, a director has an important role to play even with the author's dialogue. He needs to develop dramaturgical skills, so he can help a writer eliminate whatever is unnecessary, clarify anything that's obscure, and help to focus the structure so it embodies the action. He must employ the perspective of a sympathetic editor, and earn the author's trust by helping to find the most effective ways to communicate the writer's ideas. Most often, this leads to suggestions for cuts that might clarify, simplify, and strengthen the text. Sometimes, if he spots an opportunity that's been overlooked, a director may even identify a need to amplify.

Directorial Functions

To understand the variety of functions a director serves, let's break them down. First, a director should choose a performance space or stage whose size and shape will serve the needs of the play.

Then, he must envision a concept, choosing a style and period that will guide the set designer in creating an imaginative and practical environment for the action of the play. He must approve the furnishings, props, and ground plans for the settings.

He should cast the best actors he can find, who are appropriate for each role and who together possess the chemistry to bring the interrelationships of the characters to life.

He must make illuminating choices about the clothes the characters should wear, as well as their jewelry and hairstyles.

He should suggest the intensity, color, and mood of the lighting in order to convey the time, place, and context of the action.

Based on the creativity of the actors, he must negotiate when, how, and where the actors move. Then, he needs to design the relationships of each movement to another, constructing both fluidity and meaning.

Finally, he must orchestrate the pace, tempo, and rhythm in which each event occurs.

A director's responsibilities encompass all the territory between a conceptual vision and the most telling final details.

As for final details, I love a moment in Francois Truffaut's film *Day for Night*, a lighthearted spoof on the tribulations of being a director (and sort of a cinematic bookend for Federico Fellini's *8-1/2,* which depicts the personal agonies of being a director). Early in *Day for Night,* a prop man shows the director a case full of pistols. Truffaut looks them over and selects one to be used in the climactic scene of the film, which he will be shooting several weeks later. On the appointed day, the prop man returns with the gun and asks, "Is this the pistol you wanted?" Truffaut answers with resigned irony, "If that's the one I chose, then it's the one I want."

In this book, I'll suggest approaches that might help someone accomplish the demands of this complex art. I'll offer advice about choosing a play, casting the roles, inspiring the designers, conjuring performances from the actors, building the confidence of the producers, guiding the playwright, managing the stage managers, finding replacements, even enduring the opinions of the press.

But in the midst of all this advice is the core of a director's craft, so the focus will be on this central task: How can a director help actors do their best work? Nothing is more crucial to a director's success than helping actors become the living embodiment of a playwright's vision.

Above all, the playwright, the producers, and the audience expect us to guide the actors into performances that bring the play to life. Actors long for a working relationship with a director who at least won't interfere and at best might inspire. A director's most important function is to lure believable performances from the cast.

The student actors who participated in my directing classes at Arizona State University (1994–2004) listed the following qualities that actors want from a director:

- Patience
- Vision
- Creativity
- Flexibility
- Passion
- Sensitivity
- Honesty
- Leadership
- Efficiency
- Clarity
- Competence
- Organization
- Constructiveness
- Adventurousness

The Playwright/Director Hybrid

In the long evolution of the theater, the arrival of the director is a relatively recent development; but once he emerged in the modern era, few would argue that a director's services are not needed. Most of the few who do think so are playwrights.

Some writers are convinced that having no director is better than having a bad one, so they argue that the best way to avoid that danger is to do double duty as both playwright and director.

It can't be said that this never works, but by combining these two very different disciplines, there's sometimes a significant loss of depth. Dimension is a product of stereoscopic vision. An author's attempt to bypass the need for a separate director may fail to deepen what is on the page. For a spectator who hopes to get more from a performance than she'd get from reading the script, a two-dimensional experience would underscore the need for a second creative eye to deepen the perspective.

If a writer is also the director, will she be able to make impartial, critical judgments when a production is in trouble?

When problems arise, how can she decide whether they're the failures of the actors, or the shortcomings of the text?

A writer is a specialist in words, whereas an actor's expertise is in feeling, doing, being. A director's job is to translate from the writer's mode of expression to the actor's. The actor's process may seem mysterious (if not perverse) to a writer. An actor's creativity originates in her senses, emotions, and imagination, not in the rational processes of the intellect. As Meisner puts it: "An actor doesn't think; she *does*." This can be frustrating to writers, more excited by ideas.

A common mistake in directing is to bombard a cast with criticism, emphasizing intellectual interpretations that, rather than helping, actually impede an actor's creative process. While we can hope that the director is not the dumbest person working on a production (intelligence and intuition are helpful), it is not necessary (perhaps not even desirable) that he be the most intellectual. It's hard to collaborate with a know-it-all.

Another argument against the playwright/director hybrid is a matter of timing. When working on a first draft, most playwrights experience a surge of inspiration that fuels an outpouring of creativity. This "big bang" of creation is followed by the tiresome chore of revision, when second impulses rarely are as intuitive as the first. Writers who excel at rewriting are likely to be found in Hollywood revising someone else's screenplay.

Once a writer records that initial burst of inspiration on the page, her muse usually takes a well-deserved break; other aspects of her brain have to punch their timecards and get to work. Creativity is replaced by rational analysis, less tolerant of the trial and error of an actor's creative process. For a writer's muse, rehearsals are definitely overtime. As a result, many writers find rehearsals almost unbearable, producing a wistful whine: "If the actors would just say my lines as I wrote them, the play would work." Unfortunately, "Just do it" is about as effective for actors as "Just say no" is for addicts.

Yet it's at just this point (the rehearsal period) that another burst of creativity is needed. If you'll forgive a somewhat overheated metaphor, a director's charge should be to match the writer's original shot of inspiration with a second volley of creative fire, whose sparks will ignite the imaginations of the cast; and then to fan each spark until it burns with the brightest creativity of the actor's talent. Then, you have real fireworks!

A dynamic source of inspiration is needed during the rehearsal period to translate the words of a play into living actions for the actors to perform, allowing an audience to experience the play empathetically. Harold Clurman always emphasized that the *true play* is a seamless interaction of a script with the actors. A director's assignment is to bridge these very different disciplines and to blend their individual contributions into one harmonious whole: the living play.

To accomplish this, a director needs to provide the actors with an environment that's conducive to creative work. He needs to stimulate the imaginations of the cast and inspire them to create the world of the play.

He must challenge the actors to use the peaks and depths of their creative skills to explore the actions (the reasons, motives, and impulses for physical movement) and help them find the behavior that illuminates the characters' needs, dreams, flaws, and limitations—in short, their souls.

He must encourage and criticize, by being a mirror, a teacher, or a parent (sometimes even a psychiatrist), but always an accomplice.

Most of all, a director must shape and harmonize the creative contributions of the ensemble, establishing truth as a goal, respect for each other as a foundation, and the joy of creating as a shared passion.

Searching for Principles

If even the definition of a director's job seems daunting, the actual process of working with actors is almost impossible to describe. The interactive nature of collaboration is experienced as such a dynamic, spontaneous process that a description seems cumbersome and inadequate. It's a bit like trying to relate to a friend who couldn't join you at a magic show the thrill of seeing a lady transform into a tiger before your very eyes. How did she *do* that? The creativity of a living performance seems equally mysterious.

Before Stanislavski, an actor's miraculous art was attributed to an almost-magical phenomenon called inspiration. But Stanislavski discovered an approach to acting (a "system" as he called it, or a "method" as it has come to be known) that's based on axiomatic principles that attract inspiration. When he searched for the sources of creativity, he interviewed the greatest actors of his time to find out whether they shared any common characteristics. Based on this research, he concluded that inspiration is the product of three essential, interlocking disciplines:

- relaxation,
- concentration, and
- imagination.

It's hard to conceive of a good performance that doesn't employ these elements. Once he had established their fundamental importance to an actor's creativity, he devised approaches to sharpen and strengthen each discipline, such as the "Magic If" and "Public Solitude."

Unlike Stanislavski, I haven't surveyed the field of stage directors in order to catalogue the various approaches we use, nor to extract a system that codifies what is best in each of us. Such a quixotic goal would likely fail, because, perhaps by nature, directors are like feudal lords who rarely have commerce with their peers. They're reticent to share how they achieve their results. A wizard is loath to reveal his secrets.

Instead, I've examined my own work to see how I've approached the problems a director encounters and what solutions I've tried. As an occasional actor, I've had some opportunity to observe other directors' techniques and to experience firsthand how a director can help or hinder. Finally, I've seen many fine productions, always searching for hints of what might have led their directors to such wonderful results. I hope that the principles I've identified from these resources, and the systematic approach that arises from them might have a wider application.

In *An Actor Prepares*, Stanislavski invented a student named Kostya, studying the art of acting with the formidable director Tortsov. Kostya embodied some familiar traits of actors: a fear of inadequacy mixed with overweening vanity; an awe for authority mixed with rebellious individuality; a pure but ambitious idealism. His aspiration to mirror nature's most subtle creation is undermined by some of humanity's most petty obsessions. Think of him peering at his reflection, his face smeared with chocolate, rolling his eyes, flashing his teeth, trying to impersonate Othello.

Despite my hope to suggest a system for directors that's based on elemental imperatives, I haven't followed Stanislavski's example. A satiric portrait of a student director might display even more embarrassing traits: a naïve desire to emulate God Himself (or Herself) in the awesome act of creation; a benevolent dictator, whose wisdom informs and illuminates the lesser lights; and whose contributions, even if invisible, make manifest the difference between thundering success and abysmal failure.

So instead of inventing an insufferably egotistical character to stand in for me, I'm just going to present my egotistical opinions in my own insufferable way. Please bear with my somewhat didactic style. I've spent my life telling people what to do. I am Tortsov.

Finding Principles

The principles of directing seem elusive. As soon as I think of a possible principle, it's contradicted by an experience. If I recommend the virtues of a tolerant, nurturing rehearsal climate, such as cultivated by Harold Clurman, I'm confronted with the dynamic approach of Tyrone Guthrie. One of the giants in our field, he was reputed to be a domineering personality whose very presence intimidated those he worked with; yet he achieved extraordinary results. As soon as I rhapsodize on the glorious work of Elia Kazan, I'm confounded by a suspicion that his private, very personal work with actors differs substantially from the more public way I work, even though I try to emulate his artistry.

Still, I feel there must be basic *principles* we all share. It's our approaches that differ, not the underlying principles.

I admire the accomplishments of many of my contemporaries, including, but not limited to: Anne Bogart, Mark Brockaw, John Crowley, Erma Duricko, Scott Elliot, Richard Eyre, the late Gerald Gutierrez, Victoria Holloway, Doug Hughes, Moises Kaufman, Emily Mann, Joe Mantello, Michael Mayer, Sam Mendes, Mike Nichols, Jack O'Brien, Hal Prince, Gene Saks, Peter Stein, Dan Sullivan, John Tillinger, Matthew Warchus, David Warren, Robert Wilson, Steven Woolf, and Jerry Zaks.

All these directors possess at least one thing in common—a remarkable vision, which leads to our first principle:

- **Good direction grows from an original, inspired conception.**

Once a director has enjoyed the jolt of an inspired concept, it's essential that he's able to communicate that vision to others.

- **A basic element of directing is clear communication.**

These directors employ a variety of resources to achieve singular visions. We can identify the unique signature of a great director immediately. From this diversity emerges another principle:

- **A director's approach expresses a unique personality.**

Despite the variations, a production comes to life as if by magic. An audience experiences a play directly from communion with the actors (and unconsciously, the designers). This leads us to a contrary conclusion:

- **A director's work should be invisible, coming to life as if no other version were conceivable.**

A dynamic person like Sir Tyrone Guthrie could never succeed with the jocular approach of Harold Clurman. Yet, as different as their approaches might be, I'm sure they'd both endorse the importance of being prepared.

- **Good directing benefits from preparation.**

No matter what approach a director may use, he must find a way to achieve his concept within the limitations of time. When there's a plan in place that budgets the available time, everyone can commit to the goals of each rehearsal, feeling free to explore each day in depth. This principle is clear to film directors, who are forced by economic necessity to plan in detail, but it's often overlooked by stage directors.

- **Careful scheduling contributes to achieving artistic goals.**

Many would admit that one of the main frustrations of directing is trying to understand why actors sometimes have trouble doing what we've asked them to do. An obvious result may seem a simple matter to an observer, and an actor may intellectually understand what you want; but she may not know how to get to that result *honestly*. A director may need to help her discover an inner journey that will lead to the desired destination. Patience is essential.

Even when an actor tries a choice that doesn't work, it sometimes leads to a better choice. We shouldn't be afraid of being wrong. Always keep in mind that a director's success depends on the success of his cast and designers.

- **Directing is a collaborative enterprise, dependent on shared creativity.**

Mindful of the needs of actors, a director should establish a safe, creative environment in rehearsals, where experimentation is not ridiculed but valued.

- **The goal of rehearsals is to stimulate, not inhibit, creativity.**

It's difficult for actors to delve deeply if the focus of the exploration is too broad. The more specific your direction, the more rewarding the result will be.

- **Directions should always be as specific as possible.**

These principles should lie at the heart of all the work a director undertakes. They should guide every choice, every suggestion, and every decision. In summary, if you want to direct, you'll need to:

1. Generate an original, inspired conception.
2. Communicate your ideas clearly.
3. Use an approach that is suited to your personality.
4. Prepare thoroughly.
5. Schedule the available time to achieve your goals.
6. Collaborate to achieve group creativity.
7. Establish a stimulating rehearsal atmosphere.
8. Make your directions as specific as possible.

I'm two short of ten commandments, but I'm sure I've overlooked a couple. Maybe they'll occur to you.

With diligent application of these principles, a director's work will be rewarded, no matter what the process. But a process that *incorporates* these principles should make a director's artistic journey even more enriching.

Translating Principles into Rehearsals: An Overview

I've developed a process to achieve the goals I've described that's based on these principles. My approach is rooted in the needs of actors and designed to be harmonious with Stanislavski's approach to acting. Usually it's worked for me. I'll describe it as well as I can, with anecdotal references to times when my approach has succeeded and on occasion, failed.

In using this somewhat heretical approach, it's very important to develop patience, so the actors are free to explore without the pressure of achieving predetermined results.

Encourage them to take risks. Recognize and respect each actor's unique contribution. Be honest in your appraisals of the work, but temper that honesty with encouragement. Be clear in the directions you give. Be decisive when asked to make a choice or express a preference.

The main interaction between a director and a cast occurs during the rehearsal period. A rehearsal process should give actors a sense of security that will help to attract inspiration. The process begins by planning a schedule that makes the best use of the available time.

A rehearsal schedule amounts to a road map of the artistic challenges that confront a cast as they journey toward performance. Let's consider the allotment of time that's available for each challenge, assuming a four-week rehearsal period.

The road map begins with the need to communicate a concept that will inspire everyone's work on the production and establish the goals to be achieved. Then, a director needs to offer an approach that will guide the cast toward these goals. Clurman advises that the most important objective in early rehearsals is to cultivate communication and camaraderie, which are essential for collaboration.

I propose a rehearsal plan to achieve these goals that's based on dividing the script into beats of action that will focus our attention on one step at a time.

Once everyone is clear about the goals and the plan of attack, the actors need some time to do research. I set aside 15 to 20 percent of the rehearsal period (three or four days) for the actors to learn about the social, historical, and environmental circumstances of the play; to create the biographical histories of their characters and the forces that shaped their lives, and to explore their relationships to other characters in the play.

Most of the rehearsal time (perhaps 50 percent) will be spent in the discovery of the needs and objectives of the characters, and the physical life that results from them. During this part of the rehearsal process, we are exploring the motives and impulses that should lead to a design of physical movement, usually referred to as *blocking*. In a two-act play, we have about a week to arrive at a physical life for each act. In a three-act play, we need to divide the time into thirds, which limits us to only four or five days in which to stage each act. Four- and five-act plays probably would benefit from a longer rehearsal period. It's rare to hear a director complain that he has too much time.

Regardless of the length of the play, this approach devotes a substantial amount of time for the discovery of movement, instead of blocking the actors into a predetermined pattern. Mechanical blocking may only take a day or two, but unfortunately, it often remains lifeless.

The third division of our rehearsal time is devoted to what we can learn from run-throughs. The actors can now pursue their "super-objectives" (those inner forces that drive the action) to understand how those needs are expressed in tempo, pace, and timing. During this period, the director's role is limited to giving notes, attempting to encourage improvement through criticism. The cast should need only three or four days of playing through the play with minimal interruptions to discover what they need to learn.

Many directors spend as much as 90 percent of their rehearsals doing run-throughs and giving notes. They sacrifice depth and detail, because for both cast and director the focus of a run-through is spread too wide. This results in pages of intricate "corrections" that are difficult for an actor to implement organically.

Next, we arrive at the time when our work must be transplanted from the safety of the rehearsal room to the naked exposure of the stage: the oft-dreaded tech rehearsals. We have to integrate the technical elements that will help the audience to believe in the world we've created. Lights, sound, and costumes are added successively, a process that usually requires three or four days of work with the full staff of the theater.

After the agony of tech, dress rehearsals allow the actors to assimilate all the technical details that support and free their performances. Several dress rehearsals usually lead to preview performances, or a final rehearsal for an invited audience.

Previews teach us how interaction with an audience affects what we have created in the privacy of rehearsals. The responses of the audience tell us what adjustments yet need to be made. Depending on the playwright, there even may be rewrites. A director should see to it that changes at this stage are made as early as possible. The actors will need time to absorb the alterations, recover from the trauma of change, and enjoy the appreciation of the audience, whose approval heals all scars.

Once the critics' opening performance has passed, a director's obligations ease up. Only two remain: to monitor an occasional performance to see whether organic growth continues and to select replacements and understudies, who can continue to convey the life of the play when the original actors become ill or leave the cast.

The amount of time allotted for rehearsals will vary, but the steps I've described outline progressive stages that are endemic to any production. The stage is set for the formulation of an approach that focuses incrementally on the challenges actors will face in their quest to become part of a living play.

No book can hope to address all the elusive qualities in the complex, creative interaction between actors and a director. I offer only what experience has taught me, in the hope that as my methods emerge, they will make sense and be worth trying.

It's important to note, however, that there's not a single "rule" I've laid out in this book that I haven't broken from time to time myself. For example, on a number of occasions I've been unable to restrain myself from shouting at an actor. But whenever I've gone against the advice I've tendered, it's been counterproductive, a misstep. Later, I'll provide a few examples so you can learn from my mistakes.

A number of directors have adopted some of these proposals and adapted them to their own ways of working. I'm encouraged that this approach, arising from the principles of directing I've identified, has found resonance in the work of fellow weavers of our sorcerer's art. I hope that the incantations prescribed, if invoked with both diligence and patience, may bear results that an aspiring director might not be ashamed of.

Chapter Two

A Director's Vision

Everyone involved in a production wants a director to have a passionate vision that will inspire all of them to do their best work. Let's look at this "vision thing," as one of our recent presidents called it. How does one go about acquiring vision? Where does it come from? Can a director's vision be cultivated?

Almost by definition, artistic vision is a child of inspiration. When Stanislavski developed a systematic approach to acting, he made it clear that his method was not meant to *replace* inspiration, but rather to create conditions that could *attract* it. For many actors, his method was like a lightning rod. So, what are the lightning rods a director might use to attract a bolt of inspiration?

A director's vision is manifested in an imaginative production concept. A director's concept is distinct from the theme of the play: a concept is the *viewpoint* the production will employ to bring the author's theme to life.

An imaginative concept arises from the attraction a director feels for a project. This attraction is probably based on a combination of factors:

- the director's motivation for wanting to direct the play;
- the imagery suggested by the material;
- an intuitive, visceral sense of the spatial opportunities the play provides; and
- perceiving the opportunities of a specific style.

Let's examine these sources of inspiration in detail to see how they can contribute to a visionary concept.

Motivation

The very essence of directing involves making choices. None is more important than choosing the play. The main source of inspiration for everyone working on a production usually springs from the script itself. In arriving at a concept, a director first needs to understand (and be able to articulate) why she's been drawn to the play she's chosen.

A director can be motivated to direct a project for a variety of reasons, ranging from a deeply personal response to a play's theme, to a chance to direct a script that's already been chosen for production.

Although an opportunity to direct can be a powerful motivation, a director should still find a personal connection to the material. It's unlikely that a director will generate a dynamic production concept if she's indifferent to the script itself.

The theme of the play should resonate within. Choose a script you would like to have written yourself (if your special gift was to express yourself with words).

At the very least, you should feel that a play speaks honestly and presents a true image of reality, no matter what the style. If you believe capitalism has no flaws, you probably wouldn't be the best director for *Death of a Salesman*.

Sometimes, though, a script may not hook you on a personal level, but you might feel quite passionate about its cultural relevance to contemporary society. Relevance can be a powerful attraction.

My first production as a student at Northwestern University was Tennessee Williams' *Cat on a Hot Tin Roof*. I identified with all the characters, but I wasn't suited as an actor to perform any of them. Everything about the play attracted me. At the age of nineteen, I felt insecure and troubled about sexual identity, so Brick's denials of a homosexual relationship with his friend Skipper struck a chord within me. I had grown up in Texas, where football is virtually a religion and the football player is an archetypal hero. *Cat* dramatized a hero struggling with the same things I feared. I understood *Cat* in an intensely personal way.

At the same time, I attributed the placidity of the 1950s in America to an overwhelming acceptance of widespread "mendacity." I thought our sunny society was a façade, built on a foundation of conventional lies. So for me, *Cat* was a script that tugged strongly on both personal and cultural levels. I *had* to do this play or die.

By contrast, my second production was Euripides' *The Trojan Women*, a script for which I felt less personal involvement but whose powerful antiwar message fired me with enthusiasm. Social or political passion may sometimes surpass the merely personal in intensity. I ached to show the importance of this theme to my generation. I wanted my production to change people's beliefs. This intellectual passion provided the fuel for an imaginative concept.

Sometimes a script that poses a challenging problem can be very appealing. You might come up with an innovative solution to a production conundrum that has puzzled everyone else. This is the "Eureka!" effect that suggests one's singular suitability to direct a specific play. Slicing the Gordian knot can be tremendously empowering to the imagination. It's the motive behind many a young director's itch to direct *Woyzeck*.

David Steven's play *The Sum of Us* (about a gay Aussie-rules football player) poses just such a problem. I was originally slated to direct this script on Broadway, before the producer decided to direct it himself off-Broadway on the tiny stage of the Cherry Lane Theater. Here's the problem: the first four scenes of the play take place in the interior of a living/dining room of a suburban Australian home. The fifth scene takes place in a public park. How can the confines of the interior be transformed quickly into a vast, open space?

Using the designers I had already lined up for the project, the original production's solution to this problem was to put the living room on a platform that could move upstage about six feet to provide a narrow corridor downstage to suggest the final scene in the park. It was a pragmatic solution, but hardly inspired.

When I had the chance the following year to direct the play at the Pittsburgh Public Theater, I leapt at the opportunity. The original designers John Lee Beatty and Dennis Parichy were eager to tackle the project a second time, hoping to find a better solution to the problem. Employing them again, we came up with a solution that actually enhanced the play.

Faced with a three-quarter-arena stage, I decided to put an audience on the fourth side and do the play in the complete round. We would begin the production in the park, so that an audience entered to see nothing but a huge rectangle of grass in the middle of the arena. I choreographed a two-minute prologue to the play with a game of Australian-rules football, utilizing the actors, understudies, and stage crew, and thereby acquainting the audience with the sweat and roughness of an unfamiliar sport. When one of the players was injured, strobe lights began to flash. As he limped offstage, the team rolled on a large platform from the middle aisle of the fourth side; the rolling platform unfolded six panels that contained all the interior elements of the house; when fully unfolded, we had a full stage living room and dining room, complete with TV and a sofa. As the strobes and music ended, Jeff, our footballer protagonist, came in from the game exhausted, and threw himself down in an easy chair. His father entered setting the table for dinner, and the first domestic scene began. It was a tremendously theatrical transformation.

At the end of the fourth scene, as the father suffered a stroke, the strobe lights returned to electrifying music; the team folded the enormous unit back up, and rolled it off, clearing the way for Jeff to steer his dad onstage into the park in a wheelchair. This concept, inspired by a problem, endowed the play with a unity it did not otherwise possess.

As for being motivated by an opportunity, I remember the thrill of the first time a producer offered me a play that was not of my own choosing. Unexpectedly, I received a telegram asking me to direct Jerome Max's *The Exhaustion of Our Son's Love*, which was to be presented by Beth Israel in upper Manhattan. It even paid a little money (which can be another powerful motivation, especially if you're subsisting on peanut-butter sandwiches).

But no matter how tempting an opportunity may be, unless a play resonates within your imagination, consider carefully the consequences of making a commitment. Creatively, you might find yourself marooned with a stranger on a desert island, turning a rehearsal period into a bad version of reality-based television.

In my early twenties, the insights I found in Jerome Max's postadolescent comedy genuinely amused and inspired me, which made it possible for me to take advantage of the opportunity. If you can't at least rationalize an opportunity, you probably shouldn't take it.

A fortuitous casting opportunity can also motivate your choice. If you have a chance to work with an actor who inspires you, the opportunity should be seized. You probably shouldn't choose to direct *Hamlet* or *Cyrano de Bergerac* if you'll need to hold auditions for the title role. Those plays should be attempted only when you have found an actor who will justify choosing to produce the play in the first place. I had worked with William Hurt a couple of times before I realized that he was the first actor I had come across that could inspire me to direct *Hamlet*. Bill's Hamlet was truly **our** *Hamlet*.

Of course, a casting opportunity can backfire, leaving a director stranded with a concept. I scheduled a production of *King Lear* because Fritz Weaver had agreed to play Lear. An elegant actor in his seventies at the time, Fritz and I had worked together on several occasions, and he was perfect for my conception of the tragic king who loses everything. Also, contemporary attention to the tragedy of Alzheimer's disease gave me new insights into the nature of Lear's madness. Fritz was very tall, a veritable mountain of regal dignity, so I cast a rather tall group of actors to play with him. But before we began rehearsals, Fritz developed a medical problem that forced him to withdraw.

This left me with a production conceived for, and cast around, the impressive stature of Fritz—but no Lear. A casting scramble ensued that made it possible to get the play on, but my pint-sized replacement was surrounded by a cast that towered over him. In addition, he had played Lear four times previously, and he rejected any exploration of Alzheimer's. My concept wasn't realized, because Fritz had been my inspiration. It still turned out pretty well, but I'd love to stage it again with a tall Lear, who'd be willing to explore his madness in a fresh vein.

A career opportunity can also be a motivation. If a director loves opera, a chance to direct at the Met could prove irresistible, and probably would fuel a ton of inspiration. The problem is that such a career opportunity can also have the opposite effect: it can be so intimidating that it freezes the imagination. If you get a chance to direct a play on Broadway, it will take a lot more than the mere opportunity to assure success. Opportunity can stimulate exciting ideas, but sometimes it can be a poison pill to inspiration.

To summarize, a director's motivation for directing a play is the first cornerstone that can generate a dynamic production concept. Motivation arises from

- a director's personal passion,
- the relevance of the theme to contemporary society;
- a challenging production problem, or
- an artistic or professional opportunity.

Ideally, more than one of these factors will interact to give birth to an inspired concept, and if you can articulate your vision, it should inspire a cast to follow your every direction.

Imagery

The action of the play expresses the theme, but sometimes what really attracts a director to a script is not so much *what* the author is saying, but *how* he says it. A playwright can use a variety of tools to convey his ideas, including symbols and metaphors. These poetic devices affect us indirectly, in subtler, more emotional ways than the thematic dramatic action. An audience can be very moved by symbols and metaphors, and they can ignite the imagination.

A director's attraction to a writer's use of symbols, which *stand* for something else, and metaphors, which *suggest* a related image, will influence his design choices—the setting, costumes, lighting, and sound—to produce a concept that reflects the author's imagery.

The symbol of that eponymous creature at the heart of Ibsen's *The Wild Duck* strongly figured in my choice to make it the third play I directed. In that play, Hedwig is a vision-impaired child who cares for the unfortunate wounded bird, unaware of how it predicts her own destiny. The innocence of a wild creature, confined by injury to captivity, is a symbol that touched me in a mysterious, yet compelling way.

Another concept that was inspired by a metaphor was due to repeated references to ghosts in O'Neill's masterpiece, *Long Day's Journey into Night*. Referring to his morphine-addicted Mother, who is moving about upstairs as the night wears on, Edmond laments, "By now, she'll be nothing more than a ghost haunting the past."

The imagery of the past haunting the present led me to ask Ming Cho Lee to design a set that provided mysterious reflections (using a highly polished floor, scrim walls, and a distant mirror in the foyer) so that other ghostly selves continually shadowed the actors. To heighten these ghostly reflections, I asked Laura Crow to design clothes in subtle, monochromatic shades of summer whites.

The final glimpse of Mary, lost in her euphoric fog, dimly seen through the walls of scrim, as she drifts down an enormous staircase, trailing a long white wedding veil is one of the most indelible images I have ever conceived. This visual image, which was never imagined by the writer, happens *offstage* in O'Neill's script, but it grew from my tingling response to the metaphor of ghosts, and my instinct to let the audience *see* it.

Colors and textures can also become elements of a production concept. Peter Brook's legendary staging of *A Midsummer Night's Dream* is an example of a concept based on the use of color. In Brook's conception, his design team fashioned an all-white stage, all-white props, and all-white costumes to create a world of lovers on the eve of marriage. There have been many interpretations of *Dream*, but none are more memorable than Brook's wedding-white concept.

If one is struck by the blackness of a villain's soul or the crimson of bloodshed, these colors can become metaphors of evil or murder in a production of *Macbeth*.

The different textures of silk, or glass, or rough-hewn wood, or steel can inspire a concept that invites a new way to experience a play.

My production of Edward Albee's *Who's Afraid of Virginia Woolf?* for the National Theater of Japan incorporated a raked stage of slick black Plexiglas. During the "exorcism" sequence, when George intones the *Dies Irae* for the death of their imaginary child, the glass floor was illuminated from below to crystallize the metaphor that George and Martha's world was built on illusion.

Sometimes a script will suggest sounds or music that might inspire a director's vision. Here are a couple of examples.

Lanford Wilson and I spent one entire night in the early days of Circle Rep painting audience platforms black and coating them with polyurethane.

We listened to a radio as we painted, inadvertently inhaling the exotic fumes. In the middle of the night, Arlo Guthrie began to sing his paean to the railroads, *The City of New Orleans*:

> Good morning America, how are you?
> Don't you know me? I'm your native son:
> I'm the train they call The City of New Orleans,
> I'll be gone 500 miles when the day is done.
>
> "City of New Orleans" Written by
> Steve Goodman. Jurisdad Music
> o/b/o itself & Turnpike Tom Music.

Lanford said he'd like to write a play about the loss of the railroads as a metaphor for the changing values in America. I dizzily exclaimed, "Far out! Do it."

He wrote that play about six months later, enlarging the metaphor to include our American penchant for destroying our history by razing our architectural past. Set in the lobby of an old hotel scheduled for demolition, it was called *The HOT L BALTIMORE,* a title that suggested the significant image of a burned-out "E" in a derelict neon sign.

The Guthrie song that had inspired the playwright led me to a concept that used music to frame the whole production. The night desk clerk of the hotel has been listening to the radio, which means the actors playing the hotel staff had to be onstage before the audience began to come in. As *The City of New Orleans* plays, the day shift arrives, and at the changing of the guard, the radio is snapped off and the play begins.

The first act ended with the night shift turning the radio on to drown out a climatic comic melee. The music of the radio soared up into the house speakers, and continued throughout the intermission, going back into the radio and turned off again as the second act began. It was a fresh concept: using music rather than lights to act as a curtain, framing the action. The "sound track" of the original production became such an integral part of the audience's experience of the play that it was years before anyone tried to produce the play without utilizing a similar approach.

Jonathan Kent's 1994 Broadway production of *Medea* (starring Diana Rigg) stunned audiences at the climax of the play with a deafening sound of clashing steel as the huge metallic walls of the palace fell away. I suspect that this unforgettable sound was one of the sources for his unique concept.

Sometimes light and shadow can inspire a director's concept. When I visited Berlin as the guest of the West German government before the fall of the Berlin Wall, the directors had tired of using their state-of-the-art mechanics. Every small theater in the country was outfitted with revolving stages, hydraulic lifts, and complex stage equipment, far more sophisticated than most American theaters dreamed of. As a result, the German artists were enamored of simplicity. I saw many expressionistic productions that used a single source of light to project enormous shadows on a background. This extreme use of light and shadow expanded the scale of simple human activity to larger-than-life significance.

I stole this approach to light and shadow for my production of Arthur Whitney's *A Tribute to Lili Lamont* (starring Leueen MacGrath). Lili was a frail, pale remnant of an ex-movie star, in a white satin gown. She has been retrieved from obscurity and brought to a meeting of her fan club in a city basement. As she descended the stairs to greet her adoring fans, she was lighted from below. Her huge shadow flickered behind her, magnifying the aura of this tiny woman into the gigantic star her fan club remembered. This slightly expressionistic approach gave the whole play a flavor of the *film noire* look that would have been popular when Lili had been a star.

The blinding illumination of the final scene in Richard Eyre's production of David Hare's *Amy's View,* which featured a ritualistic baptism of Dame Judi Dench, was undoubtedly central to his theatrical coup. I couldn't wait to find a *coup de theatre* for my next production. If you're inspired by another director's concept, be sure to steal from the best.

Actually, my next production provided me an opportunity for just such a coup. The parallels between Shaw's *Saint Joan* and Lanford Wilson's *Book of Days* made me feel that it was urgent to include pyrotechnics in my concept for the latter play. We already had incorporated imagery of wind (there is a tornado) and water (there is a baptism), and the dialogue rhapsodizes about the land. Fire was necessary to complete the imagery of the four elements. Ruth, the young amateur playing Joan in a local production of Shaw's play, discovers that she has been the cause of someone's death. After trial and error, through three productions, at last I found just the right place to let Ruth's guilt momentarily, in her mind, burn her at the stake.

Lanford Wilson's *Burn This* also suggested incendiary images of light and shadow that led me (with my lighting designer Dennis Parichy) to use every opportunity to light a cigarette in the dark, as at the opening curtain; to light candles for a New Year's Eve celebration; or to use the deep shadows of the final scene to suggest the darkness that had settled upon Anna and Pale's prospects for a lasting relationship. The final image was of the two of them huddled together over an ashtray, burning Larry's note, which has brought them together for a future as uncertain as the flickering flame.

Even a quality as ephemeral as mood can suggest a concept. The enigmatic atmosphere of Harold Pinter's *Old Times* led my designers and me to create a starkly elegant salon, sparsely furnished with two divans. As the play starts, a cycloramic beige curtain covers the back wall. Deeley and Kate reminisce about Anna. Then the huge drape opens, exposing an enormous wall of glass, looking out over an abyss of darkness, and revealing the mysterious Anna center stage, standing in front of that glass wall. Without benefit of an entrance, she begins to interact with the couple as if she has emerged from their subconscious. Is this triangular contretemps actually happening? Or are they all stranded between the intersecting planes of reality and memory?

In *Old Times*, the mood dominates. The multilayered performances of my wonderful cast (Irene Worth, Raul Julia, and Beatrice Straight) sustained the tension of this fascinating enigma, interlaced with acerbic wit.

A concept can evolve from any aspect of imagery that gets ideas flying:

- dramatic symbols and metaphors;
- colors or textures;
- light and shadows;
- music or sounds; and
- even a predominate mood.

By feeding the imagination with the possibilities of imagery, you can nurture the emergence of an intuitive concept.

Even more than intellectual insights, a concept that's expressed in vivid imagery may communicate more clearly to your designers and cast than a well-reasoned thematic passion. Of course, it is essential to distinguish the images the audience must experience from those images that should be used only to inspire your collaborators. Stanislavski advised actors to "cut 90 percent," because not everything needs to be shown to an audience. You must edit yourself. Too much imagery can overwhelm a play. Let the playwright's work be the main attraction. Don't upstage the play with excessive imagery. Simplify. Less truly can be more.

But the power of imagery should not be underestimated. One summer at the Playhouse in Eagles Mere, Pennsylvania (where Miss Krause took her best students for a summer of producing challenging theater), I directed my first production of Schiller's *Mary Stuart* with Penny Fuller in the title role. A tall, lean actor named Wayne King played the sheriff, whose main function was to accompany Mary to her execution. I gave the sheriff a large wooden staff, and in suggesting the tempo of his cross, I reminded him that every time his staff struck the stage it would be like the axe falling on Mary's neck.

The following summer, I was working in the box office when a patron came to the window to buy tickets for the current production. Chatting amiably with me, he remarked that he hoped the show would be as good as the one he saw last year. "And which one was that?" I asked. He replied, "We saw *Mary Stuart*, and it was a wonderful production. I'll never forget the way the sheriff led her to her death, and with every step, his staff sounded like an axe falling on her neck." I was too astounded to take credit. It never occurred to me that the image I suggested to an actor would actually be experienced and remembered by the audience. Imagery is a powerful instrument.

Pay careful attention to what you want an audience to experience in the opening moment of the production. A striking image sets up the audience's entrance into the world of the play, and can become a key element of a concept. The same can be said for the last image. What do you want to leave them with?

A concept bridges the experience of a play from the first image to the last, often relating the two. I've mentioned how the primitive flicker of burning the note at the end of *Burn This* echoes the sophisticated flicker that lights the first cigarette. Metaphorically, we have traveled from the safety of a shallow relationship to the dangers of basic desires. The image lingers.

Space and Scale

A director should have a visceral response to the potential uses of space. Space should turn you on. If a director does not possess this innate sense, I'm not sure it can be taught. We can, however, look at some aspects of spatial relationships in the hope that their potential to excite a production concept will awaken something in your basic nature. Think about what a play needs in terms of its physical relationship to an audience. Several components should determine this relationship.

Intimacy

First is the question of intimacy. How close should the audience be for a play to achieve its optimal effect? Some plays *require* intimacy to be fully appreciated. The details of behavior in a good production of a play by Chekhov are greatly enhanced by proximity to the audience. Theatergoers need to be close to enjoy the nuances and subtleties.

On the other hand, an episodic saga like Ibsen's *Peer Gynt* surely would benefit from a less intimate proximity. The audience needs distance to appreciate the scope of the play. It's hard to imagine the virtues of an intimate *Aida*, whereas the pleasures of Noel Coward's *Design for Living* likely would be lost at a distance.

Of course, we must recognize that Peter Brook used unexpected intimacy to extraordinary effect with his 1983 production of *Carmen* at the 299-seat Mitzi Newhouse Theater at Lincoln Center. Some future director may show us the insights to be gained from an intimate *Aida* or a distant Coward.

Perspective

A parallel concern is the perspective from which a production should be seen. Would the play benefit from having the audience seated all on one side of the action so everyone shares the same perspective? If a play involves magic or illusions, a singular audience viewpoint is almost essential.

Some plays, though, may benefit from a production that allows an audience to experience it from different viewpoints. Then a proscenium stage will not be the best choice. The original production of *The HOT L BALTIMORE* was staged in a two-sided arena, and it gained immeasurably from the fact that members of the audience had to cross the "hotel lobby" to reach their seats. They became part of the action by virtue of their intimate proximity and multiple perspectives. It enabled them to believe they were sitting right in the hotel lobby, sharing the actors' sense of reality.

Your considerations of intimacy and perspective will lead to a fundamental choice: What kind of stage gives the play its best chance to communicate?

The proscenium stage frames the action of a play, giving everyone in the audience essentially the same perspective. Although the size of the theater determines the degree of intimacy, a proscenium arch divides the audience from the stage, providing a distance that promotes the magic of theatrical illusion.

Of course, you can have the best of both worlds with a proscenium stage in an intimate space. Many of the most successful productions at Circle Rep were staged in such an arrangement, with the audience on one side; but the theater seated only 160, so no patron experienced the play from more than eight rows from the stage. My favorite theater in America, although I never staged anything on it, is the beautifully intimate proscenium stage of the Krieger Theater at Washington's Arena Stage.

In contrast, the Ahmanson Theater in Los Angeles had two balconies and seated 2,067 when I last worked there. The stage could provide wonderful scenic opportunities, but it presented serious problems for a play that should be experienced intimately.

Nevertheless, the resources of a proscenium stage (with its fly-space and wings) offer a director almost infinite scenic possibilities. Most of the Broadway theaters are proscenium houses, which to some degree accounts for the trend toward spectacle in productions like *The Phantom of the Opera* or *The Lion King*.

Some directors may feel constricted by the confinements of the proscenium stage. One such was Frederick Henry Koch, Jr., who built the first arena stage at the University of Miami in 1946. Since then, the arena stage has evolved through several permutations. It started as a complete theater-in-the-round, where the audience entirely surrounded the action on the stage. This arrangement provides the maximum of both intimacy and multiple perspectives.

A two-sided arena allows similar opportunities for intimacy, while limiting the perspectives to only two viewpoints. In another variation, the Irish Rep in New York has an L-shaped theater, with the stage in the corner.

In 1979, the great contemporary German director Peter Stein staged the first act of *As You Like It* in a reversal of the arena arrangement, with the audience in the center of a space, surrounded by the action. It was a stunning concept, with the audience crowded claustrophobically into the center of a small room. When the Duke banished Rosalind, the whole audience was banished along with her. Everyone was ushered through a narrow opening in the wall, into a long tunnel, which opened out into an enormous space that represented the forest of Arden. The theater was a gigantic film studio, with a huge lake in the middle, surrounded by real trees. This was the best example I have seen of how contrasting spaces can inspire a dynamic concept.

I had tried, with less success, a similar configuration (with the audience in the center surrounded by the action) for a production of Molière's *A Doctor in Spite of Himself* in 1971. Influenced by the hallucinogenic world of the Beatles, we concocted a world that looked like a poster by Peter Max. It may have been a forgettable concept, but at least I was experimenting with more than just altered states.

A three-sided arena is an arrangement that offers some of the virtues of an arena (intimacy, multiple perspectives), with the bonus of scenic elements from the proscenium. Personally, I find this arrangement an awkward compromise; the center section of the audience, which faces the scenery, has an unfair advantage over those seated on the sides, looking across the stage at each other. Different perspectives should offer everyone equal opportunity. Unless you're really backstage, it's no fun peering from the wings.

Nevertheless, three-sided arenas became the most popular arrangement in the last quarter of the twentieth century, especially after it evolved into the more graceful thrust stage, and many regional theaters employ it. Pioneered by the designer Jo Mielziner among others, the thrust was regarded as the ideal combination of arena and proscenium. The audience curves around a stage that thrusts out from a proscenium area, providing intimate proximity, while reducing the injustice of a favored perspective. Only a cynic would say everyone has an equally poor seat. This theater design returned the theater space to the semicircular shape of its origins in ancient Greece, so it has a good pedigree for offering theater as it was initially meant to be experienced.

Of course, there are also amphitheaters, aquatic theaters, and all kinds of variations, from reconstructions of the Globe to the majestic ruins of Epidaurus. The ever-diminishing demarcation between theater and spectacle means we can expect the nature of theater spaces to continue to mutate. In Las Vegas, Cirque de Soleil now has a stage completely underwater.

The latest experimental trend has been toward the use of site-specific spaces. These are areas not initially intended for theatrical use, but which are adapted to enhance the experience of a particular play, for example, staging Lawrence and Lee's *Inherit the Wind* in an actual courtroom or *Billy Budd* aboard a ship. In the 1980s a rash of plays erupted with site-specific settings, including *Tony N' Tina's Wedding* in a church and *Tamara*, a melodrama set in Fascist Italy, which used the many rooms of a Masonic temple in fascistic Hollywood; it required the audience to follow the action from room to room.

Circe Rep was essentially a black box theater, meaning that within the four walls, a variety of possible configurations were available. A director was given the choice of where she wanted the audience and the stage to be, depending on how she wanted to use the space. This flexibility in staging became one of the hallmarks of Circle Rep production. For many years, we changed orientation, from proscenium to four-sided arena, to thrust, to L-shaped at the director's whim. Each visit to Circle Rep was an adventure for the audience, because we designed not only a set for the play but also the whole space for the production.

I remember particularly the audience's surprise, arriving to see James Farrell's *In The Recovery Lounge* (designed by Thomas Lynch). People found themselves entering a long, antiseptic hallway, complete with acoustic ceiling and recessed fluorescent lights, which took them to wide, swinging doors that opened onto the set—the day room of a hospital. It was as if there *was* no theater or set—it was all an environment.

Many university theaters and small nonprofit groups offer the joys of a black box, wherein you may use any of the opportunities I've mentioned to stimulate a production concept. In a black box, your use of space is limited only by your imagination.

In many instances, however, you may not have a choice about where a production is to be presented. In those cases, space has a more limited role in formulating a production concept. But even if the type of stage is a given, the consideration of how to use the space in an innovative way can still provide stimulation. Maybe you should put the audience on the proscenium stage in an arena configuration. Dean J. Robert Wills utilized this solution in staging Jane Martin's *Vital Signs* on the sizable proscenium stage of the Galvin Playhouse at Arizona State in 1997.

Scale

Another spatial consideration that might inspire is the scale of the production. Scale involves the size, shape, and height of the stage. The most vivid example of this I can remember was Robert Woodruff's thrilling staging of Charles Mee's adaptation of Brecht's *Caucasian Chalk Circle* called *The Golden Circle* on the stage of the American Repertory Theater at Harvard. The first scene featured a low-hanging front curtain that oppressed the action with a low ceiling. Later, that curtain rose to a full height, and opened on the sides as well, to reveal an enormous space that featured a rope bridge spanning the upper area, at least twenty feet above the stage floor. As the soldiers chased the escaping women who bore the child across the swinging bridge, the action brought the audience to the edge of their seats, as surely as any high-wire act in the circus.

When we moved Albert Innaurato's *Gemini* from Circle Rep to Broadway, scale was an important consideration that changed the production concept. The action of this operatic, slapstick, coming-of-age comedy takes place in the backyard of a Philadelphia row house. Circle Rep had a ceiling over the stage that measured only about twelve feet. The brick façade of the ground floor of the house filled nearly the whole space. The Little Theater on Broadway (now renamed the Helen Hayes) has a proscenium that arches about eighteen feet above the stage, more than doubling the vertical space an audience could see. We had the opportunity (and challenge) to make imaginative use of this additional vertical area.

As the Broadway supervisor of the production's move to Broadway, I suggested to Peter Mark Schifter, the original director of *Gemini,* that we should add a second story to the house, so the audience could see the whole structure. We also added a cyclorama that emphasized the height of Bunny's climb up the telephone pole, contributing both to the drama and the hysterical comedy of the moment.

The shift in scale underlined the humanity of the characters in their adolescent search for love, while allowing them to reach the operatic comic excesses the author intended. The enlarged production concept engaged a whole new audience (the so-called tunnel crowd, referring to audiences coming from New Jersey) and enabled the production to run for four years, becoming the fifth longest-running nonmusical play in Broadway history.

The scale of a production is not dictated by the dimensions of the stage alone—or by the size of the cast. The larger the audience, the grander a concept for a production may need to be. Certain outdoor epics, like Paul Green's *Unto These Hills,* which is staged every summer in Cherokee, North Carolina, play to audiences that number in the thousands. An opportunity to stage a show at Radio City Music Hall with over 5,000 seats could inspire you with its vast scale alone.

The Ground Plan

The most important expression of a production concept is the horizontal use of the space: the ground plan. The director's concept influences the set designer's use of the stage space, and together they need to make sure the design accommodates the needs of the action. If you allow a designer to dictate the ground plan, you have evaded one of your fundamental directorial responsibilities. You may as well let the designer direct the play, because the ground plan provides all the opportunities and limitations for movement.

A ground plan is a blueprint of the use of horizontal space. It affects an actor more than almost any other aspect of a director's concept because it delineates the physical world he will inhabit. The actor is dependent on the director's ground plan to provide motivational elements that will justify where he moves.

For example, if there is a window down right and if an actor feels a need for introspection, he might choose to move to the window to contemplate the sky. A fireplace may invite movement arising from a need to feel safe and cozy. A bar offers an opportunity to cross the room to get a drink when a character feels the need. The position of a door has different motivations for behavior, depending on *where* the door leads—outside to a dark alley, for instance, or into the sexy ambiance of a bedroom. The arrangement of these motivational elements offers the opportunities for movement and behavior, from which an actor can discover a character's physical life.

Actors also depend on the director to be aware of the sight lines in designing a ground plan. No actor wants to be worried about the audience missing his best moment. Sometimes the problems presented by sight lines demand such creative solutions they can inspire a whole concept.

There is an inherent sight line problem in Noël Coward's *Private Lives,* unless it is staged on a proscenium stage, for which it was conceived. There is a wall dividing the veranda in the first act that prevents Eliot from seeing Amanda. When I directed the play on the extreme thrust of the Repertory Theater of St. Louis, my designer David Potts and I had the challenge of solving a knotty problem. If Eliot couldn't see Amanda, neither could half the audience. Our solution was a curving *Art Deco* hotel on a revolving stage that first favored Eliot's terrace, so all could see, and then revolved an eighth of a turn to favor Amanda's terrace for her scenes. When the two former lovers discover each other, of course, the stage could be equal, because they were free to move downstage of the wall of plants that separated them. It worked like a charm, and after the intermission, the revolving stage made the change to Amanda's apartment in Paris a joyous visual journey for the audience.

Make sure the set design observes architectural integrity, because it directly affects both the actors' and the audience's ability to believe in the play's environment. A stairway should conceivably lead somewhere; so a ground plan that asks an actor to come in from outside, turn right twice, and head upstairs toward the door from which he has just entered is not believable. That's not the way houses are constructed. A bathroom is also not likely to be located on the same wall as the front door. (The plumbing would freeze!)

The most common mistake with architectural integrity is to locate a sofa parallel to the front of the stage, rather than considering its relationship to the angles of the walls (and doors) of the room. Such an arrangement instantly undermines an audience's belief, and creates a sense of artificiality. Although some styles may benefit from such a sense of artifice, realism is not among them.

In one example of poor spatial design, the floor plan for a production of a Pulitzer Prize-winning play on Broadway had the *back* of a sofa planted squarely in *front* of a burning fireplace! In another Pulitzer Prize-winning play, the position of the furniture required the actor sitting on the downstage sofa to turn completely upstage to converse with the other actor sitting on a chair behind her. In the real world, people arrange their furniture to encourage interaction. It's only in the theatrical world that the relationship to the audience takes precedence over the logical communication of the people in the room.

A director may sometimes find inspiration for a production concept from considering the physical needs of a climactic moment, or a turning point in the action. In William Inge's *Come Back, Little Sheba,* Doc comes back in a drunken rage to terrify his wife with an axe. The moment was so dramatic in my imagination that I wanted the audience to experience her palpable terror. My desire to heighten this turning point led me to ask John Lee Beatty to design a set with a steep staircase in the middle of the stage, so that when Doc chases her, brandishing the axe, Lola could be momentarily trapped on a landing high above the stage floor, bent back over the railing. This climactic moment was part of an over-all conception that sought to use space and scale to expand the action of the play with poetic metaphors, lifting it out of a mundane "kitchen sink" style.

The central location of the staircase meant that actors had to cross upstage of it to go from the front hall to the kitchen, momentarily passing out of the audience's sight. This "peek-a-boo" architectural arrangement subsequently inspired some of John Lee Beatty's best set designs, including those for *Talley & Son* and *A Delicate Balance.*

Space is the material through which a director sculpts meaning. It can be a dynamic stimulus for a concept.

Style

A fertile source for a directorial concept is to imagine how a particular style might illuminate a play.

Unfortunately, the term *style* is often misunderstood. Many people use it to mean something artificial or exaggerated. That is a limited and arbitrary definition of style. After all, even *realism* and *naturalism* are styles.

The word *style* comes from the Latin term *stylus,* a pointed instrument used to write on wax tablets. As an extension, style is a manner of expression, based on the definitive characteristics of an individual, a period, or a culture. In theatrical terms, style is the lens through which an audience experiences a play: the manner in which the action of the play is expressed.

When you encounter a play you like, imagine how you want the audience to experience the play. Many production concepts are rooted in the choice of a style.

Before considering a production style, it's important to identify the literary genre in which the play was written. Playwrights use literary styles that express both their individual perspectives on reality, as well as being a reflection of the times and cultures in which they write.

The first consideration is the style of the period—the time the play was *written* and the literary genre that expressed that time. Then, we must think about the time the play *dramatizes* and the literary voice of *that* era. For example, Shakespeare was an English dramatist in the Elizabethan era, when the principal literary devices were the use of iambic pentameter (called *blank verse*) and a Renaissance fascination with mankind as the center of the universe. But in *Julius Caesar,* he wrote about the events of the year 44 B.C. in the Roman Republic, an era that believed in the power of fate and the insignificance of man.

Given that disparity, a director must decide what time period or genre can best express the actions of *Julius Caesar* to a contemporary audience. She may elect an Elizabethan approach to the play, on a stage modeled after the Globe, with the actors costumed in doublets and hose, wearing hats and ruffs, and carrying rapiers and daggers, and with an emphasis on beautifully spoken poetry. An Elizabethan concept would allow us to see how the play was probably performed in Shakespeare's time.

Or she could choose to design a space that suggests the marble structures of ancient Rome, with the actors in togas, their hair cut short and combed forward, wearing wreaths and sandals, carrying torches and short broad Roman swords, and with an emphasis on the turbulent action of history.

Or she might decide the play would be served best by a contemporary interpretation in modern dress, set perhaps in Paris during the Nazi occupation, with a psychological emphasis on motives and rationalizations—an existential angst, played with an understated naturalism, as if the play had been written by Albert Camus or Jean Paul Sartre. This worked for Orson

Welles. Daniel Sullivan's recent Broadway production with Denzel Washington created a postapocalyptic world, reminiscent of the devastating imagery of the ruins of classical Iraq.

Or a director might choose any other imaginative variation of time, period, place, culture, and literary genre that conveys how she sees the play. Tyrone Guthrie brought new acclaim to Shakespeare's neglected tragedy *Troilus and Cressida* by playing it as an Edwardian comedy. Peter Brook produced *King Lear* with an existential edge, as if it had been written by Samuel Beckett.

Stylistic departures should never be arbitrary. Essentially, I agree with the purists (and all playwrights) who argue that a director's first obligation ought to be to produce the play as the writer conceived it. Many people will not concede a director's prerogative even to *have* an alternative vision.

In those cases where the script is being produced for the first time, it's true that a director's primary duty is to try to fulfill the playwright's vision. A first production still offers a director plenty of freedom in terms of imagery, space, and emphasis to stimulate a creative contribution, but her goal should be to make conceptual choices that will serve the writer's vision.

However, once a play has been seen as its author intended, a novel directorial concept becomes a legitimate way to revisit the play with fresh insight.

I have mentioned my rather abstract production of Edward Albee's *Who's Afraid of Virginia Woolf?* in Japan. My concept was based on my conviction that the original Broadway production had used all its courage in doing such a dangerous (for the time) play. I thought the play, which owes a debt to the sophisticated comedies of Noël Coward as well as to the abstract absurdities of Eugene Ionesco, should be liberated from a mundane, realistic set, confined within walls full of bookshelves.

By the time I was directing the play some twenty years after its premiere, I was sure that nearly everyone had seen the traditional approach to the play. Mike Nichols' movie with Elizabeth Taylor and Richard Burton had enjoyed worldwide distribution. As an artist, I saw no reason to simply duplicate the bland realism of previous productions. I wanted the audience to see the essence of the play, rather than its realistic trappings: the philosophical metaphor of history versus science and the shocking existential metaphor of the barrenness of modern love. Furthermore, I was directing the play in Japan, a society that prizes abstractions in art as well as technology.

The production was rewarded with popular and critical success in Tokyo. At a press conference after the opening, a reporter asked Edward Albee what he thought of this rather daring interpretation. With that acerbic wit for which he is so justifiably famous, Edward said he thought it was fine, if one had already seen the play the way it *should* be done.

Fair enough.

Curiously, the stylistic things that make a director's concept work for a general audience may give the critics ammunition. For example, in my recent production of *Cat on a Hot Tin Roof* for the Repertory Theater of St. Louis, a key element of my concept was the timelessness of the play. I didn't want the audience to view the actions of the production from the quaint perspective of the 1950s, which conjures up beehive hairdos and oversized fins on the fenders of automobiles. I wanted to emphasize the classical aspect of the script, which is written in Aristotelian unity of time and place: everything happens in one setting, in continuous time from beginning to end. Furthermore, Brick's relationship with Skipper is the embodiment of the Greek ideals of perfect love, the love between two men; as Maggie describes it: "It was one of those beautiful, ideal things they tell about in Greek legends."

David Potts designed a beautiful abstraction of a bedroom in a Southern mansion that was framed by two enormous marble colonnades, which suggested a different realm from the realism of the fifties, evoking instead the plane of Greek tragedy.

To achieve a sense of timelessness, I deleted the presence of the servants and the children, and focused the lean, taut action on the larger-than-life conflicts that captured the universal struggles of the characters with life-and-death matters.

I also updated any script references that buried the action in the specific period of the fifties: Big Daddy's wealth became $100 million. Margaret's reference to "twilight sleep" became "an epidural." The description "death was the only icebox" became "death was the only place cold enough to keep it." Naturally, all the strong language of the present was utilized instead of quaint euphemisms like "friggin'" and "crap," replaced with the more potent "fucking" and "bullshit." All this, the audience assimilated or praised, much of it passing unnoticed because the changes put the play into terms so familiar in the present that they were invisible.

However, to critics expecting the 1950s setting of the play, several changes to the present stuck out quite noticeably. Brick's ankle cast was the blue contemporary medical device, rather than the white plaster of yesteryear. When Brick turned off the stereo (not the hi-fi), he used a remote control, as we all do daily. When Brick's memory of a phone call from Skipper is jogged by a telephone ringing, the ring of his brother's cell phone provided the reminder.

These elements gave critics an angle they could write about. Because most of them they appreciated the power of the play in this production, they scrambled to find an angle to criticize. One critic noted that attitudes toward "homosexuality and cancer have changed a lot in the last half-century." If the play is timeless, she questioned, "Isn't 1955 just as 'timeless' as 2005 is?"

The answer is obvious to anyone under fifty: the present seems timeless because it's the time we live in, without consciousness of time. Whenever we look at an earlier period, the style distances us from the experience. The bell-bottomed look of Carnaby Street fashion that announced the revolutionary 1960s looks quaint and slightly ridiculous to today's eyes. The "cat's meow" style of the 1920s flapper emphasizes how much times have changed.

But contrary to her assumption that *attitudes* have changed, in 2005 (as in 1950) not one single active professional male in a major sport has publicly acknowledged his homosexuality, in spite of estimates of up to 100 closeted gays in the NFL alone; nor has any in the fifty years since the play was first produced. Today's professional football player's attitude toward homosexuality is virtually unchanged from the disgust expressed by Brick in the play.

It's true that cancer is no longer the hushed, taboo topic it was in the 1950s, but it still is feared as a deadly diagnosis: there's still no cure for metastasized tumors.

For anyone experiencing the play for the first time, especially anyone under fifty, the present tense of the action made it seem immediate and relevant to their lives. Only the critics care about such things, and even they welcome an angle to write about. Basically, if your concept has any element that stands out from the text, even if it enlivens the experience of an audience, the critics almost certainly will analyze it.

My production of *A Streetcar Named Desire* for the Arena Stage offered the challenge of creating the first major production of that great play in the round. But ignoring the circumstances of the play's staging, the *Washington Post* critic objected to the street life of New Orleans being introduced so vividly, attributing it all to my invention, which he claimed demonstrated "Mason's mistrust of the play." Actually, I had merely honored the author's numerous stage directions that describe the street life surrounding the play; I had added nothing. But because the play was being produced in an arena configuration, the street action occurred directly in front of the audience, rather than far upstage behind the set, as on a proscenium stage.

Mindful of this new lens through which the audience would experience a familiar play, I had carefully choreographed the major actions of the play, such as Stanley's rape of Blanche, to be experienced within the surrounding violence, which is what I think Williams intended. I sent the critic the pages of the author's stage directions, which described in detail exactly what he had seen in my production. But that just resulted in a rebuttal article entitled "How the Director Made Top Billing," in which, although he dutifully admitted the scenes he had criticized as "added" were an essential part of the action, he continued to insist they were distracting. He implied that because the staging occurred in the round, they should have been deleted. In other words, despite my concern to be true to Williams' stage directions, my staging didn't conform to his idea of how the scene should be seen and he was unwilling to consider a new perspective. As he correctly observed at the conclusion of the article, "Directors must bear responsibility for concealing their artful power." Remember the principle: a director's work should be invisible. Violate it at your own risk.

By contrast, when I changed the period of Tennessee Williams' *Summer and Smoke* from the turn of the century to the Roaring Twenties, the critics didn't even notice, because the choice was so right it was an invisible alteration.

Another factor that affects the choice of style is consideration of a director's resources. These include:

- *Budget:* There's no point in conceiving a production that uses masks if you can't afford the materials to make them.
- *Artistic Options:* A concept that envisions the use of live music or puppets must have available musicians or puppeteers.
- *Sponsors:* The style of a production should be appropriate to the audience and the circumstances of presentation. For example, it would not be wise to do a nude version of *Romeo and Juliet* for a youth group sponsored by a church.

Finally, style is a matter of *emphasis* on the previously mentioned sources of inspiration: personal passion, social relevance, imagery, space, and scale. The importance a director assigns to each of these elements will lead to a style that best conveys the play.

A Brilliant Concept

William Ball, who was the artistic director of the Actor's Conservatory Theater in San Francisco, came up with an exemplary concept for Shakespeare's *The Taming of the Shrew*. We can use this famous production, which is available on videocassette and DVD, to review the aspects involved in a directorial concept. Get it, and watch how they inspired the production.

In terms of motivation, Ball's primary inspiration came from a fascinating problem. In our postfeminist age, how can a director justify Petruchio's offensive abuse of Kate and how can a contemporary audience tolerate her submission? This knotty problem inspired him to a delightful conception that helped make the play seem not only acceptable, but also even *relevant* to a modern audience.

The key was to envision the play performed as *commedia dell'arte*, an Italian renaissance style that uses stock characters and improvisation based in broadly physical slapstick. By making the supporting characters into caricatures, he made any physical pain they suffered as funny as the tortures the Coyote suffers at the hands of the Roadrunner in cartoons. In other words, he created a world in which abuse is funny because it has no real consequences. When Kate was thrown about, the actress let herself become as limp as a rag doll, so the violence was childish and funny. Furthermore, women could delight in her strength and independence, as she gave her macho suitor as good as she got. With a wicked sense of humor, she inflicted as many sadistic blows as her husband-to-be.

As for color and texture, the director chose to present this world in pastel shades, clownish clothes, and ridiculous masks that emphasized the harmlessness of it all. Petruchio was costumed as a parody of macho manliness, often bare-chested, always in skintight pants that sported a huge codpiece. I have no doubt that having the muscular and athletic Mark Singer in the company presented an irresistible casting opportunity that may have influenced Ball's decision to do the play.

The director altered the space in an ingenious way. Although the production used a conventional proscenium stage, bleachers were set up to surround the action, where the whole cast could laugh and applaud as spectators. This helped to give it a theater-in-the-round feeling, uniting audience and cast in a sense of intimacy.

He also used silly Spike Jones–type music and sound effects: honking horns, rim shots, cymbal crashes, and bass drum beats to punctuate the farcical action.

The concept was centered on one basic idea: Kate and Petruchio fell in love at first sight. In the midst of all the ridiculous behavior, real human love was the redeeming feature. So despite all the rough games they played, this couple was headed for a happy ending from the moment they laid eyes on each other.

In the world this director created for the play, an audience could accept everything in good cheer, because it was removed from reality by the good-natured acrobatic style of a *commedia* troupe and because true love conquered at the end.

Once one has seen the A.C.T. *Shrew*, it is difficult to imagine it ever being done any better. And that is the highest praise for a concept a director can hope for.

Of course, not every production will be as successful as *Shrew*. For an example of a concept that didn't quite work, see Appendix B, A Flawed Concept.

Chapter Three

Preparation

When a director has come up with an inspiring concept and everyone is excited by the clarity and urgency of his vision, the paramount question becomes *how* to achieve it.

An approach is needed that uses the principles of directing as guidelines to bring a play to life. It begins with preparing a plan.

Although it may seem self-evident that it would be a good idea to be thoroughly prepared for an artistic journey, some directors actually never plan a schedule. They leave everything up to the inspiration of the moment, and rehearse whatever seems to *need* rehearsing most on any given day. This *ad hoc* approach produces an irregular, uneven rhythm that chugs along from one dire emergency to another. It's based on a misconception: that because inspiration is serendipitous, organization is antithetical to genius. These directors argue that a rigid schedule might inhibit creativity. How could they know in advance what will need to be rehearsed?

Well, *all* the scenes in the play will need rehearsal, so a director should plan to give each part the attention it deserves. He can always leave some slack in the schedule (an occasional T.B.A.) to make sure the unexpected can be dealt with, and panic avoided. Some work will go easier and quicker than expected, and he'll gain on the schedule. Some will be more difficult or slower, and will need more time than he supposed. A schedule can be adjusted; if the time is well considered, it can accommodate surprises without abandoning the map.

Some film actors try to justify not learning their lines because it might inhibit their believability. Wouldn't it be more *real* to wing it? It's hard to swallow this excuse. The guest hosts on *Saturday Night Live* sacrifice credibility

34

(and laughs) when their eyes wander to read the cue cards during a skit. As desirable as spontaneity is, most artists find the opportunity for spontaneous inspiration *increases* with solid preparation.

Film directors understand that having a detailed plan to shoot a movie gives them a better chance to capitalize on an unanticipated opportunity. There's a brilliant moment in *On the Waterfront* when Marlon Brando picks up a tiny white glove Eva Marie Saint has accidentally dropped. He playfully tries it on his huge hand. Their director, Elia Kazan, had thoroughly prepared them to play the truth of the moment, so the actors had no need to stop the scene, and say, "Oops! She dropped her glove!" Their preparation was rewarded with a tender moment of spontaneity that makes the scene unforgettable.

Before exploring how the principle of good preparation can translate into a productive rehearsal plan, let's look at some basic things a director needs to consider in order to be well prepared.

Finding a Project

A director's personal involvement with a script helps to inspire a concept, but it's also the first thing to consider when choosing a play. The play should resonate in terms of a director's life experience and compel a desire to communicate its truths.

Of course, libraries are full of plays from every historical period, so how do you find one that speaks to you with a special urgency?

Although you can't judge a book by its cover, you *can* rely sometimes on the appeal of a play's title. The author has given a lot of thought to make the title reflect the central image or theme of his play.

So, skim through titles, and allow your imagination to be pulled by the title, like the moon pulls the tide. *A Streetcar Named Desire* intrigues far more than its original title, *The Poker Night*. Lanford Wilson's title *The HOT L BALTIMORE* was much admired by critics, who were intrigued to discover its meaning. It's far more enticing than the original title: *Memorial Day*. Two titles that especially appeal to me are Tennessee Williams' *Talk to Me Like the Rain* and Wilson's *The Great Nebula in Orion*. It's also evident that once you find a writer whose work appeals to you, you should read all the plays he's written to find the one that means the most to you. It's no coincidence that Williams and Wilson also offer my favorite titles.

Apart from the immense number of published plays, how should you decide whether to direct a new, unproduced script? Look for a project that truly appeals to you, in either its theme, subject, characters, dialogue, or imagery.

When you come across a script you want to consider, find a quiet, unin-terrupted time to read the play for the first time. Pay close attention to the stage directions. As you read, try to visualize the settings that are described. Watch for the specific locations and the time of day, season, or year. Imagine the characters as they are introduced: their ages, physical description, clothes, and mannerisms.

When you read the dialogue, try to "hear" the voices of the different characters as they begin to interact. Watch for the first sign of conflict. Look for what is being avoided, as well as what is said. Take note when a character changes the subject, and ponder what that behavior reveals.

As you get caught up in the action, let the play come to life in your imagination. Believe in what is happening and try to visualize it. Be as open-minded and uncritical as possible. Try to sense the moods of the scenes and to appreciate the overall style.

When you've finished reading the script for the first time, reflect on how it engaged you. Were you moved? Did you laugh? Did it disturb you? Did the play ring true?

If it doesn't, the play will seem manufactured and artificial. You'll be aware of the writer's manipulation, forcing the characters, urging the story forward. The play may ring hollow or even false, straining for effect. Does the script leave you wondering, "How can I make this work"?

Directing shouldn't be a question of making a play "work." Beware of the temptation to "save" a faulty script with brilliant direction. This is a hard and painful lesson to learn. It took me years of directing before I realized that a good production of a mediocre play is still a mediocre experience for the audience. "I loved the production, but the play sucked" is hollow praise. It fails to register that the reason the director wanted to direct the play was because he believed in its value. If people criticize the play, they're criticizing the director's judgment.

A director's contribution is limited, and it's important to accept that your work always will be seen in terms of the play you've chosen. Choose a good script, and concentrate on fulfilling the author's vision to perfection. If a script doesn't grab you, don't do it. Keep looking.

Choosing a play is like falling in love; you'll know when the right one comes along.

Absorbing a Script

The sources of inspiration previously discussed help a director come up with an inspired conception. But, how do you give your imagination a chance to explore those resources? For one thing, your imagination will need time to fully absorb inspiration from the play. Also, several creative rereadings of the script will pose specific opportunities to challenge your imagination to glean new insights.

Once you decide to take on a project, it's a good idea to carry the script wherever you go. Just having the script with you stimulates your imagination on some unconscious level, even before you begin to think about a concept. Allow yourself to idly daydream about the play whenever you have a free moment—when you're going from one place to another by subway, car, plane, or train. Daydream about the play even when you're in the shower.

The longer a director knows ahead of time he's going to direct a project, the more time the script will have a chance to stimulate his resourcefulness on a subconscious level and begin to "cook" creatively.

Reread the play as often as possible. Each reading will bring new insights, as you focus on different aspects of the play.

First, concentrate on the places; look for pictures in magazines or on television that recall the setting of the play. It's like scouting locations for a film. Later, when you have accumulated a supply of images, even if they emerge only as vague feelings, you can begin to translate your initial instincts into a concept, aware of the needs for space, scale, proximity, and perspective.

In 1984, as I read and reread William M. Hoffman's beautiful play As Is, two instincts leapt into my consciousness. The play was about a mysterious, threatening new disease, which had just acquired the acronym AIDS. Very little was understood about the disease, and almost everyone was afraid. Many "uptown" audiences still regarded off-Broadway as a dangerous, bohemian adventure in a dark, dank basement; I felt it was important that the stage space be clean and uncluttered, even antiseptic. I wanted the audience to feel safe from a fear of contagion, so they would be unafraid to experience the humanity of the play.

At the same time, I didn't want to allow them the safety of darkness that a proscenium stage affords, because it was also important for them to feel uncertain about the future. AIDS, as we now know, threatens everyone, not just a special group. I wanted to wipe out any preconceptions people might bring, and make them feel that we all (actors and audience) were going to explore this frightening subject together.

These conflicting impulses led me to imagine the open space of a classical stage. I thought in terms of pillars and arches, architectural elements that would give the play a timeless, elegant, dignified platform from which we could illuminate the human condition of a real-life tragedy unfolding around us. To connect the audience to the action, I envisioned a short flight of steps across the front of a raked stage, leading down into the audience. The actors, who transformed into many different characters, would sit on the steps like a

Greek chorus, taking part in the action as required, and watching the action along with the audience when they weren't actively involved. The steps erased the division between the audience and the stage. No one would feel entirely safe. These instinctive choices served the play, the subject, and the audience.

The next time you read your script, concentrate on the characters. Make associations between the people in the play and people you've known in real life. Keep a watchful eye for details of behavior in the people around you that remind you of people in the play. Watch for clothes and accessories as you come across them in magazines or movies. Later, these stored images will help you pinpoint the colors, textures, and fabrics to construct a concept.

After you have cast the play, reread the play again, only this time, imagine the voices of the actors you have chosen. Now the dialogue gains a new life in the mind. Let your mind play with the degree of intimacy the audience should feel to the actors. Think about the size of the world of the play. You may begin to sense some general notions of movement or stillness.

At this stage, Clurman advises directors to note marginally the objectives lying beneath the words. Doing this may help you to analyze the fundamental action that drives the play, but keep in mind that without the intuition of the actors, you can only guess what the inner desires of the characters might be. You should resist the urge to get out chess pieces to block the physical action, or even to imagine the movement in too much detail. It's premature to design blocking without the contribution of the actors, who are the best judges of when their characters *need* to move.

Beats of Action

The keystone of preparation is to establish a foundation of concentration that will help the actors build the life of the script. The whole of the play is impossible to assimilate at once; we need to focus our attention on smaller parts.

When you decide that a few pages of the play can be considered as a unit, you've begun in a fundamental way to direct the play. The actors will be impelled to create *within* the units you've delineated. This subtle form of containment will endow the actors with a sense of freedom. Because you've already controlled the area of concentration, it should reduce your temptation to be obtrusive during the actors' exploration. In a way, it protects the actors' work from overt manipulation and meddling.

What should be the basis for delineating these units? Aristotle observed that the three interlocking elements of drama are action, character, and dialogue. The playwright expresses the first two by using the third. But for actors, the dialogue is a given result, not to be altered. An actor is focused on discovering how the character and the action *produce* what is spoken (and unspoken).

Character, on the other hand, is the result of both the actions that shape it and the dialogue that expresses it. A character is defined by what she does and says. The action describes how she *changes* as a result of the events she experiences in the play.

Character and action are inextricably bound together, like two sides of a quarter: they are two views of the same reality. Think of George Washington as the character, the eagle as the action. Heads or tails, it's still a quarter.

Drama, by definition, involves conflict; conflict is the crux of opposing actions, even if the actions are interior, and no more than desires. A dramatist uses action to construct the architecture of the play. When a character enters, departs, or breaks a silence, the playwright has indicated that something *new* is happening.

A director needs to focus the attention of his actors on the units of action he perceives in the structure of the script.

There are several reasons for doing this. Defining these units provides the actors with specific areas of concentration. Dissecting the action of the play will help you to understand the structure: how the play gets where it's going. These units, or *beats*, will have the practical value of helping you make a rehearsal schedule.

The action of a play is often divided into acts, when the lights dim or a curtain closes to indicate discrete units (with an interval between) that the writer wants us to experience separately.

Sometimes the action is further broken down into scenes, punctuated by dramatic changes of lighting, such as a brief blackout. These divisions serve a similar purpose, grouping events to be considered together, often bounded by a unity of time and/or place.

Within each scene, you should look for even smaller divisions, when something changes and the scene moves on to new concerns. I refer to these small units as beats for two reasons.

First, there's an apocryphal story that when Stanislavski visited America, he was asked about his directorial approach. He described how he divided the play into small *bits*; but due to his Russian accent, it was understood as *beats*. Because my directing approach owes a great deal to Stanislavski's system of acting, I retain the term as a fitting *homage*.

The second reason is that a *beat* is a rhythmic term; beats are the basic units of musical structure. Adopting this musical term to apply to the structure of a play, we are reminded of Stanislavski's observation that, "All art is striving to become music."

To find the beats of a scene, the first things to look for are the entrances and exits of characters. These events mark what are called *French scenes*, and they are the bare bones of structure that the playwright has used to signal the progressive action of the play. When a character leaves the stage, there must be a reason. Most often, it's because some action onstage has been fulfilled, or some new offstage action is about to commence. Conversely, an entrance marks the end of an offstage action, and the beginning of a new action onstage.

Of course, not every entrance or exit automatically means a new action has begun, but it's the first symptom to look for.

Skim through the dialogue, with which you should be familiar from your repeated readings, and track the action of the play, watching for one key element: change.

- Does the *subject* of discussion change?
- Does the *mood* change?
- Is there a silent moment where the *subtext* changes?

Take special notice of stage directions, such as (*Pause*) or (*She moves to the window*). Stage directions often indicate the completion of one unit of action, and the beginning of another. Again, not every stage direction signals a transition, but new beats often coincide with stage directions.

Sometimes though, a new beat will begin in the middle of a paragraph of dialogue, with no stage direction in sight. The key is to locate the change of intention that indicates a new unit of action, whether the author has marked it with an entrance, an exit, a stage direction, or not.

Depending on how the script is formatted, most beats of a manuscript typically measure about four pages in length, although many times one page (or even half a page) may comprise an entire beat. Sometimes a beat will last five or six pages to arrive at a culmination. If a beat goes on for as many as eight pages, I usually just divide it in half for convenience, to keep the focus manageable.

On the other hand, don't make your beats too short. There are changes happening on every page; we're trying to identify which changes are the significant ones that structure the action. If most beats of a script are of only one or two pages, it would indicate a very choppy rhythm in the writing. A director's beats should correspond to the flow of the writer's arc of action.

The next step is to identify each beat's main event by giving it a descriptive name. For example, the action in the first act of *The Seagull* can be described by the names of the beats:

Bt.1: Half-hour

Bt.2: New Forms

Bt.3: Courting

Bt.4: The Audience Enters

Bt.5: The Play

Bt.6: The Critics

Bt.7: Nina's Reception

Bt.8: Masha's Confession

Look at the sample character/beat chart for *The Seagull* in Appendix C to see how the titles of the beats suggest the entire journey of the play.

Naming the beats makes them easier to identify than referring to them by number. Scenes develop names quite naturally in rehearsals. "Let's rehearse the fight scene" is an inevitable development. Anticipating the inevitable, you can subtly mold the actors' perceptions by naming the beats before rehearsals even begin.

Once you've divided the action into beats, you have told the actors: "Something starts at this point, goes on to this point, and then something *new* begins." The actor can concentrate then on how to bring to life the action segment you've defined.

You've also told the playwright: "These are the units of action I see in your play." If your divisions are perceptive, you'll gain confidence from the writer. By marking these simple divisions, you can bring together these two disparate elements, playwright and actors, into a harmonious working process.

In the winter of 1964, I was preparing to direct my first play by Lanford Wilson, *Balm in Gilead*. This play is a complex work with some thirty-six characters in multiple scenes, many of them played simultaneously. Subsequently, I have directed fifty-nine productions of twenty-eight plays that Lanford has written. *PLAYBILL* says it's the longest continuous collaboration between a playwright and director in the history of the American theater. The foundation of our long artistic partnership can be traced to that moment in our first rehearsal when Lanford heard me divide his play into beats. From the accuracy of my divisions, he knew he'd met a director who truly understood his play. From this confidence arose that elusive commodity, *trust*.

A Character/Beat Breakdown Chart

Once the scenes are marked, it's useful to transfer this information to a chart that depicts a visual graph of the structure of the play. One of my associates, Erma Duricko, refers to this as the scan sheet. There is detailed practical advice on how to construct this handy tool in Appendix C. For an illustration of these instructions, look at the character/beat breakdown chart for *The Seagull.*

The completed chart provides a visual graph of the play's structure. The physical flow of the characters shows how the individual beats string together, weaving various strands of the drama into a dramatic fabric.

In many plays, particularly those of Shakespeare, the climactic scenes bring onstage almost all the participants to conclude all affairs of the drama. With a scan sheet, you can see at a glance how the subplot of Laertes, Ophelia, and Polonius first serves as an alternating counterpoint to the actions of Hamlet, Claudius, and Gertrude. The subplot then becomes entangled in the main action and is resolved late in the play by three large events: Polonius' murder, Ophelia's drowning, and Laertes treachery in the duel scene. The empty spaces that follow Ophelia's suicide evoke the return of the X's that stand for Laertes' vengeful presence.

Or in *King Lear,* one might note that the absence of Lear's fool is soon followed by Cordelia's return. Many scholars believe that this resulted from the same actor playing both roles.

Jack O'Brien dramatized their relationship to the action in his excellent production of *King Lear* at the Old Globe in San Diego by casting the role of the Fool with a woman, an idea I shamelessly incorporated when I directed the play a number of years later. Steal from the best!

Naturally, a director already may be aware of these elements from the academic study of structural dramatic analysis; but the character/beat chart *visually* dramatizes the structure of the action. It leads one away from mere intellectual understanding to the greater productivity of intuitive insight.

Of course, with a two-character play, the chart will not reveal structure, but you still have divided the play into segments for detailed concentration. And if you've named the beats, the outline maps out the terrain to be explored.

The chart's greatest value is apparent when drawing up a rehearsal schedule. Here on one page, you have before you each beat that needs your attention.

Actors need to be called for rehearsal only for the beats in which they appear. This prevents the hours wasted from sitting around outside a rehearsal room, wondering if the director will even get to an actor's scene.

You also can see when it would be wise to begin or end a block of beats to be rehearsed as a group. If an actor has only one line offstage at the end of beat 4, but then is onstage for beats 5, 6, and 7, it will make sense to call beats 1, 2, 3, and 4 as one unit (without the offstage actor) and beats 5, 6, and 7 at a separate time, starting with that offstage line.

It also allows you to group together beats that you can rehearse out of sequence. You can call a group of actors who are in several beats together, even if they're not sequential. The actors will appreciate your consideration. It shows your respect for their time, and endows them with a dignity too rarely experienced in the acting profession.

As an actor, I recall my resentment at wasting time waiting outside the rehearsal room while the director toiled with other parts of the play. If the schedule is well planned, you can avoid this abuse of the artists' time, ensuring that when an actor is called, she will be working.

Constructing a Rehearsal Schedule

Now you must plan how much time to allot each aspect of the process. Most rehearsals follow a four-week model. My rule of thumb is that a minimum of twenty-one rehearsals is needed to rehearse almost any play, no matter how short, because that number gives one a chance to establish a rhythm in the rehearsal process. Less time invites panic. Of course, more time is always welcome.

Generally, try to avoid situations in which you have less than three weeks of rehearsal in the rehearsal room (a total of 108 hours at six hours a day, six days a week), with at least an additional half-week for technical and dress rehearsals onstage.

If possible, try to get the producers to schedule a week of previews before critics are invited.

Professional theaters utilize this kind of schedule, but you can adjust it for use in any situation, retaining the rhythmic principles it's based on. Rehearsals in university theaters or amateur productions usually use more weeks, with fewer hours per night.

With classical plays, such as those by Shakespeare or Chekhov, a minimum of six weeks of rehearsal will probably be needed. These plays carry additional burdens of verse, period, and/or depth that require special skills and the time for the cast to develop them. With Shakespeare, I spend at least one full week around a table, working to understand the secrets hidden in the verse: the long vowels, the short or liquid consonants, and the rhythm of iambic pentameter.

Rehearsal Periods

One neat trick is to divide each day into two rehearsals periods. This gives you two units of time to concentrate on different beats or groups of beats. I've found that I'm able to concentrate *productively* for only about three hours at a time, so I divide my days into two rehearsals of three hours each, with a lunch break in between. This means the cast is scheduled to work for six hours out of seven, rather than the seven out of eight-and-a-half that's the normal Equity day. The actors have to vote on accepting an hour lunch break, instead of the prescribed hour-and-a-half, but in my 185 productions, I've never had a cast who didn't prefer a shorter workday, with a quick lunch.

Of course, you may find that your window of creative concentration is longer or shorter than three hours, so you can adjust this advice to suit your own needs.

Whatever the length, there are advantages to dividing the day into two segments. It doubles the units of time for detailed focus. If you have only five hours a day to rehearse, divide it into two equal segments of two-and-a-half-hours, with a short break between for a snack.

Equity permits five hours of rehearsal before a lunch break is required. Sometimes it will be to everyone's advantage to skip lunch, and plow through five straight hours. I often schedule this shorter day for Sunday, especially if I have to catch a plane before the day off.

Toward the end of the rehearsal period, Equity allows ten-out-of-twelve-hour days for tech rehearsals. The number of these days depends on the contract. The rules vary under the jurisdiction of LORT, off-Broadway, or Broadway.

Even if you're working with amateurs or students, I strongly recommend that you follow Equity's work and safety guidelines. They've been formulated over a number of years, based on what actors *need* in order to do their best work. Breaks, for example, must be taken five minutes every hour, or ten minutes every hour-and-a-half. While we can depend on our stage managers to enforce them, it's good for a director to know the rules and understand why they're important. If you're sensitive to the needs behind the requirements, your cast may be more lenient when you need to go a few moments longer, when it would be counterproductive to break in the midst of artistic discovery.

Broad Strokes

Sketch in the broad strokes of a rehearsal plan before filling in the details. Certain things change very little from one production to the next. For example, usually, the last day of rehearsal should include an "Invited Dress" to give the actors a taste of audience reaction, before paying patrons are admitted.

First, go to the end of the schedule and block off the days that must be assigned to previews and before that to the technical and dress rehearsals, which usually are determined by the producers or technical staff. In most cases, the technical and dress rehearsals will occupy about the last one-fifth of the total time allotted for rehearsal.

Now go back to the beginning of the schedule and block off the first one-fifth for research: the discussions, exercises, and improvisations that prepare the actors to undertake the written text, discussed more fully in Chapter 6, Research.

The first day of rehearsal must allow time for introductions, elections for the Equity deputy (during which the director must leave the room), costume measurements, discussion of the play, its meaning or significance, and establishing a plan of approach. Often, the first rehearsal will include a reading of the play. All this is discussed in Chapter 5, The First Rehearsal.

The Beats

So, about three-fifths of the rehearsal period is left to explore the beats, looking for impulses that lead to the behavioral life of the characters; to stage the physical action; and to conduct run-throughs.

Generally, it takes me about a week of collaborative work with the cast to block each act of a play.

Budgeting your allotted rehearsal time allows you to explore the action of the play, slowly at first, but with steady repetition that will snowball into larger and larger segments, until an entire act has been staged.

I try to schedule work on new material in the afternoon sessions and review previous work in the morning sessions. This establishes a rhythm that begins each day by repeating beats you've already rehearsed and only then going on to explore new territory. For new beats, actors need to be wide-awake, with their imaginations fully engaged. If they feel good about the work they've done in the morning review, they'll be eager to plow ahead into the uncharted afternoon.

It's just as important to include sufficient time for the review of beats, as it is to explore them anew. Repetition of what has worked in previous rehearsals allows new discoveries, refinements, subtleties, and resonance to emerge.

It's wise to begin slowly. I usually schedule only one beat for the first afternoon of staging. Once a rehearsal rhythm has been established, the actors can take on a bit more. By the third or fourth afternoon, as people become familiar with the circumstances of the play and accustomed to the approach, you may be able to explore two or three new beats in the same three-hour period. If you take the time to carefully thread a needle through the tiny eye, the whole spool will pull through easily.

Of course, each morning we accumulate more beats to review, building up larger segments of the act. By the end of the week, we should have accumulated a whole act to review.

These reviews, however, should not be viewed as run-throughs, but as accumulations that the actors should "stumble through" in a very raw and exploratory fashion. Just lay the scenes end to end, not yet looking for a through-line. Emphasize that you are all still exploring; it is not a performance. Your best advice is: "Take your time." Fight the temptation to pick up the tempo, and try to restrain the actors from their urge to perform.

It's very hard to rein in an actor's natural desire to perform, but to begin performing too soon cuts short the possibilities of new discoveries that might result from continued exploration. It's too soon to abandon the search by jumping to the gratification of performance. This issue is discussed more fully in Chapter 7, Discovering Movement, and Chapter 8, Reviewing Discoveries.

Finally, it's important to allow some time (at least two or three rehearsals) for run-throughs of the whole play, because some things can be discovered only from the uninterrupted flow of the action.

You can see that this rehearsal schedule differs dramatically from the approach of many directors, who have the cast read the play on the first day, block Act I on the second day, block Act II on the third day, and then run-through the play continuously for the remainder of the rehearsal period.

I hope you can imagine how a director (as well as the actors) might benefit from a more detailed schedule with a plan that divides the available time into units of concentration. It leads to more detail, depth, and honesty in the work.

Of course, your experience may suggest different priorities for using the rehearsal time. But whatever the variations, by allotting the available time into a schedule, you'll have time to consider each aspect of the production.

When you have completed your rehearsal schedule, print it on the back of the character/beat breakdown chart. These two pages are interlocking and interdependent, so it's best to insure that they don't get separated from each other.

A sample of a rehearsal schedule and a character/beat breakdown chart is included in Appendix C.

Stimulating Designers

Before rehearsals begin, a director should meet privately with each designer to lay a conceptual groundwork for the production. The idea isn't to *impose* your ideas on your designers, but to *suggest* the nature of the creative world you envision for the play. You shouldn't suggest solutions that presuppose a certain result; you should try to inspire the designers to find their own visions of how to achieve your goals.

The set designer needs to know what you feel about the play: why and how it moves you, its moods and textures. Describe the kind of experience you want the audience to have. Make clear any special requirements you feel the play demands, like a staircase, or a door Up Center, or running water in the kitchen. Sketch out a rudimentary ground plan to illustrate the type of movement patterns you envision. It's a good idea to talk to your designer with a pencil and pad at hand, because an image may convey much more than a word. But be careful not to limit the imagination of your partner: don't design for the designer. Pose the problems: let the designer solve them.

Nevertheless, insist on the elements you and the actors will need so you don't wind up with a pretty but impractical set that you must play in front of. Remember the time to make changes is *before* construction begins.

The lighting designer needs to know what you feel are the most important elements of light for the play. Are the time and place, the style, mood, or image more important? All of these aspects of light are needed, but the *value* of each element will vary from play to play. Do you want a practical source onstage that motivates the light? How important is the direction of light sources, such as sunset or moonrise? Do you need to establish a light-hearted mood that invites laughter in a comedy? Should the audience be able to see everything at all moments, or are some shadows permissible, even desirable?

I'm told that the very dark night scenes in Gerald Gutierrez's brilliant production of *The Heiress* on Broadway with Cherry Jones came about by a fortuitous accident. Apparently, the lighting board crashed during a dress rehearsal, leaving the stage in virtual darkness. Gerry said to his lighting designer, Beverley Emmons, "This darkness is exactly how it should be played!" It was as bold as anything I've seen on Broadway, and one of many memorable productions by the brilliant and much-missed Mr. Gutierrez.

Don't forget any *special effects* you need, such as fog, sunsets, stars, rippling water, or a rising moon. Again, don't talk about likos, fresnels, varilights, "inkies," or wattages. Just describe the *effect* you need, and let the designer provide the *technical expertise* to fulfill your vision.

Once you've begun to stage the movement, encourage the lighting designer to come to as many rehearsals as possible, so she'll be able to see where and when movement requires a change of focus. The lighting designer is to the stage what the cinematographer is to the motion picture: she focuses the audience's attention on the composition the director wants them to see.

Sit down with the costume designer and thumb through magazines or picture books together. Your designer will want your reaction to clothes before she begins to sketch. Ask to see samples of materials, as well as renderings.

Be sure the costume designer and the stage manager establish a clear line of communication so fittings can be scheduled or rescheduled, and so the designer can keep up-to-date on discoveries and/or changes you and the cast make in rehearsal.

Be sure to mention *special requirements*, such as fight scenes, garments that need to be rigged to be ripped, or blood-stained, or quick-changed. Will the shoes need to be soled with rubber to soften the noise, or to provide traction on a raked stage?

Remember to consider the particular and peculiar attributes of each actor: request the designer to make the leading lady's hips look thinner, if heavy hips are not desirable for the character. Can the leading man be made to look like he has broad shoulders?

Make clear that you expect the costume designer to work closely in collaboration with the actors. Few things are as important to an actor as the clothes she will wear onstage. The actors need to be happy with the fit, the colors, and the fabrics. If an actor hates green, it's legitimate to ask the designer to consider an alternative. If an actor is allergic to wool, what optional material could give a similar effect? Of all the considerations, an attractive and comfortable fit is most important.

The treatment of hair is also a vital concern in your conference with the costume designer: its cut, length, style, color, and curl. If an extreme difference is required, would a wig be a better solution than torturing the actor's natural hair? Some actors love wigs; others hate false hair. John Malkovich centered his creation of the character Pale in *Burn This* on a shoulder-length wig that entirely changed his persona.

Don't forget mustaches and beards. Can an actor grow the facial hair that's desirable for the character or the period? Or can believable substitutes be attached with spirit gum? When I'm directing a period play, such as *Hamlet* or *Mary Stuart*, I grow a beard along with the fellows in the cast to share in their experience. I try never to ask an actor to do something that I would not do.

Evaluation of costumes is not my strong point, but my longtime assistant, Rand Mitchell, has a very sharp eye. I rely on his advice, along with the actors' requests and the designer's ideas.

Encourage the sound designer to think of every sound that might give dimension to a scene. Don't say "no" too fast. Let the designer create the sound, and try it. You can always cut it later. Of course, it is reported that Chekhov, impatient with Stanislavski's abundant sound effects, said he was going to write a play in which the characters remark on how there's not a single sound to be heard.

A composer will need to know the length of each musical cue, as exactly as possible, especially if it underscores part of the action and dialogue. Discuss the kind of instrumentation you think would convey the mood of the music you need. You might even refer the composer to existing pieces of music that capture the sort of mood or feeling you want his new composition to convey. Incidental music plays a supporting role and should be kept simple. The cues are often surprisingly short—timed in seconds, not minutes. When you have assembled a substantial portion of the play, invite the composer to attend a run-through, so he can imagine how his music can support what you and the actors have created.

In short, try to stimulate the imagination of your designers to flesh out the bare bones of your conception with color, tone, body, substance, sound, and texture. Get them started in the right way, then let them create. Whenever possible, work with designers who know their specialties better than you do. Be flexible. Listen. Welcome any good idea from any source.

The most important aspect of your work with designers is to establish a collaborative effort to achieve your vision. Inspire each artist to contribute her best work toward an organic, seamless whole. If you have assembled a fine team of collaborators, you will be free to concentrate on your main creative task: helping the actors.

It's impossible to overemphasize the importance of the designer's contribution to the experience of a play. I've mentioned my production of *The Seagull* a number of times because the rehearsal process was one of the best experiences of my career. I had a lovely translation by David French. I had a great cast that included Ethan Hawke, Laura Linney, Jon Voight, Tyne Daly, Tony Roberts, and Joan MacIntosh. My producer Tony Randall had given us a six-week rehearsal period in a huge suite of rooms that adapted beautifully to our imagined environment, and we had every prop we would use from the first rehearsal. We had beautiful clothes by Laura Crow, and they were provided to us onstage a full week before tech rehearsals began. Richard Nelson created lights that shimmered with the magical moods of the play, and Peter Kater composed a fully orchestrated score, symphonic and filled with Russian feeling. But the production was one of my most painful failures, because of a lack of shared artistic vision with my set designer.

At our first meeting, I suggested that I wanted the production design to be in the gentle, organic style of *art nouveau*. My scenic designer asked me what I meant by "art nouveau." I showed her several books that illustrated the graceful curves of entwining vines that typify the style, but her question should have alerted me to the fact that this was not the right designer for my concept.

The resulting set was stolid, heavy, and impractical, and at the same time, sketchy and incomplete, as if there weren't a big enough budget to complete the set. Rooms suddenly evaporated into exteriors without doorways to divide them. My stars joined me in appealing to Tony Randall for expensive amendments to the units, which didn't really solve the inherent problems of a misconceived set.

When we opened, the crudeness of the set suggested a poor, threadbare traveling company (such as Nina might have acted in), and it completely undermined the delicate, deep, and intricate life we had created in the rehearsal room. When Chekhov's plays are well performed, it's as if they're not acted at all, but have the rough unfinished surface of real life. In the context of a cheesy set, our rough edges looked like the worst kind of amateurism.

I paid for my mistake with the harshest criticisms I have received as a director, in spite of having my best rehearsal period ever.

Setting Up a Rehearsal Room

One of the most important things a director can do to ensure a good rehearsal is to make the rehearsal room a stimulating place to work. The atmosphere of the rehearsal room is essential to creativity. It should be comfortable, invite seriousness of purpose, and entice the imagination.

As soon as you and your set designer have finalized a ground plan, the stage manager should tape out the exact measurements on the rehearsal room floor. With your stage managers' help, the goal is to create an environment within the rehearsal room that is as close as possible to what the actors will experience onstage. If platforms and steps are needed, bring them into the rehearsal room, even if they are not to perfect scale. If there will be a wall between two rooms, try to find something to stand for the wall. If there is a door, define it as the space between two chairs. If the stage will be carpeted, find a rug to rehearse on. Get all your rehearsal furniture as soon as possible. Don't put everything off until you are onstage. I hate surprises.

As I mentioned, Tony Randall's National Actors' Theater gave my cast and me exemplary rehearsal conditions for *The Seagull*. Not only did we have a full six weeks of rehearsal, including a week onstage in full costume, but we also had every single piece of stage furniture that we were going to use, from the *first* day of rehearsal. What a joy that was! Within your own circumstances, try to give your cast this kind of treat.

With the help of your stage managers and assistants, stock up on all the props you anticipate might be needed. Have clean, drinkable water for the actors to pour and drink as soup, vodka, or coffee. Provide the actors with rehearsal props so an actor never has to pantomime a prop. Provide whatever you can in the way of rehearsal clothes, particularly coats, scarves, gloves, or anything that might affect an actor's timing.

You should provide exercise mats, so that you can request warm-ups before each rehearsal commences.

Make sure the room has the necessary heating or air-conditioning, for optimum working conditions. The rehearsal room should be clean and sanitary, but not antiseptic.

Transform a neutral rehearsal room into a living environment for the play to inhabit. You will be in this room for four weeks or so. Make it your home.

Finally, install rehearsal lights so you can suggest the mood and times of the play. You can get six or eight PAR lights with flexible clips and a couple of household dimmers at almost any hardware store for minimal expense. This will enable you to turn off the overhead (usually fluorescent) lights and make it "magic time" when the actors get on their feet to create. If there is a fireplace in the play, get a portable electric heater to provide the heat.

In other words, personalize the rehearsal room. Make it come to imaginative life as the environment of the play. The more you stimulate the imagination of the actors, the more they'll be inspired.

To bring a play to life, you must create a world in which the characters live out the actions of the script. Make it as easy as possible for the actors to imagine the circumstances you ask them to create.

When you've accomplished all the preparations outlined in this chapter, you'll be ready for the real work to begin.

Chapter Four

Casting

Casting may involve the most important decisions a director must make, and is often reckoned as 90 percent of a director's job. While it's hard to overestimate the importance of selecting a good cast, 90 percent may be a bit inflated. Even Harold Clurman exaggerates a little when he advises (only half in jest), "Choose a good script, cast good actors—and you'll all be good directors." Remember Yogi Berra's prescription: "Success is 90 percent sweat, and the other 50 percent is talent!"

Let's settle for the proposition that if a director wants to bring a script to life, she'll have to do it through her actors. That places an enormous burden on finding the right people for the roles. Directors who say they don't like actors mystify me. That's like a chef disliking fresh ingredients.

When directors cast for a production, what are we looking for? Probably the most important qualities are

- talent,
- experience,
- skill, and
- discipline.

Most of all, a director needs to find actors who can convince an audience they *are* the people in the play. It's better to choose a gifted, skilled actor who may not be quite the right type over an inexperienced actor whose physical characteristics are exactly what the script calls for. So in an audition, the first thing to look for is basic belief: when the actor speaks the lines, do you believe that the words are *his* words, expressing his thoughts and feelings?

Format of an Audition

If possible, make the entire script available to everyone who'll be auditioning at least three days ahead of time. If a complete script can't be provided for each actor to take home, at least make sure a script is available for reading in an accessible casting office.

If *sides,* which are portions of scenes, are going to be used for auditions, the sides should be given to actors to take home and prepare. We want each actor who auditions to have every opportunity to do his best work so that we can find the best actors for the parts. If an actor has both the script and the sides, he can really prepare to do his best.

I love how Jeff Daniels describes his acting approach to auditions: "The way I see it, the director has a problem, and I'm there to see if I can help him solve it."

Choose sides that are three to four minutes in length—long enough to see different colors of a scene but short enough to be practical. For the initial reading, it's better to choose scenes that occur early in the play, saving more complex scenes for callbacks, when actors can explore a scene collaboratively.

Avoid choosing climactic scenes that are the result of a complicated journey through the play. It's not productive to ask an actor to audition with Masha's breakdown at the end of Act IV in *Three Sisters.* On the other hand, because it is essential that the actor you cast has the ability to reach the emotional intensity that's required, such a climactic scene may profitably be included in a callback.

The sides should be marked clearly so actors know exactly where the scene will begin and end. Any cuts in the scene should be clearly indicated. Allow actors to go all the way through the selected scene, no matter what. Even if the reading starts off terribly, you never know when some tiny spark might emerge toward the end of a scene that shows you an actor is capable of more than he's yet shown.

Unlike some directors, I allow every actor to read the same amount in the initial audition. This egalitarian spirit establishes that each person should have the same chance to win the role. The pain a director might suffer from sitting through an incompetent reading is minor compared to the injustice of short-changing anyone of an equal opportunity.

It's wise to select scenes that involve more than one character, because the cliché is true: much of acting is reacting. Monologues limit what you can discover about an actor because you're robbed of the opportunity to watch him listen and respond. Two-person scenes are best, but some plays have scenes only with multiple characters. In that event, for auditions you can cut the extra characters from the sides to make it easier to read as a two-person scene.

To alleviate the boredom of repetition, select two or three different sides for each character. Actors then can choose which scene they prefer to read, and that gives you and your casting associates a welcome bit of variety.

Everyone should be treated with courtesy, respect, and, if possible, charm. A director's fair and equal encouragement in casting is as important as a doctor's bedside manner. I often receive notes from actors thanking me for being gracious and caring in auditions. You want to encourage every actor to give the best audition he can, so your cast will be the best you can find.

The Résumé

A résumé is, in a sense, a brief autobiography, reflecting how an actor sees himself. The roles he chooses to list will give you an idea of the range of characters he feels he can cover. The extent and kind of training he lists will suggest the sort of skills he's acquired.

General background information is also helpful. What schools or universities has the actor attended, and with what teachers has he studied? Has he had vocal training? Movement? Dance? Mask-work? Mime? Have his roles included a variety of types, or do they expose a narrow range? Has there been a diversity of experience, or has his background been limited to musicals, classics, or contemporary plays? If I'm casting a new play by Lanford Wilson, I'd be cautious about using someone whose repertoire has been limited to roles in *Oklahoma!* and *Once Upon a Mattress*. Conversely, if I were casting a musical, I'd have some hesitation about using someone who's appeared only in the plays of Eugene O'Neill and Arthur Miller, even if he has a nice voice.

Not all actors can sing and not all singers can act, but when I taught a remarkable group of kids at Carnegie-Mellon University for one semester, it convinced me that there *are* singing actors, where no compromise is needed in either discipline. Within six months of graduation, half of them were in Broadway shows. This was confirmed again when I directed the fine actor/singer Michael Hayden, as comfortable in *Carousel* as in *All My Sons*.

Dancing, on the other hand, is more exacting. Few actor/singers have bona fide dance credentials, which imply classical dance training. If they haven't studied ballet, most musical actors will profess only "to move well."

It may be useful to ask about the hobbies or special skills the actor includes on his résumé. They might provide insight about how his personal history might give him a special connection to a character.

It's also important to look on the résumé for the actor's age, height, and weight; if it's not listed, ask the actor "How tall?" Physical statistics may be helpful when you begin matching two actors for callbacks, if they've been seen initially on different days. Even though it certainly happens in real life, for aesthetic reasons you may prefer to avoid casting a Juliet six inches taller than her Romeo.

When I was recasting Lanford Wilson's *Fifth of July* for Broadway, two actors from my original Circle Rep cast were unavailable. William Hurt, who originated the role of Kenneth Talley, was about six feet two and Helen Stenborg, who played Aunt Sally, was about five feet six; it was easy to believe they were members of the same family. But when we had the chance to bring the play to Broadway, Bill was making his first film in Hollywood and Helen was starring opposite her husband Barnard Hughes in another Broadway production. When we had to recast, Christopher Reeve replaced Bill and a fine actress named Mary Carver replaced Helen. Unfortunately, Mary (who played Chris' aunt) was about five feet tall, and Chris towered over her at six feet four. Side by side onstage, not only was it hard to believe they were from the same family, the difference in size also made it hard to believe they were even of the same species! Ever since that potentially fatal mistake, I've kept careful track of the height of each actor who auditions.

Asking an actor his (or especially, her) age can be a risky business, because age may be regarded as sensitive information. Of course, an actor's *actual* age is not important, but whether he can believably *convey* the age of the character. As a result, many actors balk at revealing their true age, and that's their privilege. If you decide to ask, you may see an unguarded moment. It's a sneaky way to throw a curve that forces a spontaneous, unrehearsed reaction to your rude behavior. He may tell you it's none of your business. Some actors have a ready response: "How old do you want me to be?" In that case, you learn only that the actor is experienced, witty, and knows the score.

The same problem may surface with the question of weight. If an actor doesn't mind telling you, probably it'll be listed on the résumé. If it's not, it may not be worth risking the actor's goodwill by asking. Let your eyes give you an estimate.

Eventually, every director comes across dishonesty on a résumé. Young actors sometimes expand their experience by claiming to have appeared in a production, when actually they've only worked on a scene in class, or to have played a lead, when in fact they carried a spear. I've seen résumés that claim an actor appeared in a production I directed and I clearly know that they didn't.

How you deal with such dissembling depends on how serious you are about working with the actor in question. If you'd like to hire the liar, I'd recommend confronting the falsehood in a genial way to resolve it. Even if you're not interested in casting him, it would be a kindness to warn about the dangers of deception on a résumé. You might suggest that if he has faith in his talent, an actor has no need to exaggerate experience.

Make note of the extent and kind of study the actor reports. I've found that actors who've trained in certain skills (the Meisner Technique, for example) are able to adapt to my way of working more easily and with greater depth than others. A background at a school that features extensive voice training (like Julliard) might make an actor seem more attractive if you're casting *Much Ado About Nothing* or *Private Lives.*

You even might find yourself impressed by actors who have studied with a particular teacher. For example, over the years, I've discovered that many of the actors I've enjoyed working with have studied with William Esper, either in his private classes or at Rutgers University. Often his students seem to have grasped the art of "living in the moment," which means I won't have to spend precious time in rehearsal, rehashing basic acting techniques. This doesn't mean that all good actors have studied with William Esper or that all actors who have studied with him are good. But on a résumé, the mention of such study encourages me to take a special look to see if *this* actor is the one I'm looking for.

Types

Elia Kazan, who was my directing hero, pointed out that all casting is type casting, not in the sense of external characteristics, but in finding the actor who has an "inner river of experience" that resonates within the character.

It's important to remember, and to remind both playwright and producers, that it's far more advantageous to cast a skilled actor rather than a type. Wigs, makeup, clever costuming, and especially the miracle of characterization can transform an ordinary Jane into the most charming of leading ladies.

I recall watching the great soprano Elizabeth Schwartzkoff sing the role of the tall, beautiful young blonde Countess in Mozart's *Marriage of Figaro* at Chicago's Lyric Opera. Backstage after the performance, I eagerly waited for the enchanting diva to autograph my program. Then, from her dressing room emerged a tiny German *haus-frau,* barely over five feet tall—a warm, but wrinkled face, her graying hair covered with a babushka. In that instant, I realized that beauty on the stage truly *is* in the eye of the beholder. The illusion lies in the hands of the artists. We can make audiences believe almost any actor is beautiful or handsome if the circumstances are right: the size of the house, the lighting, the costume, the makeup, and most of all, the *acting.* That's the magic of the theater.

When I directed Jessica Tandy in *Foxfire* at the Guthrie Theater in Minneapolis, she stunned audiences with her instant transformation from a woman in her eighties to a girl of sixteen, accomplished by removing her apron and whirling around, twirling it overhead. You would swear you could see the wrinkles melt away.

Few better illustrations of the advantages of casting against type could be offered than the Circle in the Square revival of Sam Shepard's *True West* (directed by Matthew Warchus) in which Philip Seymour Hoffman and John C. Reilly alternated on successive nights in the roles of two brothers, opposite in every way. They were both electrifying in both roles. Hoffman is a gentle, sensitive actor, while Reilly is larger and coarser. Yet, having seen them both play both parts, I felt that Hoffman was better as the brutish brother and Reilly as the sensitive writer. Casting *against* type proved superior in this adventurous production.

Jonathan Hadary's performance as the obese Herschel in Albert Innaurato's *Gemini* is another example of casting against type. Herschel is meant to be an adolescent genius, monstrously overweight, and hoarsely asthmatic. When Jonathan played him, he was in his late twenties, slender, and with the melodious voice of a singer. He played the character in padding, an enormous "fat suit" that his performance made completely credible. The important thing was that this gifted actor understood the isolation of genius, and could imagine how that could be exacerbated by obesity. Had we insisted on finding an actor with the right weight, we would have been deprived of this extraordinary piece of acting. Subsequently, by the way, an actor much closer to type replaced Jonathan. Wayne Knight, a very heavyset, hoarse actor (memorable in *Jurassic Park*) was also good in the part, but there was more genius in the original casting.

Aristotle Onassis proved that "tall, dark, and handsome" isn't the only kind of sex appeal. Many handsome leading men lack the magnetism John Malkovich displayed in the original production of *Burn This,* in which he became a matinee idol. As in this case, I often cast against external type if I feel the brilliance of the talent and the inner connection with the part justifies the risk.

In contemporary America, it's increasingly important to be free of racial prejudice in casting. If race is not specified, we should welcome an opportunity to cast a role with a talented black, Asian, or Hispanic actor. I began doing exactly that in 1965, casting an excellent young black actress Robbie McEnnery in the role of Sasha in Lanford Wilson's *The Sandcastle,* and I've continued to cast interracially throughout my career.

But in casting, you have to consider family relationships. Some audiences may have difficulty, for example, believing racially mixed siblings in Chekhov's *Three Sisters.* Color-blind casting in this instance could distract from the period and environment of Russia under the Czar. If we choose to cast in such a manner, we must be able to justify the liberty we are taking with Chekhov's original intentions.

But if your concept of *King Lear* occurs in a mythical time or, say, in the outback of contemporary Australia, then casting a black actor in the role of Edmund, the bastard son, might add a new dimension, if the rest of the family is white, or vice-versa. I think it could be argued that such casting fulfills, even enhances Shakespeare's intention.

When we were casting the part of the Amerasian teenage girl Geri in Lanford Wilson's *Redwood Curtain,* we never considered casting anyone who was not both of Caucasian and Asian races, because that racial mixture is essential to the circumstances of the play.

Yet not everyone feels so limited. When the British star Jonathan Pryce was cast as the Eurasian lead in *Miss Saigon,* it created a heated contretemps between the producer Cameron Mackintosh and Actors Equity Association. To some, it may seem just as logical for a Caucasian man to play the Asian half of this Eurasian character as for an Asian actor to play the Caucasian half. But as talented as Jonathan Pryce is, I doubt he ever could convince an audience that he's a teenage Amerasian girl looking for her American father.

On the other hand, Jonathan Pryce played a brilliant Matt Friedman opposite Hayley Mills in my London production of *Talley's Folly.* In spite of being British and ten years too young, Jonathan found Matt's middle-European Jewish traits well within reach. Having admired Judd Hirsch's original portrayal, he was able to build on Judd's inspiration.

Setting Up Auditions

Whenever possible, auditions should be held in a clean, neutral space that is large enough to accommodate everyone who needs to be there, but not so large as to be overwhelming. I prefer to avoid holding auditions on a stage because of the inevitable intimidation and the restricted intimacy it offers between director and actor. I also recommend avoiding small offices with desks and office equipment, because such places are usually too confining to be psychologically comfortable.

The number of people watching the audition should be kept to the absolute minimum, but all the following have a role to play in casting: the director, the playwright(s), the producer(s) or artistic director, the casting director, and the reader(s). No assistants, family members, or pets should be allowed (except, of course, your A.D.).

Your readers should provide each actor a chance to engage in the interplay of the scene. Avoid at all costs a stage manager reading the lines in a bored monotone, offering no eye contact. The sex of the reader is not critical, but it's helpful to have both male and female readers if the scenes are between different sexes.

The role of the reader is to help an actor achieve the best reading of which he's capable. A reader should pick up cues quickly, and speak the lines audibly and simply. A generous, sympathetic nature is an asset. Readers should be positioned near the actor, with their backs to the evaluators, so we can see the face and reactions of the actor who's auditioning. Even though readers should be flexible enough to follow the lead of the actor, they must be careful to avoid the temptation to *compete*.

In auditions, I never sit behind a table, because I don't want anything between the actor and me. I want to give each candidate my full attention and concentration. Most playwrights and producers welcome the safety of hiding behind a table, which is fine for them. I prefer to sit at the side of a table where I can take notes without having furniture between us. This position allows me to interact easily with the person auditioning.

Arrange the pictures and résumés in the order in which actors will be seen. You can check out the main points on the résumé during your introductory chat with the actor, and then pass it on to the playwright and producer. By the end of the audition, the picture should be returned to you, so you can make an initial selection. Put it in one of three stacks: Not Interested, Maybe, or Callback.

But the meaning of the stacks should remain obscure to the actors who are auditioning: don't label them.

It is also useful to have plenty of pens, pencils, and paper available so that whoever needs to make notes can do so. I like casting directors to provide us with lists of the actors we're going to see, with enough space between each name for brief notations. I use a check by the actor's name to indicate that I saw the audition but she's not what we're looking for and an X by those I'm interested in calling back.

Sufficient time should be allotted to each audition for

1. introductions,
2. a brief conversation to allow the director and actor personal interaction,
3. asking questions arising from interesting points on the résumé,
4. answering any questions an actor may have relating to the character or the scene,
5. time for the actor to relax and prepare,
6. the reading of the scene itself, and
7. a brief wrap-up, as the actor prepares to leave.

It's hard to accomplish all this in less than ten minutes. I usually schedule no more than five auditions per hour, which leaves a ten-minute break, and gives me a cushion of comfort in case I feel the need for a little more time with a particular actor. At this rate, you can keep on schedule and not inconvenience people waiting to see you.

An Audition Format

Let me describe the moment-by-moment path I recommend for an audition.

An assistant should introduce each actor to the director, and then return outside to monitor the arrivals of others.

You should *always* stand to be introduced, and offer to shake hands. Then, introduce the other people in the room, including their positions with the production that justify their presence. End by introducing the readers.

Invite the actor to take a seat in the middle of a well-lighted area, and ask a couple of questions about points of interest on his résumé. This gives him a chance to relax and talk about himself, something almost everyone enjoys doing.

You might want to ask if he's read the whole play or only the sides. If the actor hasn't read the whole script, briefly describe the circumstances of the scene, and how the scene fits into the play as a whole. If the actor has read the play, just offer to answer any questions he may have. Be sure to pronounce any unusual words or names that appear in the scene.

I then *always* say these magic words:

> Please feel free to do as much or as little as you like. If you feel like moving around, feel free. If you prefer to sit, that's fine too. Now relax, take your time, and begin when you are ready. I want you to be happy with your audition.

During the reading, don't let anyone in the room distract in any way. For example, eating and smoking should be prohibited, as well as reading newspapers or other material.

Give your full attention to the actor and try not to take too many notes, because excessive writing also can be a distraction. If for any reason there's an interruption, invite the actor to begin again. Sometimes, he will stop and ask permission to start over. I *always* grant this request, and remind him again to relax.

Watch for the actor's connection to the material: his creation of the surrounding environment; the interaction with his partner, the reader; and your belief that the spoken text comes from the actor's thoughts, reflected in his eyes and in the expression of his mouth.

Also, you should ask yourself:

- Has the actor followed your instructions and achieved relaxation before beginning?

- Can you see spontaneous creativity as he explores the scene, or is it all cut and dried according to some pattern he's worked out ahead of time?
- Does the actor show sensitivity to the humor and style of the piece?
- Are impulses flowing, and the emotions unforced?
- Can you sense the actor's commitment to standards in his work?
- Is there some degree of personal investment in the character?
- Does he speak the lines as written, or is there an improvisatory approximation of the dialogue?
- Are the actor's voice and diction appropriate to the scene, and the size of the audition room? How about your eventual performance stage?
- What details of the actor's approach seem to make the scene come to life for him?

At the end of the scene, say something positive and reassuring (even if it's a little white lie) like, "Good. Very nice. Thank you."

As the actor is preparing to leave, check on any information you might need, such as his height or the name of his agent. It's good to recount the scheduled dates of rehearsals and performances. I usually try to give actors an idea of *when* they might expect to hear about a casting decision. If I have *loved* the audition, I let the actor know immediately how much I was moved or amused and that I will want to see him again in a callback (even though callbacks may not be finalized until the end of the day).

Finally, shake hands again, and thank him for coming in.

You should treat each actor with courtesy, dignity, and respect. Try to make each actor feel that you are his ally and that you want him to give the best audition he can. After all, it's the truth. You are looking for the best cast possible, so be sure that each actor gets a chance to show why he is the best casting for the role. Your goals should be to be fair to each actor, and to give each an equal opportunity to shine.

Never discuss or permit a discussion about an actor's reading while he's in the room. A minute or two should be allotted between each audition, so the playwright, producer, and director may exchange quick observations about the reading before the next audition begins.

Keep in mind that in an audition, the director is also being judged. If you conduct the audition with the same tone of mutual respect and adventure that you hope to establish in rehearsals, actors will want to work with you. Neither the playwright nor the producer should be allowed to disturb your opportunity to work with the actor.

At the end of the day, go through the stacks of résumés you've set aside as Maybe or Callback, and discuss each choice with your collaborative partners. At this point, you can return the Not Interested stack to the casting director, but until a cast is selected, keep the pictures of all actors who are still in the running. You may want to review them at home, looking at faces in combinations.

Callbacks

It's a good idea to select two or three candidates for each part from the initial auditions and call them back for a second reading. Few actors do as well the second time, but this is so universally true that it makes the callbacks an invaluable opportunity for reassessment.

The purpose of callbacks is to see the leading contenders in closer proximity to each other, so you can compare the assets and drawbacks of each reading. It's a time to clarify what you liked about each audition and to assess who has the better potential to play the role as you imagine it.

It also gives you the opportunity to look at chemistry, the interaction of pairs or groups of characters. For example, if you're casting three brothers, you will probably look for some physical resemblances, harmonious textures, or coloring, and want to compare ages, heights, and weights. Of course, not all brothers bear a clear resemblance to each other, but the audience must believe their kinship. This concern gave my casting of *Cat on a Hot Tin Roof* a freshness, because John Lepard, who played Gooper, could easily have been the older brother of Jason Kuykendall, who played Brick. The similarity between their appearances emphasized the vast difference in their characters.

For callbacks, I often ask actors to read in pairs, so I can see how combinations work. Sometimes, you will want to mix and match those combinations, and as long as you don't overstep the generosity of the actors, they will usually accommodate your request.

In the callbacks, if you have any suggestions based on the first audition, give them before the reading begins. If there are qualities you are looking for specifically, be sure to mention them.

Reaching a Consensus

Both the playwright and the producer must approve each casting decision, but first the director should make his choices for each part. I find it useful to pin the pictures of my first choices on a wall, along with alternatives, so we all can envision how different combinations could work. It helps to group together the faces of the cast you're proposing.

In the event of disagreement, remember that the director is the one who's responsible for getting good performances. It's important to listen to objections and to hear their reasons, but your job is to convince the producer and playwright that your casting choices are the actors you need to achieve the results you all desire.

Don't be stubborn, but neither should you be weak and vacillating. Leadership is called for, and this is a test of your ability to communicate, persuade, and compromise. Diplomacy is the key. Each participant has a power of veto, but *you* have the responsibility to deliver the performance.

Your goal is to persuade your colleagues to let you have your way. Sometimes you have to decide which casting is worth a fight and where you can take the chance of being wrong. Your Hamlet must be the director's choice, but perhaps the producer's favorite Osric has merits that could make a profitable contribution to the production as a whole. Choose your battles wisely.

Contact the actors as soon as a decision has been reached. Otherwise, you may find your choice for the part has taken another job. You'd be wise to call first the actor who's being offered the part and to contact the others only after the job has been *accepted*. Actors appreciate it when you take the time to inform them personally of your decision, and it shows the respect you have for their work. Unfortunately, I don't know anyone who does this. As Boyd, the cynical director in Lanford Wilson's *Book of Days* sneers, "Yeah, I'm known for my compassion." And so are we all—*not!*

With a good group of actors, well chosen for their roles, the director's job seems a good deal less impossible.

Chapter Five

First Rehearsal

T he first day of rehearsal is the hardest. With the exception of opening night, which is completely unbearable, the first rehearsal offers the most trying test of a director's nerves. It sometimes seems like the main objective is just to get through to a second rehearsal without anyone quitting.

Actually, it's a bit more complicated than that.

The first rehearsal is the director's best opportunity to

- identify the goals for the work you are about to undertake,
- outline the process by which you hope to reach those goals, and
- establish the standards of discipline the process will demand.

The first rehearsal is a great chance to articulate the principles on which your goals, your process, and your standards are based. A statement of principles requires an honest self-examination that would make Socrates proud. It's likely you'll feel a little embarrassed because by publicly sharing your most profound beliefs, you risk ridicule or cynicism. It feels so uncool to be deeply honest about your highest artistic ambitions.

Many directors simply do an end run around this hurdle, but that just results in no principles being established at all. Instead, the standards of the marketplace become the unspoken guidelines for rehearsals. When problems begin to crop up, they will arise from aiming for commercial and material success. That's one reason our contemporary theater seldom reaches the eloquence of uncompromising principle that's visible in any painting by van Gogh.

Establishing Principles

The theater, like America itself, is a melting pot of people with vastly different experiences, goals, and dreams. Some people become actors in the hope of becoming stars, with the fortune they imagine accompanies such fame. Some are driven to become actors by low self-esteem, even though it may be disguised as vanity, or even arrogance. Other actors may possess an amazing sort of selflessness, but can express themselves only by creating a human disguise.

So don't assume that all the actors in your cast are motivated by the same dreams. You are the one person who can focus their attention on what *really* matters, and rouse them to new heights of creativity. Ideally, our job is to inspire every actor to give the performance of her life.

During my first rehearsal, after the general greetings and formalities have been observed, I usually begin with a statement of artistic principles that goes something like this:

> I believe that acting is behaving truthfully in imaginary circumstances. As a director, I will never ask you to do anything more, although I may ask you to behave truthfully a little faster or a little louder.
>
> In the art of acting, we have to examine our own lives with uncompromising clarity, so we can use our personal experiences to illuminate the souls of the characters.
>
> Artistic creativity originates in the unconscious regions of our psyche, where our dreams and fears are born. Because creative impulses are not subject to our direct command, we have to lure them out indirectly, using Stanislavski's "Magic If."
>
> We have only three resources we can offer for our imaginations to explore:
>
> * personal experience,
> * vicarious (or observed) experience, and
> * spontaneous creativity, whose treasures lie hidden in the present moment.
>
> First, we have to explore how our personal experiences relate to the play, and then courageously contribute our deepest, most private images to the creative work.
>
> Then, we can start watching for people who might serve as models for the characters. The behavioral details we pick up from these observations can ignite our imaginations. We need to find relevant psychological, sociological, and artistic material that we can read with creative curiosity, to increase our understanding of the country, time, and social context of the play.

During rehearsals and performances, we must always be alive in the present moment, and in touch with our acting partners, always available for spontaneous inspiration.

There are six imaginary circumstances that we must consider each time we begin to work:

- Where am I?
- When is it?
- Who am I?
- What do I want?
- Why do I want it?
- How am I going to try to get it?

I believe, as Stanislavski tells us, that inspiration is the result of three interlocking phenomena: relaxation, concentration, and imagination.

I believe our responsibility is to create a living play, and using the script as a road map, to *live* the lives of the characters onstage, not just represent them.

I believe "interpretation" in acting is to make the play and the character *real* to yourself.

I believe the theater is a collaborative art, and that our shared goal is to create an ensemble of artists who inhabit the *world* of the play.

These statements, when spoken from the heart at the first rehearsal, can kindle a remarkable response in many actors. If you've cast a company with genuine artists, not merely types, these words express lofty goals they've seldom heard in the hard world of professional survival. It can be refreshing, stimulating, and liberating for actors to dedicate their work to artistic goals, rather than to the commonplace goals of agents, opening nights, and critical reviews.

It's good for an artist to be pure of purpose and demanding in discipline. I often quote Jim Tuttle, a teacher of acting in the Sandy Meisner mold, who advised:

"*Give* everything you have for your art, and demand everything you *need.*"

The word *ensemble* is tossed about fairly frequently. It should mean more than just teamwork. True ensemble work comes from establishing a bond of mutual trust and respect within the cast. Trust must be earned, and the first step is to establish a goal the cast can share: to live in the world of the play. Everyone should demand the best of themselves and each other.

Of course, your principles may (and probably should) differ from mine. If you share them, by all means use them. But it's far more important to articulate your own.

You may want your cast to aspire to a whole different set of principles. For example, you might say:

I believe theater ought to be as thrilling as a circus, with the actors, like aerialists, daring to risk all on the high wire of the present tense. I believe an audience ought to be kept on the edge of their seats, gripping with white knuckles the arms of their chairs. I believe artists of the theater should make bold, vivid choices, rather than passive, safe, timid interpretations.

Or:

I believe theater should be fun, and that's why they call it play! I believe you should feel more alive onstage than anywhere else. I believe the theater is an evanescent art that bubbles with the fleeting spirit of life, and that the essence of the theater lies in the living moment. I think the most memorable moments in the theater rarely occur *on* the lines, but *between* them, in the thrill of improvisation that risks all the *plans* of rehearsal on the *actual* experience of the instant.

Or:

I believe the stage is a forum for the glory of the spoken word. I believe the theater is a world of ideas, and the actor should express these ideas through the clear, precise, glorious enunciation of language.

Or:

I believe the theater is a world of imagistic gestalt. I believe that the stage offers an opportunity for visual experiences of the imagination that can never be duplicated by the mundane reality of the movies. It's a canvas for heroes and heroines, of abstraction and insight, for dreams and imagination.

Or:

I believe the theater is a temple to the truth of human experience. The script is the inspiration of a prophet, and the actors are priests, leading the audience through a transcendental enlightenment of empathy and understanding.

Your credo will be found in deep self-examination. Dig for it. Strive to express it.

By the way, I endorse all of the above beliefs, and I invoke any of them at my first rehearsal if the exploration of the artistic terrain suggests the need.

Setting Standards

To achieve the idealistic principles you've posed, you'll need to establish standards of discipline for which you'll hold your actors responsible.

Certainly first among these is the need for promptness. When a cast has come together, prepared to work, few things can be more deflating than the absence of an essential member of the team. The minutes of waiting that tick by seem like hours, as creativity is kept penned up at the starting gate. Promptness is basic to establishing an atmosphere of mutual respect, and there are few excuses that can repair the damage caused by the disrespect of tardiness. Stanislavski dismissed his company from rehearsal rather than start late.

Voice, movement, and emotions are the actors' instruments. If we value actors as artists, we must encourage the vocal, physical, and emotional warm-ups that are essential before playing. Recognizing the potential for injury, no dancer would dare perform without first limbering up his muscles. Similarly, no actor should attempt to impersonate another human being without first warming up the suppleness of his own body. No singer would attempt an aria without first singing some scales. Likewise, no actor should try to delve into the subtleties of characterization without exercising "the tip of the tongue, the lips, and the teeth." Sanford Meisner pointed out that the first quality of a good actor is good diction.

The keys to good vocal production are relaxing the jaw and locating the source of sound in the body, supported by the diaphragm. Deep, efficient breathing is closely related to relaxation. Relaxation is central to emotional work, so the awareness and control of breathing is a gateway to creativity.

Encourage your cast to warm up before every rehearsal, whether at home or when they arrive. Make sure that mats are available for the cast to use, if they choose to come early and warm up in the rehearsal room.

The story of a mishap illustrates the need for warm-ups. One of the best actors I've worked with is my old friend, colleague, collaborator, and successor at Circle Rep, Tanya Berezin. We were presenting Edward Albee's *Who's Afraid of Virginia Woolf?* at Saratoga Springs in upstate New York, but Tanya's extraordinary creation of Martha (opposite Tony Roberts as George) was hampered on opening night. Without warming up before her first entrance, she stepped off a six-inch platform and due to tension, pulled a ligament in the arch of her foot, just as she delivered the famous line: "What a dump!" The result was her Martha literally hobbled through the remainder of the performance. Her limp severely affected her concentration and the quality of her accomplishment. The role of Martha is not improved with a cane. Don't, as I warn my casts, *ever* take that risk!

The third discipline I expect of actors is unusual but also quite essential. Before we begin to explore the beats to discover a physical life, I require my actors to learn the lines for the beat that is scheduled for rehearsal. Let me explain why.

First, the script is a "road map" of the experiences we're going to explore. Before you undertake a road trip, it's a good idea to know the map. The author's lines are the guidelines for the experiences that lie beneath the text. There is every reason to begin our journey of exploration by memorizing the clues we've been given: the dialogue.

Secondly, the actors will be encouraged to use rehearsal props and rehearsal clothes right from the beginning. Naturally, their hands need to be free to use these indispensable elements.

Thirdly, the actors need to explore where the lines come from, and they'll need their eyes to search for motivation, focusing on the eyes and behavior of their fellow players, *not* on *a script*.

Finally, a director must detect the impulses that arise from the needs of the characters. Impulses suggest a potential for movement that best expresses the action of the scene. In order to see these impulses, we need the actors to explore each beat moment by moment, with their imaginations fully engaged in believing the circumstances of the scene.

It's a rare play that would require a character to carry a script and read his thoughts from it. If a person is reading from a manuscript, the best physical life would be to sit comfortably and never move. For most plays, the script must be *absent* in order for a director to see where impulses really come from.

Once you spot an actor's *impulse* to move, you can advise him *where* to move. Take an actor's impulse, born in his experience of the circumstances, and *transform* it into a move that advances the scene. In this way, the movement is truly organic to the work of the actor and cannot be achieved independently of the actor's contribution.

Once the actors understand this, they cheerfully trade off their scripts in exchange for moves that are genuinely meaningful to them, rather than arbitrarily assigned.

By the time we have discussed all this discipline at the first rehearsal, it's usually time for a break. You may need one too. Take five, if you like.

Dividing the Play

Following the break, I distribute the rehearsal schedule/character-beat breakdown chart and take the actors through the script, marking exactly where each beat begins and ends. We all go through this together, slowly and clearly, marking our scripts as we go. Using *The Seagull*, it sounds something like this:

> At the top of page 11, before the first stage direction (*Curtain Rises*) mark Beat 1, beginning with Medvedenko's line, "Why do you always wear black?" and call it "Half-hour."

On page 13, near the bottom, see Yakov's line "Yes, sir." and the stage direction (*Exits*)? Mark Beat 2, beginning with Treplov's line "How's this for a theater?" and call it "New Forms."

Wait until each cast member has marked her script accordingly, before going on to indicate the next beat.

Once you've gone through the entire script and everyone has marked the beats, go over the character-beat breakdown chart, and explain what the X's and O's mean. Make clear how the beats on the chart correspond to the beats we've marked in the script and how the beats are called on the rehearsal schedule. In my rehearsals, if a character has an O, they're not called the first time the scene is called, but must come to all subsequent rehearsals of the beat.

Ask the actors to identify any conflicts they might have with the schedule so you can try to accommodate their needs. If the stage manager has gathered potential conflicts from the cast *before* the first rehearsal, you'll be aware of them as you make the schedule, so very few adjustments will be needed. But some new conflicts may have arisen, and you can alter the rehearsal schedule to accommodate those unexpected changes.

By showing your concern for people's time and commitments, you establish an up-front respect that allows you to demand that everyone adhere religiously to the schedule everyone has agreed to.

Showing the Renderings

If at all possible, your designers should be at the first rehearsal. Their sketches of the settings and/or costumes can communicate more clearly than words to start the actors on the road toward imaginative creations.

Giving the designers a chance to present their renderings to the cast also emphasizes the collaborative nature of the work process. It should inspire the actors to achieve the same level of beauty they see in the designers' work.

The set renderings show the actors what the environment of the play will look like to the audience. This first sight of the sets should be a visual experience that will guide the cast's own visualizations throughout rehearsals.

The costume sketches, of course, are central to an actor's curiosity, because these will be the clothes of her character. If an actor sees the character differently from the designer, it's important for both to have an early occasion to discuss and resolve different interpretations of how the character should look.

John Lee Beatty's sketches of his sets often include an idea of the kind of lighting that he anticipates Dennis Parichy will provide. This comes as a result of working together over a long period of time. But even if the designers are strangers, the set designer's sketch showing the light sources and tone can be helpful in the communication between a director and the cast.

If you know pieces of music you plan to use in the production, the first rehearsal is a good time to play them. Music can unify the cast with a shared experience and incidentally, soothe the director's savage breast.

Walking the Ground Plan

Once the set designer has shown her drawings of the set, walk the cast through the diagram on the floor that the stage managers have taped out.

Using the rendering as a reference, point out where the windows, doors, and platforms shown in the drawing are depicted by the outline of the set that's taped on the floor. If there are multiple sets, make sure everyone understands which color of tape relates to which act.

As you walk through the set with the cast, discuss the surrounding environment. The door that's pictured on the rendering is represented by a slash of tape on the floor. Point out which way the door swings and on which side the handle will be found, demonstrating in pantomime how the door opens. If you don't know, the designer should clarify it for you as soon as possible. Describe where the door leads to in relationship to the rest of the house, or the town or countryside around.

Indicate which direction the town is from here, or the lake, or any other element that is discussed or might be imagined in the play.

Describe the environment specifically, so the actors can imagine with their senses the sounds, the smells, the temperatures, the breezes, the nature of the light, and the direction of the sunrise or sunset. In other words, using the rendering as a starting point, invite the actors to begin creating the three-dimensional, five-sensory environment that the ground plan taped on the floor merely outlines, just as the script only outlines the experience of the play.

The actors' imaginations must give dimension to thin pieces of painted canvas that represent, perhaps, a thick stone wall. The environment of the play should inhabit the rehearsal room in three dimensions, so the ensemble's work springs from a shared creation of the world around it.

The lines taped on the floor must *become*, in the actors' imaginations, the walls and platforms they *represent*. An actor who stands within a space outlined on the floor should be able to imagine herself alone in a room, while people on the other side of those lines are in another place.

Discuss with the cast the *fourth wall*, through which the audience will see the play. The actors need to resolve the question: "If the audience isn't there in the play, what *is* there?" After a discussion, the cast might try an exercise in which each actor creates one element on the fourth wall, seeing it, touching it, and describing it. Then the next actor relates to each element created before him, and adds his own creation. Creating together in this playful game provides collective solutions to a problem they share.

Discussing the Play

The real work of the first rehearsal is to direct the cast toward the work that will follow. It's an ideal occasion for you to discuss your ideas about the play.

Describe what the play is about and share your feelings about why it's important to do *this* play at *this* time or for *this* audience. You can base your discussions on the relevance of the play to our lives, the excellence of the author's artistry, or just why it will be fun to work on.

Basic Research

Every play has a context within larger social and political circumstances. As Hamlet describes it:

> the purpose of playing, whose end, both at the first and now, was and is, to hold, as 'twere, a mirror up to nature, to show virtue her own feature, scorn her own image, and the very age and body of the time, his form and pressure.

The cast needs to understand the context of the play within the fabric of the society that surrounds it.

You should spend about 20 percent of your rehearsal time on research that will equip the actors to bring the text of the play to life, and you should kick off basic research in the first rehearsal by describing the general circumstances that surround the play.

Two circumstances are central to all plays: Time and Place.

> Where does it take place? Pay detailed attention to the places where the action occurs: the continent, country, region, state or province, city or village, house or building, rooms or spaces.

> When is it? Consider the century, the years, the seasons, the months, and days covered by the action, as well as the specific hours of the morning, afternoon, twilight, or night.

Aquaint the cast with the historical period in which the play was written, as well as the period the play depicts.

The basic facts of time and place should be placed in a context of social circumstances:

- the geography, weather, vegetation, and natural resources of the locale,
- the racial origins, language, and history of the population,
- the sources of commerce, form of government, education, religion, and social conditions (such as housing, wages, cost of living, social security, and health) of the time,
- the cultural life and institutions, the literature, music, painting, sculpture, even the museums and monuments of the civilization the play embraces.

To prepare for your first rehearsal, consult the *Encyclopedia Britannica* for this sort of information, which can be supplemented with the use of an atlas and an almanac. Of course, on the Internet, Google can point the way to a kaleidoscope of source material.

Involve the cast in collectively exploring the world of the play. At the first rehearsal, you might assign each actor a specific topic to research in detail. At subsequent rehearsals, each actor can report on her special topic, and the cast can pool its research. In my production of *Three Sisters,* for example, the actor playing the schoolmaster, Kuligan, reported on the Russian educational system, while Vershinin researched the Russian military under the Czar.

In addition to these "dry" facts, encourage the cast to read biographies of important people of the era and to indulge in novels or short stories that capture the social fabric of the time. Sometimes, movies that re-create a bygone era can be a source of inspiration and information. If a film has been researched with painstaking exactitude, as were Stanley Kubrik's *Barry Lyndon* and Martin Scorsese's *The Age of Innocence*, a cast researching the same period might benefit from seeing such a movie together.

Of course, one must beware of the "Hollywoodization" that is common, for example, in the films of Cecil B. de Mille. In the recent films of *Troy* and *Alexander*, the designers cheerfully admitted they ignored research when they could imagine something more "interesting."

But Laurence Olivier's film of *Henry V* accurately shows the contrast between the Elizabethan age, when the play was *written,* and the earlier time of Agincourt, which the play *depicts*. Kenneth Branaugh's *Henry V* dramatizes the same fifteenth century from a very different perspective, but with similar accuracy.

Music of the country and the period of the play may communicate a lot about the texture of the civilization. Paintings or photographs also may provide the actors with delicious details that spark the creative imagination. Victoria

Holloway is a director who asks her cast members to collect a scrapbook of images that are helpful to their work. These are all useful tools of research.

Biographies

The actors should investigate the specific circumstances of each character.

- Who are they? (In terms of both genetics and environmental influence?)
- How and when did the characters meet?
- What is the nature of their relationships?
- What shared past do the actors need to create together?

Actors should become acquainted with their characters on an intimate and personal level before they begin to speak their words.

At the first rehearsal, assign each actor the mission of creating her character's biography. An actor once asked, "How long should it be?" The answer is, of course, "As long as it *needs* to be," whatever it takes to suggest an imaginative, yet factual foundation of a character's life.

A character biography should begin with a history of the character's parentage. In some cases, it might be necessary to think back even further in the family lineage. For example, I would expect an actor who's playing Prior in *Angels in America* to invent a whole family tree.

An actor needs to imagine the major events in the character's life:

- from birth through childhood and early influences;
- through his education, detailing important catalysts along the way, such as a significant teacher, pastor, coach, uncle, or sibling;
- through crushes, courtships, marriages, divorces, the birth of children;
- the experiences of the death of loved ones in his life;
- the choice of career, employment history, and so forth, right up to the moment we meet the character in the play.

Advise your cast to pay special attention to significant turning points in the character's life, when goals change, when hopes are deferred, when the sting of disappointment is experienced, and when particular fears or phobias are generated.

Encourage the actors to imagine who their characters' heroes are—who stirred the character's imagination and stimulated emulation. One actor I worked with described this as figuring out who the character was "understudying."

Exploring the specific likes, dislikes, and tastes of a character can give an actor insights into her nature: her favorite food, song, sport, smell, movie star, novel, hobby. What is her deepest fear, most repulsive image, or most hated activity?

If an actor pursues her character to the most intimate level, her investigation can even lead to esoteric destinations, such as the character's masturbation fantasies. This is not the business of the director, but anything the actor finds helpful must be respected.

Personalization

The most critical stage of creating a character is to personalize the inventions. As an actor makes up the story of her character's life, she should endow the history of that character with as many specific events from her *own* life as possible. She should bestow any actual experiences that parallel those of the character. She should use the images of the faces (and smells, and texture of the skin) of her father, mother, sisters, brothers, and lovers to whatever extent they apply. Encourage your actors to use their own histories whenever they are relevant to their creations.

By now it should become clear that the characters in the play have had some experiences for which the actors can find no parallel in their own lives. Actors are stimulated by differences they see in their characters, as well as similarities. Both can kindle empathy and understanding.

Some differences can be explored through improvisation, so that the experiences of the actors and those of the characters *blend* into an organic creation, no matter their origin.

For example, if an actor is playing a suicidal character but has never attempted suicide in his own life, improvisation can be a bridge to understanding the character's desperation.

In the following chapter, I'll describe how one such improvisation gave my cast of *The Seagull* an indelible personal experience of suicide.

Of course, Sanford Meisner downplays the importance of characterization, in order to help actors concentrate on the far more important discovery of truthful actions and responses. It's true that many actors, particularly untrained amateurs, get so wrapped up in their *character* that they forget to explore their actual experience in the circumstances.

We must remember that when Stanislavski proposes that we should imagine all circumstances in terms of "If this were true, what would I do?" that it is essential to focus on the "I", not some imagined response of the character in the play. Stanislavski put it very directly, when he observed, "Always and forever, you are playing yourself onstage."

Still, many actors are genuinely inspired by characterization, and if it leads to spontaneous and truthful behavior, characterization must be regarded as an important source of creativity. Stanislavski recommends first exploring the play in your own personal terms, and then adding the elements of characterization late in the rehearsal process.

Emblems of Identity

At some point in the first rehearsal, I empty my pockets on a table and invite everyone to analyze my identity from the things I carry in my pockets. When the police arrest a suspect, this is the first order of business, not only for the obvious reason of checking for weapons but also because, as Sherlock Holmes could tell you, we can deduce a person's fundamental identity from detecting the details of such evidence. Alvina Krause, who taught me acting at Northwestern University, used to repeat this dictum:

> Heredity deals the cards, environment plays them, and the resulting hand is laid down for all the world to see.

Identity isn't limited to your driver's license. A human being is a collection of values, and these values are embodied in choices. So the essential things that we choose to carry with us provide important clues to our nature. These "props" are emblems of our identity, as surely as certain fossils speak of dinosaurs.

When the actors have understood how identity is expressed by choices, ask them to imagine what objects are to be found in the pockets and purses of each character. What keys, cosmetics, drugs, instruments, cards, money, mementos, amulets, and supplies are considered essential enough to this character's identity that she *always* carries them.

What rings or necklaces or anklets or earrings are worn, and where did they come from? Those items that were gifts carry emotional value as well, because they symbolize the emotional life of relationships. Your grandmother's wedding ring is not just an article, but also an expression of value. The gifts we treasure bring special meaning to our lives as well as to those of fictional characters.

When actors consider such personalized values, they can begin to live within their characters or as one actor put it, to wear their underwear.

Ready to Start

You should approach the first rehearsal thoroughly prepared. Too much is at stake to improvise. Take time to think about the journey ahead, and to collect your thoughts, so you can *extemporize.*

At the first rehearsal, you are Henry V addressing your troops before a battle in which their very lives and fortunes may be at risk. Certainly, the mood in the rehearsal room will reflect the same uneasiness before a battle that Shakespeare paints so well:

> Now entertain conjecture of a time
> When creeping murmur and the poring dark
> Fill the wide vessel of the universe.

At the first rehearsal, the director must provide "A little touch of Harry in the night."

In order to be up to this challenge, I pray to the great god of battle by outlining my thoughts on the eve of the first meeting. Even Lincoln used the back of an envelope to frame his thoughts on the Gettysburg address. One size does not fit all. Each play demands specific preparation.

Appendix E is a verbatim transcript of my first rehearsal of *Summer and Smoke*.

The Read-Through

If you've conducted a successful morning rehearsal and everyone has returned for the afternoon, and if you feel it's important for the cast to read the play together, the second half of the first rehearsal day may be as good a time as any to take the plunge. Resist reading the play just for the hell of it or because it's expected. If the play is known to all (as may be the case with an old play), little is gained from going over familiar territory. Read only if you feel reading the play has a clear artistic value to the cast.

There are many reasons that could be cited as legitimate artistic needs to read the play:

- to hear the particular music in the language of the play,
- to experience the overall arc of action that might not be evident to the individual actors,
- to share the sense of style or tone,
- to get an accurate sense of length that might provide the director and author an opportunity to look for possible cuts, and/or
- to give your design colleagues a chance to hear the play in a unified way that may affect their own contributions to the production.

There are other reasons to read a play that ought to be resisted:

- to reassure the producers they have made a wise choice of play and/or cast,

- to give the company a self-congratulatory opportunity to celebrate their employment, or
- to give extroverted actors a platform to show off their "brilliance."

You must evaluate what's to be gained from reading the play and weigh it against what's likely to be lost. A reading can have the adverse effect of pressing actors into giving premature "performances." Avoiding that, the actors may read in an uninspired, flat mumble that distorts the experience of the play. It may give actors with small roles dismaying evidence that their parts are smaller than they realized and that playing these cameo roles may be a career mistake. It may give cast members a disagreeable opportunity to judge each other's "performance" and to compare jealously how much better a role could be cast.

In short, it often inhibits the finer artists and encourages the hacks to shameless displays.

Still, there are legitimate reasons for reading the play together, and if you decide to do so, it's important to guide the actors carefully through a first reading.

Assure the cast that its reading is not a performance, and won't be judged as such. It should be regarded as an exploratory expedition. Encourage cast members to read simply, audibly, and clearly, but not to push for emotions or effects. Ask them to make sense of what they read and to minimize acting pauses. A first reading should be brisk, light, and simple, looking for the overall progression of the play.

At the same time, we have to acknowledge that a first reading can be a unique opportunity for actors to learn about the play by giving them their first chance to speak the lines aloud in the context of the whole. This is a moment of "artistic *gestalt*," in which an actor's first impression may leave an indelible imprint. For this reason, it's important to allow the actors' imaginations full freedom to fly if inspiration is somehow sparked.

These seemingly contradictory, paradoxical instructions demonstrate both the danger and the potential inherent in the company's first reading of the play together.

End of the Day

By the time you've accomplished all these things, you and the cast members may feel as if you've undertaken a great adventure together, and perhaps that it's too late to turn back now. As you remind them of their calls for tomorrow, you should be able to sense the excitement in the room. It has been a long day, but you have given them a great deal to think about. If you have done your job well, they'll all be back.

Top: Balm in Gilead *by Lanford Wilson, La Mama, 1965: Neil Flanagan, Gregory Rozakis, Mary Thomlin, Savannah Bentley. Photo by Frederick Eberstadt. The first full-length play produced off-off-Broadway, and the first of the historic collaborations between Lanford Wilson and MWM that have lasted forty years.*

Bottom: The Haunted Host *by Robert Patrick, Caffe Cino, 1964: Robert Patrick, William M. Hoffman. Photo by James D. Gossage. MWM got strong performances from two famous playwrights in their early years acting off-off-Broadway.*

Top: The HOT L BALTIMORE *by Lanford Wilson, Circle Rep, 1973: Rob Thirkield, Zane Lasky, Conchata Ferrell. HOT L ran for 1,166 performances and won the NY Drama Critics' Circle Award for Best American Play and MWM's first Obie.*
Bottom: The Sea Horse *by Edward J. Moore, Circle Rep, 1974: Edward J. Moore, Conchata Ferrell. The third hit from Circle Rep within a year won the Vernon Rice Award for Best Play. Photos by Ken Howard.*

Top: Knock Knock *by Jules Feiffer, Circle Rep, 1976: Daniel Seltzer, Nancy Snyder, Neil Flanagan, Judd Hirsch. MWM's Broadway debut on his birthday, February 24, 1976, earned him his first Tony nomination for Best Director. Photo by Herbert Migdoll.*

Bottom: Gemini *by Albert Innaurato, Circle Rep, 1977: Reed Birney, Jonathan Hadary. Photo by Ken Howard. A slim Hadary played the obese Herschel to perfection, defying ideas of typecasting. The play ran for 1,788 performances, the fourth longest in Broadway history.*

Left: Fifth of July *by Lanford Wilson, Circle Rep, 1978: Danton Stone, Jeff Daniels, Amy Wright, Nancy Snyder. Photo by Ken Howard (print courtesy Billy Rose Theatre Division, The New York Public Library for the Performing Arts, Astor, Lenox and Tilden Foundations). The first of what would become "The Talley Trilogy."*

Bottom: Fifth of July, *New Apollo Theater, 1980: Swoosie Kurtz, Christopher Reeve, Danton Stone, MWM, Jeff Daniels. Photo by Martha Swope. Kurtz won the Tony for Best Supporting Actress and MWM (staging the curtain call here) had a third Tony nomination for Best Director.*

Talley's Folly by Lanford Wilson, Circle Rep, 1979: Judd Hirsch, Trish Hawkins. Photo by Gerry Goodstein (print courtesy Billy Rose Theatre Division, The New York Public Library for the Performing Arts, Astor, Lenox and Tilden Foundations). Talley's Folly *transferred to the Brooks Atkinson Theater, where it won the 1980 Pulitzer Prize for Drama and the NY Drama Critics' Circle Award for Best Play. MWM had his second Tony nomination for Best Director.*

Top: A Tale Told *by Lanford Wilson, Circle Rep, 1981: Michael Higgins, Fritz Weaver. The third in the Talley Trilogy followed the other two to the Mark Taper Forum in Los Angeles, but never made it to Broadway.*

Bottom: Talley & Son *by Lanford Wilson, Circle Rep, 1985: Helen Stenborg, Lindsey Ginter, Jimmie Ray Weeks, Farley Granger. This much-revised and retitled revival earned Obies for Stenborg and Granger. Photos by Gerry Goodstein (prints courtesy Billy Rose Theatre Division, The New York Public Library for the Performing Arts, Astor, Lenox and Tilden Foundations).*

The Farm by David Storey, Circle Rep, 1976: Nancy Snyder, Trish Hawkins, Jack Gwillim. Photo by Ken Howard. After a successful run at the Academy Festival Theater in Lake Forest, Illinois, MWM replaced Richard Gere with Jeff Daniels for the Circle Rep run in New York.

Top: Serenading Louie *by Lanford Wilson, Circle Rep, 1976: Michael Storm, Edward J. Moore. Photo by Ken Howard. MWM received his third Obie, and remounted the play for the Academy Festival Theater, with Tony Roberts replacing Storm.*

Bottom: Who's Afraid of Virginia Woolf? *by Edward Albee, Circle Rep, 1984: Tony Roberts, Michael Ayr. MWM restaged this avant-garde production for the National Theater of Japan in Tokyo with Alan Feinstein replacing Roberts. Photos by Gerry Goodstein (prints courtesy Billy Rose Theatre Division, The New York Public Library for the Performing Arts, Astor, Lenox and Tilden Foundations).*

My Life *by Corinne Jacker, Circle Rep, 1977: Christopher Reeve, William Hurt (seated). Hurt received an Obie for his performance, and the cast included Reeve, Jeff Daniels, Douglass Watson, Nancy Snyder, and Tanya Berezin. Photo by Ken Howard (print courtesy Billy Rose Theatre Division, The New York Public Library for the Performing Arts, Astor, Lenox and Tilden Foundations).*

William Hurt in three memorable roles at Circle Rep.
Top left: Hamlet *by William Shakespeare, 1979. Hamlet was the quintessential collaboration between an actor and director in the longtime collaboration between William Hurt and MWM.*
Top right: Childe Byron *by Romulus Linney, 1981. Hurt played Lord Byron as "Mad, bad, and dangerous to know."*
Bottom: Richard II *by William Shakespeare, 1981. Although this Celtic production was a "flawed concept," Hurt was a moving Richard. Photos by Gerry Goodstein (prints courtesy Billy Rose Theatre Division, The New York Public Library for the Performing Arts, Astor, Lenox and Tilden Foundations).*

Hamlet *by William Shakespeare, Circle Rep, 1979.*
Top: Michael Ayr, William Hurt. This is the beginning of one of the best fight scenes ever staged by the legendary B. H. Barry.
Bottom: Timothy Shelton, Douglass Watson, Beatrice Straight, Lindsay Crouse. Seen here in Ophelia's mad scene, Lindsay Crouse played opposite William Hurt in Hamlet, Childe Byron, *and* Richard II.
Photos by Gerry Goodstein (prints courtesy Billy Rose Theatre Division, The New York Public Library for the Performing Arts, Astor, Lenox and Tilden Foundations).

Hamlet *by William Shakespeare, Circle Rep, 1979: William Hurt, Beatrice Straight. Photo by Gerry Goodstein (print courtesy Billy Rose Theatre Division, The New York Public Library for the Performing Arts, Astor, Lenox and Tilden Foundations). A classic of the closet scene, this photo features two Academy Award winners in a powerful moment.*

Mary Stuart by Friedrich Schiller, Circle Rep, 1979. Left: Timothy Shelton, Tanya Berezin. Right: Stephanie Gordon, Ken Kliban, Burke Pearson. Photos by Gerry Goodstein (prints courtesy Billy Rose Theatre Division, The New York Public Library for the Performing Arts, Astor, Lenox and Tilden Foundations). Pitting two "Queens of Circle Rep" against each other, this production played in rotating rep with Hamlet. Neither Berezin as Elizabeth or Gordon as Mary were conventional typecasting.

Childe Byron by Romulus Linney, Circle Rep, 1981: William Hurt, John Dossett. Photo by Gerry Goodstein (print courtesy Billy Rose Theatre Division, The New York Public Library for the Performing Arts, Astor, Lenox and Tilden Foundations). Intense performances by Hurt and Dossett portrayed a tender but scandalous love affair before either actor had achieved stardom.

Angels Fall *by Lanford Wilson,
Circle Rep, 1982.
Left: Danton Stone, Tanya
Berezin.
Below: Nancy Snyder, Fritz
Weaver.*

*Photos by Gerry Goodstein (upper print courtesy Billy Rose Theatre Division, The New York Public
Library for the Performing Arts, Astor, Lenox and Tilden Foundations).
First performed at the New World Festival in Miami's Coconut Grove Playhouse, the production moved to
the Longacre Theater in New York, where MWM received a fourth Tony nomination for Best Director.*

Angelo's Wedding *by Julie Bovasso, Circle Rep, 1985: William Hickey, Scott Glenn.*
Photo by Gerry Goodstein (print courtesy Billy Rose Theatre Division, The New York Public Library
for the Performing Arts, Astor, Lenox and Tilden Foundations). This production showed that the col-
laborative process can prove to be a rocky road; it had to be canceled before it opened due to the
author's backstage harassment of the actors.

As Is by William M. Hoffman, Circle Rep, 1985: Jonathan Hadary, Jonathan Hogan. Photo by Gerry Goodstein (print courtesy Billy Rose Theatre Division, The New York Public Library for the Performing Arts, Astor, Lenox and Tilden Foundations). The first play about AIDS, As Is transferred to the Lyceum Theater, where it won the Drama Desk Award for Best Play and got MWM his fifth Tony nomination for Best Director.

Burn This *by Lanford Wilson, Mark Taper
Forum in Los Angeles, 1987.
Left: Joan Allen, John Malkovich.
Below: John Malkovich, Jonathan Hogan.*

*Photos by Jay Thompson (Prints courtesy of Center Theater Group/L.A.). Joan Allen won the Tony
Award for Best Actress, but John Malkovich became a movie star after this incendiary performance.
Burn This was remounted a year later at Steppenwolf in Chicago, and transferred to the Plymouth
Theater on Broadway.*

The Destiny of Me *by Larry Kramer, Circle Rep at the Lucille Lortel, 1992: Jonathan Hadary (stand-*
ing), John Cameron Mitchell (seated). Photo by Martha Swope (print Billy Rose Theatre Division, The
New York Public Library for the Performing Arts, Astor, Lenox and Tilden Foundations). This play,
which won the Lortel Award for Best Play, was the prequel to The Normal Heart. *Both actors are play-*
ing the same role: Ned Weeks.

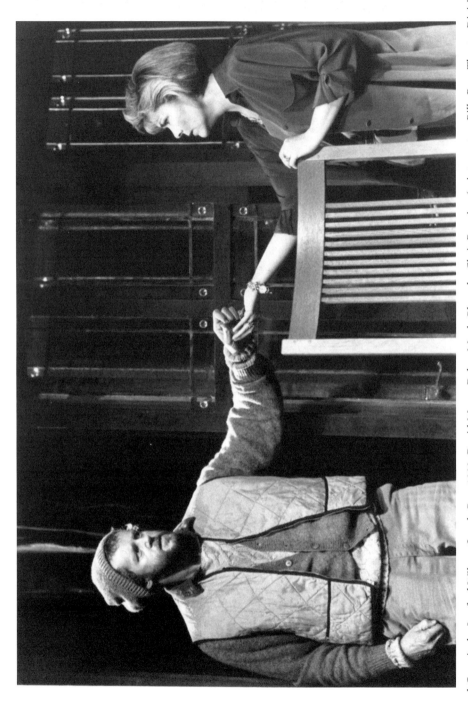

Redwood Curtain by Lanford Wilson, Seattle Rep, 1992: David Morse, Debra Monk. Photo by Chris Bennion (print courtesy Billy Rose Theatre Division, The New York Public Library for the Performing Arts, Astor, Lenox and Tilden Foundations). When Redwood Curtain transferred to the Brooks Atkinson in 1993, Jeff Daniels replaced Morse, and Debra Monk won the Tony Award for Best Supporting Actress.

Sunshine *by William Mastrosimone, Circle Rep, 1989:*
Left: Jordan Mott, Jennifer Jason Leigh.
Below: John Dossett, Jennifer Jason Leigh.

Photos by Gerry Goodstein (prints courtesy Billy Rose Theatre Division, The New York Public Library for the Performing Arts, Astor, Lenox and Tilden Foundations). MWM and Jennifer Jason Leigh visited the girlie booths on the old 42nd Street for research that produced an authentic performance.

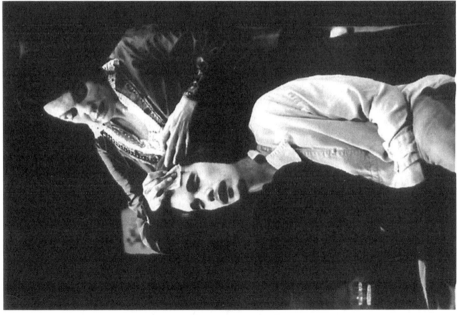

The Seagull by Anton Chekhov, Lyceum Theater, 1992. Left: Ethan Hawke, Tyne Daly. Right: Tyne Daly; Jon Voight. Photos by Joan Marcus. This production was staged for Tony Randall's National Actors Theater. The all-star cast also included Tony Roberts and Joan MacIntosh.

The Seagull by Anton Chekhov, Lyceum Theater, 1992. Ethan Hawke, Laura Linney. Photos by Joan Marcus. Considered to be his finest rehearsal experience, MWM discusses at length the use of improvisation as part of the research process.

Foxfire by Hume Cronyn and Susan Cooper, Guthrie Theater, 1981. Left: Jessica Tandy. Right: Hume Cronyn. Photo by Bruce Goldstein (print courtesy of the Minneapolis Historical Society). MWM considers Ms. Tandy the best actress he ever directed, but his conflict with Mr. Cronyn at a dress rehearsal led MWM to withdraw from the production before Broadway, in spite of rave reviews in Minneapolis.

Old Times by Harold Pinter, Academy Festival Theater, Lake Forest, Illinois, 1977: Beatrice Straight, Raul Julia, Irene Worth. Photo by Lisa Ebright. This was a dream cast. The setting is one of many John Lee Beatty did for MWM. He won his first Tony Award for the set of Talley's Folly three years later.

Picnic *by William Inge, Ahmanson Theater, Los Angeles, 1986: Jennifer Jason Leigh, Gregory Harrison. This was Jennifer Jason Leigh's stage debut after MWM had seen her in* Fast Times at Ridgemont High. Picnic *featured an all-star cast that also included Michael Learned, Rue McClanahan, Conchata Ferrel, and Dick Van Patten.*

Summer and Smoke by Tennessee Williams, Ahmanson Theater, 1988: Christopher Reeve, Joaquín Martínez, Wanda de Jesus. Photos by Jay Thompson (prints courtesy Center Theater Group/L.A.). Costar Christine Lahti was pregnant while playing Miss Alma, and had to be replaced after opening by Gemini star Carol Potter. MWM's first production of this play at Eastern Michigan University in 1976 was when he discovered Jeff Daniels.

Private Lives by Noël Coward, Repertory Theater of St. Louis, 2002: John Pasha, Mary Proctor, Don Burroughs, Stephanie Cozart. Photos by J. Bruce Summers. MWM had more fun with this production than any other. He thought it was much funnier (and more honest) than the acclaimed Broadway production the same year.

Long Day's Journey into Night by Eugene O'Neill, Arizona Theater Company, 1998: (foreground) Kim Bennett, Jason Kuykendall, Lawrence Pressman, (behind, on stairs) Ruth Reid. Photo by Timothy Fuller. MWM considers this his all-around best production, with a set by Ming Cho Lee, lights by Phil Monat, costumes by Laura Crow, and music by Peter Kater.

107

Above: Boris McGiver, Allan Campbell, Matthew Rauch.
Right: Miriam Shor.
Below: Tuck Millican, Kelly McAndrew, Boris McGiver
(in background: Matthew Rauch, Miriam Shor, Hope
Chernoff).

Book of Days *by Lanford Wilson,' Signature Theater, 2002. Photos by Rahav Sagev. Originally commissioned by Jeff Daniels for his Purple Rose Theater in Michigan (where it was directed by Guy Sanville), this drama provided sharp criticism of the close relationship between politics and the religious right.*

Cat on a Hot Tin Roof *by Tennessee Williams, Repertory Theater of St. Louis, 2005.*
Top: Joneal Joplin, John Lepard, Jo Twiss, Mary Proctor.
Bottom: Molly Schaffer, Jason Kuykendall.
Photos by J. Bruce Summer. Gooper and Mae were depicted as three-dimensional characters, rather than the usual cartoonish treatment. Kuykendall gained thirty pounds to play Brick, the ex-football hero. This production followed MWM's debut production by forty-six years, and emphasized elements of Greek tragedy.

Richard II *by William Shakespeare, Circle Rep at the Intermedia Arts Theater, 1981.*
Top: Gary Berner, Danton Stone, William Hurt (kneeling), Michael Ayr, Edward Seamon, Richard
Cox (in mask), Jonathan Bolt, Jimmie Ray Weeks, Ken Kliban, John Dossett.
Bottom: (foreground) Richard Cox, William Hurt, Richard Seff, John Dossett (background) Jimmie
Ray Weeks, Jordan Mott, Edward Seamon.
Photos by Gerry Goodstein (prints courtesy Billy Rose Theatre Division, The New York Public Library for
the Performing Arts, Astor, Lenox and Tilden Foundations). Staged on a huge proscenium stage of an old
vaudeville house, this production never jelled in that environment, so MWM decided to save his actors from
the critics by not inviting reviews. The upper photo shows the use of masks, illustrative of the Celtic concept
that didn't work under these circumstances.

Chapter Six

Research

The 20 percent of rehearsals we spend on research can be the most exciting part of the whole process. Before they have to start moving around and speaking dialogue, cast members need some time to get acquainted with their characters and their circumstances. On my rehearsal schedules, I describe this period of work as "Improvs," although in fact, improvisation is only one of the ways to discover a creative path into the play. Let's go through some of them.

Discussions and Field Trips

Research rehearsals usually begin with discussions. Each cast member gets a chance to share with everyone what he's learned about the subject he was assigned at the first rehearsal.

Also, the actors may be eager to discuss some of the discoveries they've made while inventing biographies for their characters. It's not a good idea for an actor to divulge *all* his secrets, but discussion can help him focus his ideas.

Ask a couple of questions, and then let the actors take over, so they can express their feelings about who the characters are, and how they came to be that way.

When you make the schedule, call the actors in groups that will benefit from sharing exploration. These groupings may be based on family ties, relationships, or on similar circumstances.

For example, when we rehearsed *The HOT L BALTIMORE*, the actors playing The Girl, Suzy, and April were grouped together because these characters share the same job: they're prostitutes. The actors were able to share

111

research about the psychosociological causes that might lead a woman to enter the "oldest profession"; they took field trips together where they could safely observe women working "on the street" and absorb details of their behavior. By doing their research together, camaraderie was established among them, and that remained subtly evident throughout a long run of performances.

The night clerk Bill, the manager Mr. Katz, and the bookkeeper Mrs. Oxenham also researched together, because they run the hotel. On field trips, they interviewed hotel employees and managers, and learned how to operate a hotel, from using the switchboard to sorting the mail, from registering the guests to enforcing the rules of the establishment.

When characters are members of a family, it's especially important for the actors to create their family together. They need to agree on their shared histories of mother, father, aunts, uncles, and siblings. Although each actor prepares his own private biography, the cast members need to discuss how to fit their individual ideas into a cohesive family, who've accumulated a lifetime of shared experiences.

If two actors are playing a married couple, they'll need to agree on when, where, and how they met. If they don't know each other at the beginning of rehearsal, they'll need some private time together, away from the scrutiny of other cast members, to develop the unique nature of their married relationship. They'll have to create a shared life of intimacy, for better or for worse, for richer or for poorer. The first steps toward intimacy may be only talking about their roles, when they can appreciate each other's creativity, and begin to build a trusting relationship.

These discussions should remain imaginatively creative. Discourage everyone from being too cerebral or analytical. Keep the creative spark alive among them.

One of the goals of the research period is to help an actor to make an important transition: from thinking of the character as "he" or "she" to thinking in terms of "I."

Usually, discussions lead to a need to explore relationships or circumstances more actively. Then, discussions should yield to exercises that allow the actors to create together in more than just talk.

In both *Childe Byron* and *The Night of the Iguana*, actors had to play poets. It seemed a natural exercise to assign each actor to write poetry during the rehearsal period, as part of their personal research. If an actor is playing a photographer, he should take pictures daily. If playing a doctor, he should visit a hospital and observe the behavior of the medical staff. He should also interview a willing medic about procedures as well as more personal issues such as the motivation for becoming a doctor and any details of experience from medical school through internship. In both *Cat on a Hot Tin Roof* and *Angels Fall*, the actors playing doctors benefited from the participation of a generous medical adviser.

Relationship Exercises

Often when a couple of actors are cast as lovers, they're actually meeting as strangers at the first rehearsal. A useful introduction to quick intimacy is the baby exercise.

From six to eight months old, a child is filled with curiosity about everything and everybody. Babies have what is called polymorphous perversity; they delight in exploring everything within reach, with total freedom, lacking all inhibition.

This exercise should be performed privately, and only after you've created an atmosphere of trust. I might ask only one stage manager to remain with the couple and me.

After a good physical warm-up that includes ample elements of relaxation, ask your two actors to remove their shoes and sit facing each other on the floor (or on an exercise mat). Invite them to imagine they are babies, only six months old. They have not yet learned to talk, but they can make sounds that express their mercurial feelings, which may quickly change like tropical storms, from giggles to bawling, and almost instantaneously, to smiles again.

As the actors explore each other's mouths, eyes, hair, skin, hands, feet, breasts, thighs, and belly buttons, they'll be plunged into an immediate intimacy.

When two people are in love, they echo the joyful discovery of a baby's behavior. Being in love takes us back to that universe of innocence ("Trailing clouds of glory," as Tennyson puts it) in which everything is beautiful, desirable, and edible. Maybe that's why lovers call each other "Baby."

After physically exploring each other with curiosity and intimacy, the actors should feel free enough from conventional reticence to begin to create a close, playful relationship.

Now the actors will be ready to improvise the characters' first meeting. This is particularly important when the characters have had a relationship for a long time.

For example, the actors playing Masha and Kuligin in *Three Sisters*, should explore how they met, what they shared, and what their attraction was based on before the degeneration of the marriage that's so pitifully evident in the play. Most marriages begin with great hope. The partners have convinced themselves that their love will conquer all. Life sometimes teaches us otherwise.

Only an improvisation can give actors a hopeful experience in the past, on which the present circumstances of the play can be built. The audience won't *feel* the tragedy of Masha's and her husband's barren relationship unless the actors *know* what's been *lost.*

Another exploration you may find useful is the ubiquitous mirror exercise, in which two actors imagine their partner to be their reflections. Virtually everyone in the theater has done this classic at one time or another.

Facing each other and duplicating every move, the actors transfer their identity. They yield their will to their own "reflection" and connect with their partner in a way that transcends the external movement and concentrates their attention on the inner origins of motion and intention. If two people can tune in to each other in this exercise, it can form a basis for a deeply trusting relationship.

The mirror exercise was indispensable in my rehearsals for Larry Kramer's *The Destiny of Me.* Jonathan Hadary played Ned Weeks at the age of fifty, while John Cameron Mitchell played Ned at the age of eleven. The mirror exercise gave them an opportunity to work together, equally creating the whole being of one character and his earlier/later reflection. Both were Ned.

The mirror exercise actually made it onstage in my production of Pirandello's *Enrico IV.* I added an unwritten character to the action, a silent, Fellini-esque clown who acted as sort of an Everyman to the madness of the play. She assumed various roles: from audience member to puppeteer, to the alter ego of Enrico. At one point, she assumed the role of the Countess as a young woman, and as Enrico described to the aging Countess how she sees her lost youth reflected in a glass, the clown mirrored the movements of the Countess, giving it a surreal reality that embodied the mystery and madness of the moment.

Ensemble Exercises

There are several exercises that can contribute to the development of an ensemble. Building trust among a group of individuals is a key element. Trust exercises, which were a popular innovation of the 1960s, later became so common that rock musicians incorporated them into their concerts, body surfing the crowd. It's liberating to experience trust by letting yourself free-fall into the arms of your fellow actors.

Of course, in combat choreography, trust is required even in performance. When I replaced Douglass Watson as Claudius in my own production of *Hamlet,* our consummate fight director, B. H. Barry, had designed a spectacular death dive from the heights of an upper stage. Crying "Oh, yet defend me friends, I am but hurt," Claudius pulled the dagger from his wound, and fell ten feet, head first into the surprised arms of the courtiers on the lower stage.

Although I love to swim, I had never dived.

B. H. asked us to do the trust exercise first at a height of eight inches, then at two feet, and so on until it was actually thrilling to execute at ten feet in the air. By the third performance, I was so confident in my leap that instead of merely falling I dived way out over the awaiting arms of my courtiers. Fortunately, they all saw where I was going to land, and managed to react quickly enough to be where I was coming down. I was told later that I missed the lighting instruments overhead by inches. Ah, I love to act! But a tendency to gild the lily may be why I'm rarely afforded the chance.

Other exercises might involve the whole cast to explore a metaphor physically. For example, if you were directing Miller's *Death of a Salesman*, you might ask your cast to build an organic machine, composed of mechanical parts. Each actor could create a repetitive sound and movement, joined by his collaborators doing likewise, until together they've created a whole machine of interlocking mechanisms, noises, and wheels.

The physical experience of their creation will be stored in their muscles, and the ensemble intuitively might better understand Miller's viewpoint: a capitalistic system has enslaved Willy, making him a mere cog in the social machine. This exercise may seem a little abstract for such a realistic play, but as a group "nightmare," it might unlock a spark of creativity you could never anticipate from a more intellectual approach.

For an improvisation for *The Destiny of Me,* we asked each cast member to imagine the circumstances of his inevitable death. Because all the characters have to deal death in the play, the cast gained unity from the exploration of a common theme.

Similarly, when the talented comedian John Belushi died, we were in the research portion of my rehearsal schedule for Shakespeare's *Richard II*. Even though Mr. Belushi's career had next to nothing to do with Shakespeare, I asked the cast to mourn the loss of his genius and crystallize their feelings with physical gestures. This uses an idea from Michael Chekhov's technique called the psychological gesture, and it allowed the group to find a sense of community from individual grief. We were all surprised at the depth of our feelings, but reality is a strong source of creativity.

Ensemble is the result of a cast creating a world together.

One of the best ways to start this process is to spend time together creating the environmental circumstances of the play. Encourage the company to create the sounds and smells of a summer evening, to feel the stifling breeze of a humid August night, in short, to use their senses to play together in a shared imaginative reality. Each person's imagination will be multiplied by the work of other cast members, and the whole creation will transcend its individual parts.

Alone in My Room: 1

During the workshops we conducted during our first year of training at Circle Rep, I came up with an exercise that's become a "classic" in my work ever since: Alone in My Room.

The purpose of the exercise is to achieve what Stanislavski calls *public solitude.* An actor uses his imagination to believe one simple circumstance: that he's alone in his room. The goal is to believe so strongly in this fictional circumstance that *actual reality* (of a stage and the presence of an audience) is superseded. If an actor can believe he's alone, the audience can see unconscious, private behavior, far more revealing than stage posturing that "shows" an audience what an actor wants them to see.

In this exercise, an actor uses his senses to imagine he's by himself in that place where he feels most safe: "my room," which can be a living room, a kitchen, a porch, an office—anywhere that's an extension of a person's notion of self—his nest, or in contemporary jargon, his crib. For most of us, "my room" is where we sleep, so a bedroom is a logical starting place.

First, an actor should spend an hour or more carefully observing all physical aspects of his room at home. How big is the space? Where is the door? How does it open and/or lock? Where are the windows? What do they look out on? What sounds can be heard? Feel the texture, size, and weight of the furniture. Discover the exact sensory experience of the floor or rug. Explore the smells of the room. Open the closet doors, and hang up a jacket. Locate the mirror. Find all the tiny specifics of perfume bottles, note pads, trinkets that adorn the surfaces of the bedside table. Where is the phone? What are the colors? How high is the ceiling? And so forth.

Then the actor, using his sense memories, imaginatively re-creates all these specific details in front of an audience. By concentrating on the sensory details of his creation, an actor can lose himself so much that an audience can see a degree of relaxation that occurs *only* when he is alone. His breathing changes. Inhibitions disappear.

Once his imagination is concentrated on the details of his environment, the actor should pursue a simple activity, such as looking for a lost object.

From believing he's alone doing a simple action, an actor can experience a series of impulses that sometimes leads to an external result, like impulsively saying something.

When a series of impulses leads an actor to an inner life that results in a spoken line, he comes to understand the process he must go through to explore the subtext beneath every line of dialogue. A spoken line illuminates the unconscious behavior an audience is privileged to witness.

Alone in My Room: 2

Although this exercise was devised to allow an actor to experience "living onstage," it soon became apparent that it was also a useful way to explore and experience the life of a stage character.

Just as character is expressed in what we choose to carry in our pockets, it's expressed even more vividly in the nest we make for ourselves. Whenever I'm directing a play out of town, I'm struck by a need for certain things that make me feel at home, that transform a hotel room into "*my* room." Think of the pictures, the incense, the trinkets, the telegrams, or whatever, that an actor uses to make a drafty dressing room "his own."

Those same needs exist for the characters we portray. Creating a room they've made for themselves provides a natural starting place for us to get to know them. If we know their rooms, we'll know them. What better way to begin to understand a character than to experience being alone in his room? The exercise is so simple, and has so few demands, that an actor can indulge his imagination and experience his character without intellectual analysis, by just *being* in his room.

Let the critics analyze; it's for the actor to *experience*.

I don't think I've ever directed a production in which the cast hasn't benefited from creating each character's room. It's an imaginative bridge from discussion to creating the circumstances of the play. It personalizes an actor's experience, and endows him with a confidence that comes from creating. It's exploring through experiencing.

Sometimes, with a rehearsal room that's large enough, several actors can perform this exercise simultaneously, in their own private corners. Because each will be in his own world, an actor can privately create his part of a whole house or building. Then, they'll be ready for a group improvisation, like the one from *The Destiny of Me*.

Improvisation

Improvisations offer directors an extraordinary means to explore the circumstances of a play that can be duplicated in no other way. But what exactly is an improv?

Improvisation is a free and uninhibited exploration of experience, arising from belief in a set of imaginary circumstances.

In a sense, acting is always improvisational, from the given circumstances of one line of dialogue to the next. The experience of acting truthfully is a free fall of unplanned adventure, more vivid than mere reality. That accounts for the exhilaration an actor feels when playing with true inspiration.

But remember, it's the *experience* we are exploring, not making up dialogue. There's a clear distinction between improvisation as a performing art and its use as a rehearsal technique.

The former is represented in the work of groups like Chicago's Second City. In the 1960s, Mike Nichols and Elaine May reached the peak of performance improvisation. Assuming characters and agreeing on a situation, these witty artists spontaneously created comedy that would make even a Strindberg laugh. The purpose of performance improvisation is to come up with a skit, allowing the dialogue to spring from the invention of the actors. A current example is television's popular *Whose Line Is It Anyway?*

In the 1950s, the Actors Studio experimented with this sort of improvisation to come up with *A Hatful of Rain,* which was created out of collaboration between a writer and dedicated actors. The book for *A Chorus Line* also was based on improvisation. It's an entirely legitimate process, with historical roots all the way back to Italy's *commedia dell'arte.* But it's not the sort of improvisation I am talking about for rehearsals.

For improvisation as a rehearsal technique, we are concerned solely with the internal experience of the actor. In our improvs, actors should avoid making up dialogue. No one *need* speak, unless his inner experience demands it. Even then, it's not what's said that's important, but the behavior, the motives, and the actions that arise from believing in the circumstances.

If an improvisation remains on a verbal level, it also remains on a superficial level. Sometimes an improv even should be ended when speech becomes necessary.

Improvisation shouldn't replace the dialogue of a play or substitute the words of actors for those of a playwright. For this reason, *never improvise a scene that is written.*

There's little to be gained from actors reinventing dialogue, and it's maddening for a living writer to hear. The care a writer has taken in the exact wording of the dialogue must be respected and honored. If the actors spontaneously can create dialogue that's superior to the playwright's, his script is unlikely to merit production.

The quality of the dialogue in *A Hatful of Rain* can't be compared to the beauty of Clifford Odets' *Awake and Sing.* As delightful as Nichols and May are, few would equate their wit with Oscar Wilde's. The spontaneity of improvisation may earn a quick laugh, but literary quality must withstand the scrutiny of contemplation; readers who never have heard the dialogue uttered can savor its excellence.

Remember that the script is the road map for the actor's experience. Improvisation is the journey. So it's best to leave the invention of dialogue to the writer, and the exploration of experience to the actor.

Stanislavski *did* use improvisation of circumstances to discover the reality of the actors' experience, *before* they even knew what play they were doing. He set up an improvisation in which a father discovers that his daughter has eloped with a foreigner in the middle of the night. The experience of that improv provided the actors of the Moscow Art Theater with a visceral basis for understanding *Othello,* even before they had read it. Of course, Stanislavski had the luxury of a full year of rehearsal. Today, I doubt there are many actors who would think of substituting their own dialogue for the superb poetry of Shakespeare.

But, perhaps we ought never to say never. If you're working on a play written in verse, or in a rigid archaic style (such as the drama or comedies of ancient Greece), there might be some value in asking the actors to explore the situations of the play, using their own words.

The main focus of improvisation should be to explore the circumstances that precede or bridge the scenes that are written.

Most modern, psychologically oriented dramas, from Ibsen and Chekhov to the present, set up circumstances that precede the beginning of the script, and those circumstances can be explored through improvisation with excellent results.

Chekhov *Three Sisters* begins with Olga saying to her sisters: "Father died a year ago today, on the fifth of May." Their father's death would have been a profound event for all three of the sisters, and their memories should stir Masha and Irina when Olga reminds them of it. Only through an improvisation can we re-create that event and give the actors the *shared* experience to which the dialogue refers.

Similarly, Chekhov often writes of enormous dramatic events that occur between the acts of his plays. Kostya's suicide attempt between Acts II and III of *The Seagull* or Nina's affair with Trigorin between Acts III and IV are events that should be re-created and experienced before the actors speak the dialogue that refers to them.

Objectives and Independent Activities

Sandy Meisner developed exercises that provide a wonderful framework for structuring an improvisation. Even if your actors have never studied Meisner's techniques, they can grasp the fundamentals well enough to use them in a rehearsal.

Almost every actor is familiar with the concept of pursuing an objective. In the simplest terms, it's a driving desire to achieve something. It can also be described as an *intention* or a *need* to do something.

An objective should always be an active verb, like: "I want to *borrow,* or to *punish,* or to *seduce,* or to *avoid,* or to *win.*" Sometimes the motive can be expressed as a negative: "I don't want to *lose* my apartment, so I have to *borrow*." "I don't want to be caught, so to *prevent* her from suspecting me, I must *joke* with her."

In preparing to play an objective, an actor must justify his desire so he can experience it personally. Stanislavski's "Magic If" is helpful to connect an actor's imagination to the character's desire: "If *I* wanted to seduce" or "If *I* wanted to win." "If" opens up a world of possibilities, rather than insisting that imaginary circumstances are *actually* true.

The independent activity is an exercise that's less familiar, but actors can learn enough to experience an improvisation.

You need to help them find something to do that's physically difficult to perform and that requires their total concentration: gluing together a broken vase, making a scrapbook, fixing a broken motor, or cooking a complicated recipe.

It's important that an actor *actually* works to accomplish his task, so real props are essential. It does no good to *imagine* doing the activity, because the imagination needs to be engaged in motivation, creating the necessity of actually doing the action. Accomplishing the task must require an actor's full concentration. Meisner calls it the reality of doing.

David Hare's play *Amy's View* begins with an excellent independent activity. In the first scene, Amy's boyfriend is patching a leak in a bicycle tire, and then pumping it full of air. It really has to be done at every performance. The justification should be intensified by including a time limit: why it has to be done *right now.*

When one actor pursues an objective that needs the immediate assistance of another actor who is equally engaged in an urgent independent activity, real conflict will result.

Conflict is the very stuff of drama, and the experience of conflict releases a rush of uninhibited impulses. These impulses catapult an actor into the reality of here-and-now. Reality is a great source of inspiration.

Two additional rules must be added. It's important that the actors leave themselves entirely free to respond to the behavior of their partners.

The second rule is that each actor must take the behavior of the other personally, as if everything he observes is a direct reaction to *him*. We want the actor to respond as fully to the subtext—the motives he sees in the *behavior* of his partner—as to the actual words spoken.

When an actor's concentration is focused on these rules of engagement, he often finds his fear of improvs is diminished considerably. The reward is discovery through experience.

Improvisation can build an actor's confidence in the process of taking risks, until the challenges of reaching deeper produce results beyond anybody's expectation.

A director can be most helpful by coming up with imaginative circumstances, compelling objectives, and independent activities that are truly involving. In Appendix G, there's a summary of the Meisner rules, but read *Sanford Meisner on Acting* for a deeper understanding of how to discover creativity in the spontaneous moment.

Setting Up an Improv

Designing a productive improvisation requires careful preparation. First, of course, you must decide which events or circumstances need to be explored.

Never undertake an improvisation in order to teach the actors some foregone conclusion. A genuine experiment cannot have a specific outcome in mind. If you know what the end result is supposed to be, you should save everyone's time and simply tell the cast your opinion. Of course, then you're dictating your interpretation to the cast, rather than giving them an opportunity to discover through their own experience.

In an improvisation, there is no right or wrong conclusion. There is only whatever we learn from the experience of believing in the circumstances. So, it's important to set up an improv with circumstances that are vivid and specific, with no end in sight. Find rich circumstances for a starting point, and then let the experience of the actors take the improv wherever it goes. The adventure often will surprise everyone, including the director, with unexpected illumination.

Begin every improvisation by proposing *public circumstances* that all the actors must take into account. Make sure that everyone understands the specific details of the public circumstances: time, place, and event. What is the year, month, date, and hour when it occurs? Exactly where does it take place: the country, state, town, estate, room, or space?

Also make sure the purpose of the exploration is clear to everyone:

"We're going to improvise the circumstances of your first meeting."

Or (in *The Seagull*):

"We need to explore the experiences of Masha, Treplov, and Nina when they were students in Medvedenko's classroom."

Or (in *Fifth of July*):

"Let's investigate a night fifteen years earlier, when Kenny, June, Gwen, and John plan a trip to Washington to march in an antiwar protest."

These public circumstances provide a framework, but actors respond even more vividly to *private imaginary circumstances.*

Imagination thrives on secret circumstances that the other actors don't know.

These private circumstances can include

- secret events that confer a clear point of view about the public event everyone else knows,
- a hidden objective, a secret justification for an independent activity, and
- a surprise for the rest of the cast.

After announcing the public circumstances of the improv to the whole cast, take each actor aside, out of the hearing of others, to assign private circumstances. Most actors relish this special attention and the intimacy of sharing whispered secrets with the director.

When the public circumstances interact with the private secrets, they may lead to surprises the actors experience as if it were reality.

No time limit should be set for an improvisation. You simply stay attuned to the experiences the actors are having and call an end to the improv only when a significant event has occurred or when an improv has gone off-course in a way that nothing is to be gained by continuing.

You'll need to be very patient and make it clear to the actors that they're being trusted to explore the territory of an improv to the fullest. It is for themselves. It's not a performance. It's better for an improv to last a little too long than to have an experience cut short, just on the cusp of a discovery.

When you see an opportunity to stop the improv, give the actors a chance to discuss their experience. What did it feel like? Did it work for them? What did they discover that they want to share? If the actors don't have a chance to discuss the experience and put their discovery into words, it may never quite crystallize into the insights you're hoping for. Let the cast tell *you* what happened.

Because an actor's secrets may be powerful sources of creativity for future development, no one should be *compelled* to relate what he or she was using or working on. Sometimes they'll *want* to share their private circumstances; sometimes they *won't*. Sometimes the secrets may surface during an improvisation, to the surprise of the others.

Of course, communication is a two-way street; you may participate in describing how the events seemed to you as an observer. But don't dominate the discussion; invite it.

The element of an unexpected surprise can be very powerful, experienced with the force of reality. When I was directing the New York production of Lanford Wilson's *Book of Days* at the Signature Theater, I had my cast engage in an improv that preceded the events of the play by a year.

The public circumstance was preparing a "surprise" birthday party in the high school gym for the character Martha. Everyone was involved in decorating the room, under the direction of her best friend, Sharon. Martha's son, Len, his wife, Ruth, and his fellow workers at the factory, the minister, even the town sheriff were climbing ladders, selecting music, stringing crêpe paper streamers, putting candles on a birthday cake, etc., using real props, including a delicious cake. The character Luanne's task was to engage Martha in another room in a separate improv until it was time to bring her to the party. The actress playing Martha had no idea what the other actors were up to. When she was brought in to the decorated room with candles ablaze on the cake, she was genuinely surprised at the event, just as if in real life.

However, the *real* surprise was hidden from the whole cast. The circumstances in the script indicate that a year before the events of the play, the town patriarch, Sharon's husband Walt, had suffered a heart attack. Unbeknown to the others, I told the actor playing Walt (the brilliant Jim Haynie) that once the party got underway, he should have a myocardial infarction. While everyone was having a great time eating cake, drinking punch, celebrating their successful improvisation of a birthday party, Jim suddenly grabbed his chest and keeled over in a completely convincing portrayal of a cardiac arrest.

The cast stopped acting, rushed to Jim's side, panicked by his apparent discomfort. Faces blanched white with fear. A few moments after everyone was sufficiently scared, and before anyone called 911, I stopped the improvisation, and Jim sat up smiling. The relief in the room was palpable, as everyone realized that Jim's performance was only part of their improv. But it united the cast in an experience that informed its work on every aspect of the play.

A Successful Improvisation

While working on Larry Kramer's *The Destiny of Me*, I devised an improvisation for the family in the play that I think illustrates how an improvisation should be structured.

The mother, father, and two sons comprise a psychologically intertwined family. I described an improvisation I wanted them to explore that would start a complicated journey.

To begin with, I asked each actor to create the room in which his/her character felt most at home. The brothers shared a bedroom, so I wanted them to create together the room they inhabited, beginning with the twin beds, the posters on the wall, a lamp on a bedside table, and the window between the beds (all suggested by the designer's renderings). I asked the mother to create her dressing table with three mirrors, along with the perfumes, powders, combs, and brushes that anchored her bedroom. The father was to concentrate on "his" chair, the overstuffed club chair with the telephone table behind, with a bridge lamp for reading that represented the living room.

I announced that the public circumstances of the improv would be that it was 3:30 in the afternoon on September 23, 1943, in Washington, D.C., when the kids had just come home from school. Their mother was also in her room, home early from work.

I then told them I would give each actor private circumstances to work with and a simple action to pursue.

I first took aside John Cameron Mitchell, who played the nine-year-old younger brother, Alexander. I suggested these private circumstances: the previous day, he had gone into the basement of the building and played "I'll show you mine if you show me yours" with a neighbor girl. His present activity is to write a play about Halloween for his third-grade class to perform. The teacher has assigned the project, and it must be turned in "tomorrow."

I then took aside his seventeen-year-old brother, Ben, played by Peter Frechette, and gave him his circumstances. The previous night he had a date with a girl from his class and in the heat of passion, they had intercourse without a condom in the backseat of her car, and that he might be a little worried today about disease or pregnancy. His activity grows out of the circumstance that the senior quarterback for the football team has been injured in last week's game, and the coach has challenged Ben, along with two other students, to compete for the opportunity to replace him. The coach's assignment is for all three students to come up with play plans, which will be tested tomorrow, and the kid with the best play plan will be the new quarterback.

I then took aside Piper Laurie who played Rena, the mother, and gave her the circumstance that last night, sleeping in the double bed with her husband, she had been awakened by her husband's passion. Feeling a little bit "used," she has been thinking all day that perhaps it would be better to have twin beds from now on. Her activity centers on composing an acceptance speech for an award she's won for "Volunteer of the Year" with the Stage Door Canteen, which is to be presented to her tomorrow night.

Finally, I gave private circumstances to David Spielberg, who played Richard, the father. He has three baseball tickets for the Yankee-Senators game for tonight and wants to surprise his two sons by taking them to the baseball game. But this afternoon, he received a telegram informing him that his mother has died. He must figure out how to get his family, which has no automobile, up to Bridgeport, Connecticut, for the funeral tomorrow.

I let the two boys and the mother create their rooms, and gave them about ten minutes to involve themselves in their motivated activities. Then I asked the father to join the improv, with the dreadful news.

Interwoven with the exercise of creating "alone in my room," each actor has been given an activity. Together they share public circumstances, but nurse private circumstances that are their own secrets. This dramatic situation stimulates the imaginations of the actors, so that when the unexpected circumstance of the grandmother's death is introduced, the actors must personally deal with the inevitable conflicts that occur, as they anticipate tomorrow's consequences.

The result was a very enriching experience for all involved. These intriguing circumstances engaged the imaginations of the actors, so they could commit fully to their motivated independent activities. As a result, the surprise death had the force of reality, and the family interacted with all the complex emotions, resentments, and reactions they honestly felt. The experience of the improvisation went far beyond the value that might be expected from any intellectual, analytic activity.

Imaginatively, the family collectively experienced a major event that profoundly impacted all four characters.

Life Before the Play

During the rehearsals for *The Seagull*, I set up a series of improvisations that became a part of our daily rehearsal routine. Whenever we would go through the first act (after it was staged), we'd begin with an improvisation up at the house of the dinner that precedes the opening scene.

Chekhov gives the circumstances surrounding the dinner, although details must be filled in. The famous diva Arkadina has returned to her summer estate, arriving two nights before. She's brought with her a stranger from Moscow, the celebrated writer Trigorin, who is her current paramour. The estate manager's dog has kept everyone awake by howling the past two nights, so nerves are frazzled. The actress' son Kostya is an amateur playwright, and he has announced that he will present a play this evening down by the lake for everyone's entertainment.

The National Actors Theater rehearsal rooms occupied the entire fifth floor of the Exxon building in midtown Manhattan. Suite after suite of offices and empty conference rooms stretched down the hallways, available for our use.

We installed a simple lighting system in the main rehearsal room, controlled by household dimmers. All the windows overlooking 47th Street were covered, and when we'd start on the scenes, the overhead fluorescent lights would be turned off. During the opening scene by the lake, we could suggest a sunset, dimming the lights down to the virtual darkness of twilight.

In what were the most luxurious conditions I'd ever encountered, we had all our furniture and props right from the first rehearsal, exactly as we would use them onstage.

Across from the main rehearsal room was a large conference room, where we set up a dining room table, complete with candles and lanterns. We provided the cast with a simple banquet: fruit and cakes and tea, with vodka and brandy as well. Actors love to eat! Unobserved by the director or stage managers, the cast would gather in the dining room, and improvise the dinner.

As their meal drew to a close, Trigorin, Shamraeyev, and Sorin would light cigars, and join Arkadina for an after-dinner drink. Dr. Dorn, who disapproves of cigars, would excuse himself to get a breath of fresh air, and Polina would quickly join him. Masha and Medvedenko strolled through the wild paths around the estate (up and down our seemingly endless corridors), until they decided to come down to the lake; at that point, they would enter the main rehearsal room and begin to speak the dialogue of the first scene.

When Masha and Medvedenko entered, we would signal Kostya and Sorin (who were still in the dining room) that they should head down to the lake as well, and they would contrive to arrive after Masha and Medvedenko had finished their scene. Then Nina would enter, having not taken part in the group improv, but rather privately improvising her escape from her parents' house across the lake. When Sorin left to go back up to the house, Dorn and Polina would see their signal to enter for their scene, until they're finally interrupted by the arrival of the rest of the dinner improvisation, servants and all.

This became our practice before every run-through of the first act. The actors' offstage improvisation blended right into the onstage scene, as written by Chekhov. The improv gave the actors a chance to immerse themselves in a life that flowed before, during, and after the lines of the text. It also gave them an opportunity to create the intricate relationships that develop among family, neighbors, and servants in an isolated rural setting. The richness and texture of reality they created (and brought into the first scene with them) could have been achieved no other way.

Bridging Acts or Scenes

Having established this kind of group creativity, the ground was prepared for the major improvisation at the end of the second act of *The Seagull*.

By this point in the play, Kostya knows he's losing Nina to Trigorin. His experimental play has been a disaster, and in desperation, he has shot a seagull. He presents Nina with the dead bird that symbolizes his broken heart. Appalled by this callous, obtuse gesture, Nina rejects him again, so he takes his gun and goes back down to the lake.

Meanwhile, Arkadina has been insulted by Shamraeyev's refusal to let her use the horses. In a fit of hysteria, she has vowed to pack up and leave.

While we watch Nina flirt with Trigorin, offstage Shamraeyev somehow has been persuaded to apologize, so that the act ends with a cheerful Arkadina calling from inside, "We're staying!" Trigorin goes in to join her for lunch, as Nina sighs, "It's a dream!"

I asked the actors to play on through the end of the second act, when everyone sits down to lunch. We continued the action in the main rehearsal room, all the windows open, and all the conflicts of the second act momentarily resolved.

Once the actors were in full swing, having their lunch, I asked Ethan Hawke, who played Kostya, to go into a small office that opened onto the large conference room next door, which represented our boathouse down by the lake. There, Ethan anointed his temple with "blood," and fired a blank pistol.

Naturally, the sound of the shot startled all the actors at the table. The actor who played Yakov (Danny Burstyn) came running from the boathouse into the lunch improvisation to fetch the doctor.

Naturally, the whole party went flying down to the lakeside, where they discovered Kostya, lying unconscious, his temple covered in blood. Dr. Dorn (played by Tony Roberts) began to treat him, while everyone crowded around to see. Masha (Maryanne Plunkett), who loves Kostya, fled into the woods, terrified that he might be dead. Medvedenko (Zane Lasky) pursued her, trying to comfort her. One of the marvelous discoveries of this improv was that it was under these circumstances that Masha agreed to Medvedenko's otherwise unwelcome proposal.

Meanwhile, the injured Kostya was carried back to his bedroom (all set out and prepared by the stage management), where he was put to bed, and nursed by Tyne Daly, as Arkadina.

This improvisation seemed so real that it experientially justified much of what follows in the play. Jon Voight was deeply shaken by the experience, discovering why Trigorin must leave. At the end of the fourth act, when Arkadina hears a gunshot offstage, it echoed from this previous experience, causing her startled flinch. Her heart almost stops, until Dr. Dorn covers the suicide with the lie that a medicine bottle in his bag has exploded.

When a director, with the help of an imaginative staff, can give an ensemble a fresh, unexpected jolt of experience, it makes an indelible impression, unequalled by any other approach. Certainly, the power of each actor to imagine the event described in the play is puny compared to the power of a group's creativity. Interacting with the imagination of others reinforces each actor's sense of truth. If everyone believes in the circumstances, they feel true.

Chapter Seven

Discovering Movement

When an audience sees a production, they learn what the play is about from the words the author has written, the performances of the cast, and from the live action they see.

A director's most visible contribution to the audience's experience is the stage life, embodied in the movement of the actors.

Yet all three of these sources must blend together so seamlessly that an audience is unaware of the individual components. As Harold Clurman put it, "the living play, in which the audience is unaware of where the dialogue stops and the performances begin."

How does a director go about creating a stage life that communicates both the play itself and the truth of the actors' performances?

First, he must understand that stage movement serves three masters:

- the requirements of the script,
- the impulses of the actors, and
- the enlightenment of the audience.

A director must balance his choice of every movement among these three needs. Because a lot of inspiration springs from the script itself, the information about the needs for movement begins there as well. Both possibilities and restrictions for movement can be found in the text. So first, any movement must be consistent with the script.

For example, in *Fifth of July*, Kenny is a paraplegic Vietnam vet, who has lost both his legs above the knees. To walk, he must use artificial limbs, and either crutches or a cane. He must use his stomach muscles to propel his legs.

The script vividly talks about how awkward he feels when he moves around. After a particularly exhausting cross, he wryly comments, "Cha, cha, cha."

The kind of movement and the number of crosses this character can make are limited by this given circumstance. So neither an actor nor a director may choose to have Kenny skipping rope or dancing the cancan, or for that matter, running or tiptoeing. Getting across the stage is a Herculean effort, which must not be overworked. A swift cross is just not possible. Near the end of the play, Kenny is accidentally tipped off balance and, in a terrifying moment, must fall over backward. This is a challenge for both the actor and the director, but there's really no way around the obligation.

This is a blatant example, but ordinary instances abound. If two people are on opposite sides of the stage and the stage direction reads (*He kisses her*), the script is demanding a move that will bring the actors close to each other. Which actor moves, and how, is subject to other influences, but the script *requires* a move.

Now, I don't believe a director is obligated to follow literally *every* stage direction that calls for movement. Without the aid of actors, an author has written stage directions to convey action to a reader. Sometimes an author overdescribes, like O'Neill in *Long Day's Journey*, or underindicates what's wanted, like much of Samuel Beckett's work, where almost no movement is specified.

Stage directions are meant for a reading public, but when collaborative artists bring a script to life, they don't have to treat stage directions as sacrosanct. They are guidelines, not ironclad dictates.

Naturally, a director and his actors should consider all movement the author's stage directions indicate and try to honor the author's request, unless there are strong reasons to disregard a suggested move.

The exception is when the stage directions don't originate with the author, but are the residual contributions of a previous production. It's been the practice for many years for Samuel French and Dramatists Play Service to acquire a stage manager's copy of the script that indicates all the moves of the actors in the original production.

This appropriation of a director's work is unconscionable, if not illegal, but publishers continue to violate the principle that a director's contributions to a production are his property and should not be used without permission and compensation. The Society of Stage Directors and Choreographers fights a constant battle to ensure its members of their property rights over their creative work.

When you receive a script that has stage directions for almost every line, it's doubtful that they indicate the author's original intent. If you want your work to be organic and the actors to be free to explore, it is essential that you *cross the stage directions out* before they can influence your choices.

An actor breathes life into a character, using his whole emotional, physical, and visceral being to explore the fictional reality of the author's creation. When an actor inhabits the world of a play and assumes a character's circumstances as his own, he becomes an expert on what that person is thinking, feeling, wanting, and doing at every moment. And these are the forces from which physical movement materializes.

Actors, believing in a play's given circumstances, are a director's spontaneous source of inspiration. If acting is behaving truthfully in imaginary circumstance, then the impulses that produce behavior are the core of movement.

The central premise of organic staging is that from the subtlest impulse in an actor's behavior, a director can find the motivation for a move that will express the meaning of a moment with clarity and grace.

I'll talk in some detail about just how to do that, but first consider the third factor that impels the choice of movement: the audience.

Throughout rehearsals, a director is a stand-in for the audience. In a sense, he's the first audience. He must have a keen eye for discerning how movement can tell us what's happening. The script may call for a move; an actor's impulse may dictate when a move is made; but a director must understand what the move will *mean* to an audience.

The movement of the characters and the relationship of one move to another illuminate the script. Using the raw material of the actors' impulses, a director designs movement that delivers to an audience the meaning of the play as an empathetic experience.

Looking for Impulses

The aspect of directing most difficult to describe is the actual process of finding a good physical life for a scene. A director's choices seem to be instinctual; any analysis seems labored. Like the naïve question asked of authors, "Where do your ideas come from?" it's almost impossible to identify the origin of a director's creative insights.

It's clear that a certain movement at a given moment can illuminate the meaning of a scene. Any move must be

- logical for the actor to perform,
- consistent with the script, and
- merge the spontaneous with the inevitable.

Once you spot an actor's *impulse* to move, you can suggest *where* she might go. We can take that impulse and *transform* it into a move that advances the scene. Whatever movement you come up with will be organic because it was born in the actor's impulse. The choice can't be made independently of an actor's contribution.

Of course, not every movement will originate in an actor's impulse. Some of the actor's impulses may be born from insecurity or from a desire to draw attention. A director must reject these motives for movement because they arise not from the imaginary circumstances of the *character*, but from the actual (and irrelevant) circumstances of the *actor*. It's the character's impulses discovered through the imagination of the actor that form a basis for movement that's true to the circumstances of the play.

In addition to spotting impulses that are legitimate motives for movement, a director must also be aware of movements required by the script; then, he must help the actors find motivation by discovering impulses that bring the requirements to life.

Also, for reasons of sight lines, stage composition, or directorial insight into the behavior of a character that an actor has not intuitively reached on her own, a director may request movement that helps bring the script to life. But these, too, must be justified by impulses. All movement must appear to originate in the actor' impulses and should never look as though an actor is moving because a director asked her to.

It's entirely legitimate for a director to have in mind the opening and closing images of an act, but these images also must be justified by actors' impulses that result in the desired effect. For example, in *Cat on a Hot Tin Roof*, I had a specific image of how the play should begin: Maggie enters, dabbing at her lace dress where the "no-neck monsters" have thrown a hot buttered biscuit. In the mirror on her vanity, she discovers that Brick has left the bed where she has left him sleeping off the pain of his newly broken ankle and the previous night's hangover. In a slight panic, she opens the door on the fourth wall to see if he is on the gallery (thereby establishing its location). Then, turning upstage, she hears the shower coming from up right, and her spine relaxes into a feline sensuality. This opening image involves a "dance" that the actor must perform as if spontaneously, and for which convincing impulses must be discovered.

Similarly, at the end of the second act, I wanted the actor playing Big Daddy to be upstage center, cursing the heavens with his fists raised over his head, bellowing, "Christ damn all lying sons of lying bitches!" This movement captures the image of the poem by Dylan Thomas that Tennessee Williams quotes as the epigraph for the play:

> "And you, my father, there on the sad height:
> Curse, bless me now with your fierce tears, I pray;
> Do not go gentle into that good night:
> Rage, rage against the dying of the light."

The director should encourage his cast to explore the reasons for *all* movement, no matter its origin. An organic move that arises from an actor's impulse may seem false or enforced if it's not freshly justified with each repetition. Even if a move came from an actor's discovery, if it isn't newly justified by a fresh impulse, it will seem externally imposed and false.

Before he undertakes blocking a beat, a director must be alert to the opportunities for movement that are inherent in the ground plan.

He should also be thoroughly attentive to the circumstances that influence the beat. Is there an offstage character who affects the onstage action and if so, from what direction is that character's influence felt?

For example, at the beginning of *The Seagull*, Kostya knows that from one direction, his mother and her friend, the famous author, will be coming to see his play. It's likely that side of the stage will produce nervous behavior. From another direction, he anticipates the arrival of his sweetheart, Nina. His movement in relation to her will be of a different nature. The text makes much of exactly where the moon will rise and the beauty of the vista overlooking the lake. A director must consider how these subtextual forces affect Kostya's movement, moment by moment.

It's also important to keep in mind the sensory elements you've asked the actors to imagine: the heat, the time of day, the presence of mosquitoes or gnats, the smells wafting in the air after supper, the sounds of crickets at twilight. All these elements have an effect on the movement of the actors.

Blocking a Beat

I begin each rehearsal with the actors sitting peacefully, "running" the lines for the beat we're rehearsing. This half-hour of calm gives them an opportunity to speak (quietly, in their own voices) the lines they've memorized and to hear their partners respond, turning cues into conversation.

The first time through, everyone will concentrate on remembering lines and cues. By the second time, while tossing the lines back and forth, they can begin to explore the motives for what they're saying and the meanings in what they're hearing. It gives them a chance to listen, which they couldn't do alone. A stage manager closely follows the text, helping and correcting, as requested by the actors.

We run the lines in this easy manner three or four times. Meanwhile, as the actors sit comfortably, free from any obligations for movement, I'm watching for unconscious impulses that begin to appear in their relaxed bodies. I listen to the music of the dialogue. I let it wash over me, hearing the nuances that emerge when lines are spoken.

By the fourth time through the beat, while the actors are still sitting, I sometimes get up and begin to wander as I listen, letting the cadence of the dialogue affect the muscles of my body, sensing how I respond physically to the music of the speeches. I try to do this in an unobtrusive way that doesn't draw attention to my little dance, but it's good to feel the rhythms of the dialogue in my muscles and to sense the impulses lurking there.

After running the lines several times, the actors will be eager to get on their feet, ready to inhabit the space of the set. At this point, I turn on the "magic" lights that create the mood and turn off the overhead fluorescents.

Exploration needs to be done in "real time," as opposed to stage time. For now, we don't want cues picked up; we want the cast members to take all the time they need to understand what's being said, how they feel about it, and what they want to do before speaking the next line. In real life, people take as much time as they like answering each other. There's no obligation to pick up the pace. Our work on tempo and timing will come later, but now we need to slow down enough to explore each moment, not perform it. At this point, we encourage the actors to be self-indulgent. There's a lot to consider, and it takes time to discover how everything affects our inner life. And the physical life of a scene must be based on that inner life.

The first time an actor works with this approach, she sometimes wants to write her blocking in her script, because that's the way she's always done it. We should explain that in our process there will be no need to write down blocking because the movement will originate in her impulses. If a move feels right, there will be no need to record it. Her muscles will remember it. The stage manager will keep track in her script of when and where the actor moves, and we can consult her notes if we forget exactly how and when an organic movement emerged.

Before we begin to explore the beat, I recount the given circumstances the actor needs to keep in mind: an actor must imagine *where* she is, *why* she's there, *when* it is, *who* she is at the moment, and *what* she wants. I also remind her about the sensory elements of the environment.

I suggest starting positions and assign any independent activities that should be underway as the "curtain rises." I especially emphasize, "*Take your time!*"

Sometimes, if I have some general idea of the physical progress of the scene, I may describe the areas of the stage where it would be best if certain things were to happen. If I have a specific final image of the positions I'd like the actors to achieve by the end of the beat, as I described for the end of the second act of *Cat*, I let them know the result I envision as the culmination of motives, moves, and action, so the actors can see that image as a goal. Directorial suggestions may constitute additional circumstances for actors to consider. Of course, following their impulses may lead to a different and more believable result than I've anticipated, so any such goals must remain flexible and responsive to the creativity of the actors.

Finally, I sit down and wait—patiently. The actors are now fully loaded with imaginary circumstances to explore the first moment. When they begin, I watch for an impulse that signals a need for the first move. When I see it, I rejoin the actors onstage to share my discovery. We discuss the reason for the move I saw in her impulse, and I suggest where she might go to act on it. Sometimes, as we discuss a proposed move, I try the move myself, not to demonstrate, but to see whether it feels natural. Does it feel more natural to go upstage of the chair or downstage of it? Which choice is simpler or more graceful?

I have a pet peeve while watching a production when a director makes an actor pass by an empty chair that's close to her and requires her to cross to a farther chair in order to sit. Unless there's a good reason to do so, that just doesn't make sense.

On a thrust stage, a curving cross may seem more graceful and logical than a straight line. Curved crosses may also be more beautiful if they're motivated by the train of a skirt or the flow of a cape. Circular movement may lend a sense of style that seems more true to the movement of an earlier period, when more room was required for swords, fans, and hats. But in contemporary drama, most often, the simplest, most direct route should be chosen for a cross.

If the script requires a movement for which an actor has discovered no impulse or if the director sees how a certain movement or behavior will illuminate the scene, he must describe the need for the movement in terms of the character's circumstances, so the actor can accommodate the addition in her imagination.

In other words, avoid using mechanical terms like "stage left" or "upstage" unless they're needed for clarity. Instead, describe movement in terms of the actors' reality: "toward the desk," or "go to the window," or "move away from him," or "get a drink of water" (which motivates the actor to cross stage left where a side table has a pitcher of water). These directions describe movement from the actors' point of view and will keep her in her imaginative world; stage terminology takes her out of the circumstances of her character and refers to the artifice of the stage.

Once we've determined when, where, and why an actor should move, I sit back down and ask the actors to start over, reminding them once more to take their time. The actors begin the beat again and incorporate the new move, whether it has arisen from an identified impulse or a circumstantial requirement. If the resulting movement looks right and the actors seem comfortable with it, they play on until I spot the next impulse to move. Then I stop them again and suggest where they might go.

I constantly check with the actors to see if what we've done so far feels comfortable. If it doesn't, we try something different. I'm eager to receive ideas from the actors, and unless I feel a proposed move is clearly wrong, I encourage the actor to try it. Then we evaluate together which choice is better.

Next, we begin again from the beginning. Taking their time, they play through until I spot the next need for movement. This process continues until we've explored the first full page or so of a scene; then, we take a break.

Although a description of the process may sound tedious, actually, with all the repetition, the actors begin to feel that the moves we've discovered are organic, fulfilling their internal work.

I sometimes refer to my process as rehearsing "movie style." As in a film, the actors know their lines ahead of time, the movement is explored and decided on, then there are a series of "takes" until the director and actors feel sure they've got what they want for the scene. Similarly, after we've explored any part of a beat, we could set it and then film it. But because we have no cameras, we can continue to explore and to grow. It just gets better.

After the break, we can begin on the second page of the beat, repeating the same process: slowly building up the physical life, repeating the previous moves, and exploring until the next. When we have a physical life for the second page, we go back to the beginning and play through the first two pages.

Always, I remind them to work in real time, not in stage time. We'll work on picking up speed later (in our "editing" process, to continue the film parallel), but for now, we want to take as much time as needed to explore the inner thoughts, impulses, secrets, and objectives that lead up to, and are embodied in, the physical life of the scene.

The discovery process takes much longer to go through than it will take to perform a beat once we know what we're doing and can play up to tempo. But by going too fast too soon, actors tend to skip over discoveries and rush to superficial results that will wear thin over time. Deep, slow exploration finds more richness with every repetition.

If everyone is comfortable with what we've done so far, we go on. In the same slow process, we discover what moves feel right for the third page. When we've explored it, we repeat it, and then go on to the fourth page.

Then we back up and repeat the third and fourth pages in sequence. If those feel comfortable, we go back to the beginning and slowly live through all the physical life we've discovered. By this time, we've settled into an organic physical life for the whole beat, and now we're ready for another break.

After the break, we take on the second beat, just like we explored the first. And then, if the schedule calls for it, we take on the third beat, using the same slow, explorative process, although as the actors become familiar with the routine, discoveries come more easily.

By the end of our three-hour rehearsal, we will have found a physical life that feels true and organic to each actor for eight to twelve pages, our two or three beats. In this process, a director works intimately moment by moment with the actors, sharing insights about motivations, intentions, objectives, and the interplay of circumstances and emotions. From this collaboration, a physical life is emerging that gives expression to the inner journey. It's what Harold Clurman means when he says it's good to rehearse as if there's no opening night.

Of course, in a two-person scene, a director might choose to stay out of the actors' way entirely and let them stumble through the whole beat, discovering movement on their own. Then, a director needs only to be supportive, affirming the choices that seem natural, suggesting how to fix problems they've encountered, and helping them to settle on what worked best, to "keep" it.

At no rehearsal are we merely working on blocking. At no point do I arbitrarily assign moves solely on the basis of a "stage picture."

Other Considerations

Sometimes a director may want a move for a reason that's essentially *directorial*: to tell the audience something, to balance the stage, or to create a physical dynamic that prepares for an entrance. However, it's best if he can find a way to describe the move he wants in terms of the actor's needs, not those of the audience.

I had a dreadful moment in an early rehearsal of *Twelfth Night,* in which I was playing Malvolio under David Mamet's direction. In the scene, I discover a letter, left in the garden by the pranksters Toby and Maria. I was trying to create the garden around me, discover the unexpected letter in a believable fashion, and read it as if for the very first time. While my imagination was creating these circumstances, David interrupted my concentration with an observation that seemed to come from Mars. "The audience," he told me, "won't be able to see your eyes unless you hold the letter lower."

Now this advice would be very welcome at a later stage of my rehearsal process, but at this juncture, it only interfered with my creative work. Nothing was further from Malvolio's mind than an *audience*!

Certainly, once the production moves onto the stage, a director has to make sure that an actor is seen to best advantage; but in the rehearsal room, the time for that kind of "help" had not arrived. Had David told me instead that I needed to hold the letter at a distance because I was farsighted and too vain to wear spectacles, that would have fit right in with my work; at the same time, it would have achieved the director's objective, which was to get me to hold the letter lower.

But this is the kind of mistake we all make, as the following anecdote may illustrate.

In preparing *The Seagull*, I thought I had a very good Chekhovian concept for the second act, interweaving one scene with the next. When Shamraeyev announces that the horses are ready, I thought it was just too coincidental for all the servants, coming from different tasks, to arrive through different doors at the same moment. To alleviate this coincidence, I suggested that when Trigorin has acquiesced to Arkadina's wish to leave and makes a note about "virgin pines," the servant Yakov could arrive with Trigorin's traveling cloak and Anya, the maid could come with him, bringing Arkadina's accouterments. When Trigorin sees Yakov, he says: "So we are leaving again," (so the servant's entrance justifies the line). As he stands and receives his coat, he could continue to write in his notebook: "Railway stations . . . carriages . . . veal cutlets, conversations. . . ."

Then Shamraeyev could come in, announcing the arrival of the carriage, while two more servants, Vladimir and Mikhail, would follow him on to take out the two huge trunks. (Chekhov doesn't give these servants' names, but they were what my actors decided on.)

In a low voice that perhaps only I heard, Jon Voight (playing Trigorin) muttered to me, "I have the crux of my part here. I'm not just a piece of scenery to be shoved aside. I have a moment here, in which my life changes."

Oh. Okay.

Jon's concern was that the moment when he decides what his future will be *vis-à-vis* Arkadina would be lost in the bustle of servants coming on prematurely. Sure enough, as we ran through the scene following the stage directions, the house seemed to explode all at once; the servants and relatives stormed the stage in the frenzy of departure; but standing stark still in the center of the hubbub, Trigorin fixed Arkadina with a look of such anguished resentment that his life indeed seemed in the balance. His intense fervor made the quick, passionate scene with Nina that follows seem almost inevitable. Apparently Chekhov knew what he was doing, and my brave actor saved me from directorial excess that would have upstaged the acting. We found a way to honor Jon's moment, which was far more important than my "directorial conceit."

Sculpting Behavior

Designing a physical life for the action of a play is a director's most visible contribution to a production. The audience will evaluate his work chiefly on how clear, smooth, and seamless the movement appears.

Early in my career, I was so focused on helping the actors inhabit the world of the play with believable performances that I neglected the importance of communicating with the audience. As a result, I was highly popular with actors and writers, but audiences probably couldn't see what all the fuss was about.

My awakening about the importance of staging was the result of a critic's response to my off-Broadway debut. See Chapter 12 for Walter Kerr's alarming evaluation of my "blocking," which woke me up to the necessity of assuming more responsibility for where my actors move.

Allowed free rein, many actors will prefer downstage center to any other position, and will gravitate toward that privileged spot. The result of directing with too light a touch can be to appear overly controlling. To achieve the best proportions requires a director to consider and approve *every* move, so that the actors' movement seems effortless and essential, motivated by the circumstances of the play, rather than the actor's ego.

Once I realized how important movement is as a way of communicating meaning, I began to see the larger picture. My defensive dismissal of "blocking" gave way to seizing an opportunity to illustrate a narrative through designing organic movement. Although I had always perceived the importance of the ground plan to the actors' movement, now I began to understand how valuable the scenic elements, the costumes, props, music, and lights were in expressing the meaning of the play.

More significantly, it dawned on me that the best way to help actors achieve a living performance was to guide them in finding the moves that best express their inner journey. I perceived that a director is a sculptor of behavior.

Good organic staging is akin to Michelangelo's idea of freeing the person from the stone surrounding him. For a director, the stone is the surrounding space of the stage, and he's carving the movement that gives birth to meaning.

Chapter Eight

Reviewing Discoveries

The exploration of beats I described in the last chapter, looking for a physical life based on impulses, is usually scheduled for the afternoons in my rehearsals. The mornings are reserved to review our previous discoveries. Reviewing beats is virtually as important as the initial exploration. The cast can concentrate on playing through the beats without undue disruption. As any actor will tell you, interruptions aren't helpful to an actor's process. Yet because the units of action are so short, a director has plenty of opportunity to offer advice between the repetitions. We should be able to work through a beat (or a group of beats) several times.

Review rehearsals are many people's favorite part of the schedule. The urgent work of finding a believable physical life is behind them, and the worries of opening night seem far away. It's the time we have for "play practice," as we called it in grade school.

Reviewing Beats

When reviewing the beats, actors have an opportunity for a different kind of exploration: how the moments flow from one into another. It's a matter of stringing impulses together, allowing them to strengthen into objectives.

Even though the initial exploration produced movement that felt right and organic at the time, as an actor begins to play through, he may find it feels better to simplify. He may discover that some moves are unnecessary now that he has a sense of the overall scene. He may decide that some of his impulses should be "sat on," rather than finding expression in a move. A director can help decide which moves can be cut, if they seem irrelevant or make the player uncomfortable. Often a second look can bring insights about better choices of where or when to move.

But on the whole, our concentration transfers from movement to other important aspects of the beats. We've got the moves down, and everyone is satisfied with the physical life. Now our attention can turn to what's going on inside.

During these reviews, suggest specific assignments for each repetition. It can be helpful to focus on one aspect of a scene, rather than trying to accomplish everything at once. For example, the actors might think exclusively about the environmental, sensory conditions: the temperature, the humidity, the smell, sounds, time of day, when they've eaten last, how they slept the night before, what they dreamed about.

Another review could focus on personalizing their objectives, making them stronger—what Meisner calls "raising the stakes." I devised an exercise that applies Meisner's use of repetition to the text in order to explore the actors' personal relationships to what they're saying.

The original purpose of the exercise was to restore life to a production following the deadly influence of tech rehearsals, which tend to drain creativity. But when I was directing *Long Day's Journey into Night,* I introduced the application of repetition to the text earlier as a means of exploration during the review period.

Essentially, the exercise involves repeating what has been said to you until you discover through your personal evaluation of the cue why you respond with your written line. The cue is passed through your actual experience, taken in, and repeated until it connects to your response. Using repetition to explore the dialogue is very useful in personalizing what's being said so that the written lines become an actual expression of your feelings and subtext. For a more detailed explanation of the technique, see Chapter 11 where I describe how this same exercise can reinvigorate a cast after the enervating effects of tech.

Sometimes it's productive to experiment with hidden circumstances for the actors to try, just for the hell of it, probably to be discarded afterwards. These hidden circumstances will color the main action and can offer fresh discoveries. They could include things like: What if you really needed to go to the bathroom? What if today were your birthday, and nobody has remembered? What if you have a headache? What if you'd like your partner to kiss you? What if her voice reminds you of your mother's voice? What if you just won the lottery, but don't want to mention it? What if you couldn't sleep last night? What if you're hung over?

These subtextual situations may not be part of the circumstances depicted in the script, but they might prove worth trying just to see how they color the beat. On occasion, an actor may find a wonderful underlying secret that he can actually incorporate. Other experiments will show exactly why such an inner circumstance would completely wreck the scene and by going in an extremely *wrong* direction, illustrate more clearly what is *right*.

Sometimes, an actor can unlock incredible dimension by playing the *opposite* of what seems, on the surface, to be needed. If a character is very angry, he might find lowering his voice is far more menacing than shouting.

Review rehearsals offer the best opportunity for an actor to find a personal point of view. A good example of this was John Malkovich's entrance in *Burn This*. Pale comes on in the middle of the night to pick up his dead brother's possessions. He storms into the apartment with vituperative complaints about parking conditions in New York City. Anna (played by Joan Allen), cowering in her skimpy hopi coat, listens silently, until finally she manages to get a word in: "Do I know you?"

During our review rehearsals, we were discussing the brutish behavior of Pale when John let us in on what he was playing: "She is completely rude to me. She's insensitive to my situation, I've just lost my brother, I've come to pick up his things, as I said I would, and the bitch doesn't even offer me a cup of coffee." Now, *that's* personalizing a point of view.

It's important to remember that no villain ever thinks he's behaving badly. He's just doing what he needs to do to accomplish his ends. An actor must not criticize his character. He must understand from Iago's point of view just *why* the Moor must be made to suffer.

Although unquestionably the tempo of the beats will pick up some, keep reminding cast members to take their time. These rehearsals may not be as slow as the ones when we were looking for movement, but we're still exploring the beats for hidden richness. No conscious attempt should be made to pick up the pace. There will come a time when we'll go faster, but it shouldn't be in our early review work.

We're looking for what Lee Strasberg called "the colors" of the scene. To find them, we'll need to flow without interruption but at a leisurely pace. Even outrageous comedy or farce should be slowed down to anchor the characters firmly in believable reality. It's important to note that it's not an actor's job to be funny. That obligation belongs to the author. The actor's job is to discover truthful behavior, and if the author has written it funny, the truth will be funny.

Of course, a director can aid and abet the writer with a physical life that's true to the style and humor of the play. This collusion crystallizes in what we usually refer to as "comic bits." When a character is hiding behind a bush, picks that bush up, and moves it around with him (as could easily happen in the aforementioned garden scene in *Twelfth Night*), it's the visual image that's funny, not the acting. The character is simply trying as hard as he can to remain hidden from Malvolio. He may be forced to go to ridiculous lengths, but he's not trying to be funny.

It's during review rehearsals that we begin to see group problems that need to be solved together. The timing, not the speed, of the actor behind the bush must coordinate with the timing of Malvolio's looking around, sensing something's not quite right, but unable to put his finger on exactly what's askew. Did that bush move? Don't be silly, bushes can't move. As he goes back to his letter, the bush moves. The actors need to work out together, with the help of the director, this intricate *pas-de-deux*.

Review rehearsals serve a variety of needs, depending on the style of the play. In a naturalistic drama, an actor will be working on all the complicated business he must accomplish in a scene, whether it's packing a box because he's moving or lacing up his shoes. He'll be looking for foolproof ways to get his task done, and by going through it several times, he'll develop insights about the specific requirements for props. The cast will decide how much water should be in a glass, how loose the laces on the skates need to be, where a compact disc should be placed on a shelf. The director's staff (stage managers or assistants) will keep careful track of such discoveries and pass them on to the appropriate artisans.

It's during these rehearsals that the prop master will want to begin to gather preferences from the actors. What kind of liquid would they prefer to represent red wine? Is anyone allergic to anything? It's sometimes difficult to come up with something everyone can eat with enthusiasm that the production can afford. It's part of the actor's job to convince us the crushed banana, chunks of bread, and cranberry stained apple sauce are as delicious as the *foie gras* or caviar they're supposed to represent.

The exact nature of costume pieces may come to light: whether a coat should have buttons or a zipper, whether a skirt should fasten in front or behind, whether a hat or gloves add or detract from the business.

This is also the best time for the costume designer to make appointments for costume fittings. These rehearsals are a bit more relaxed, and a director can be a little more generous with time. Work can be flexible enough to accommodate other people's needs.

A director, too, is checking whether the things she and her designers have planned actually work with the physical action that has evolved. What adjustments will need to be made that couldn't be anticipated?

In a Shakespearean tragedy, an actor may use review rehearsals to explore how his impulses fit with the verse. When we were doing *Hamlet*, we listened to a recording of John Gielgud's matchless reading. Sitting down, working on the verse, William Hurt could speak the poetry with all the skill and beauty one would expect of a Julliard graduate. But when he was on his feet, involved in Hamlet's world, the verse had a tendency to be chopped up and mumbled. It's very difficult to keep the impulses spontaneous within the rigid demands of iambic pentameter. It's during review rehearsals that conflicting elements should be resolved.

Usually, during this stage people feel confident and optimistic about how the work is going. There may be questions up ahead, but the work that's been realized is beginning to feel good. A director can make the most of this spirit of goodwill. She can relax, and let everyone have more fun. She'll find everyone is in a more agreeable mood, so she can get away with making directorial demands that would seem heavy-handed at a more vulnerable juncture.

Strive to be perceptive about the specific achievements of each repetition so you can offer constructive comments more than: "Okay! Okay, let's do it again." The repetition provides a good opportunity to make those suggestions you've been biting your tongue about.

Larger Segments

As the actors repeat the beats, the deliberate slowness eases up because they become more familiar and comfortable through the repetition of review. As a result, it's soon possible to cover more ground in the three-hour slice of rehearsal. We can begin to add more beats after they've received enough review individually. The beats can be laid end to end, and if we've rehearsed any beats out of sequence, now they can be put into successive order.

Our rehearsal schedule is fashioned to allow us to build up larger and larger segments of work. The first rehearsals following exploration for movement should provide ample review of individual beats. The next time we repeat a beat it should be joined by its surrounding counterparts.

A rehearsal rhythm is established that gradually increases the size of each section that's scheduled for review. Here's the kind of progression it provides:

- slowly exploring a beat to discover a physical life;
- carefully reviewing a beat through repetition and experiment;
- rehearsing larger segments of several beats, sequentially;
- accumulating beats into half an act;
- stumbling through an entire act;
- working on improvements in each act, with variations and exercises;

- working through the entire play, with a natural pace, looking for the through-lines of action; and
- tightening cues, picking up the pace, and working on volume and audibility.

I'll discuss these progressive stages in a subsequent chapter, but this outline shows how the process of review continues the exploration, carrying the work forward into improving what we've done.

Stanislavski told his actors: "Always and forever, you are playing yourselves." What he meant is that an actor is always exploring the imaginary circumstances of the play in terms of what if these actually were *his own*. How would *I* behave? What would *I* want? What would *I* feel?

All the initial work on a script should follow the simple guideline of exploring the circumstances from a very personal point of view. Only then, Stanislavski says, can actors shift their focus to characterization.

Meisner goes further, suggesting that there is no such thing as character separate from the actions. The actions define the character. As mentioned about the dual aspects of a quarter in Chapter 3, action and character are different viewpoints of the same phenomenon. Action creates an impression of character, while character choices dictate the inner, outer, and behavioral actions an actor experiences as he "becomes" the character.

After a cast has fully explored a substantial portion of a script personalizing the imaginary circumstances, a director can suggest ways to focus on more sophisticated discoveries, like characterization.

In attempting to improve the work, it may be useful to suggest to each actor a specific focus for a run-through. For example, in my recent production of *Cat on a Hot Tin Roof*, once we had established a physical life based on the actors' sense of truth, I suggested specific goals for the next stumble-through.

I mentioned to Maggie that Tennessee Williams had a remarkable sense of ironic humor; he was famous for attending performances of his plays and howling with laughter at what everyone had considered the most poignant moments of the play. If Blanche (in *Streetcar*) observes to the paperboy that he looks like a prince from the *Arabian Nights*, Tennessee thought this was a hilarious attempt to seduce the youngster with an extravagantly poetic pick-up line. Because Molly Schaffer had explored the whole first act of Maggie's bravery, insecurity, longing, passion, and regret, I suggested she should in this run-through go all-out in exploring the irony of everything she or anyone else said, and to see ironic humor in every situation.

As I put it to the cast, "This rehearsal room is our holy of holies. No one in the audience will ever know about the magic we employ to bring them the result they will see. Don't be afraid to explore one aspect to the extreme to see how that aspect figures in the overall colors of your work."

I suggested to Jason Kuykendall, who was working on Brick, that he should concentrate on incorporating the behavior of Jack Snow, a professional football player with the St. Louis Rams whom we had interviewed, and use his characteristically masculine gruffness throughout the act, hiding any vulnerability or sensitivity.

I suggested that Michael McCarty fully explore one single circumstance: that he felt extremely ill, as if he had the flu, and could barely make it through the rehearsal.

I asked Jo Twiss to explore the queenly aspect of Big Mama, as if she were used to having her slightest order obeyed and suffered no fools, not even Big Daddy. Big Mama's expectation is unquestioned obedience.

John Lepard worked on exploring Gooper's sense of inferiority. Joneal Joplin concentrated on Doctor Baugh's realization that he was lying to these people even with his silence. Edwin McDonough experimented with Reverend Tooker's aspiration to become a bishop in his church, based on exploiting the instinct as a businessman, which underlies almost all success in our capitalistic society.

As a result of concentrating on just one aspect of "character," and going all out in their exploration in a rehearsal experiment that no audience would ever see, the cast made incredible progress, leaping ahead with truth and insight into another dimension of the playing of the play. Simple focus is one way of truly improving the work.

As larger segments are rehearsed, this would also be an ideal time to explore the work utilizing Anne Bogart's "Viewpoints" techniques. Viewpoints allows a cast and a director to explore an individual's creative relationship to the whole. The physical awareness of working together to create layers of meaning can enrich the individual exploration that has preceded it. For an understanding of her innovative techniques, consult her book *A Director Prepares*.

In Chapter 10, I'll discuss other exercises for improving the work, once the basic truth of the circumstances of the play has been thoroughly explored.

Chapter Nine

Criticism and Notes

One of the more challenging aspects of a director's work with actors lies in communicating ideas for improvement. Generally, if the director has established atmosphere of trust, an actor is eager to hear how she's doing. Most actors want a director to offer suggestions in a constructive manner that will help them get better. These suggestions usually come after a run-through, in a session of "notes," when the director takes the opportunity to request changes that he perceives would make the performances better. Consider which approach to communicating the improvements you want works best for you.

Elia Kazan was said to have cultivated intense, personal relationships with his actors, and he used this intimacy to give notes. He would take each actor aside for private discussions, rather than give his critiques in an open forum.

For sure, there are some matters that should be discussed in a one-on-one, confidential manner. By avoiding the possible embarrassment of public criticism, you show an actor that you value her contribution and understand the parity of your collaborative partnership. Most actors will respond well to such special treatment.

Although there's wonderful potential in using such a technique, there are many instances when a different approach is needed. I use a mixture of public and private criticism for several reasons:

- Open critiques recognize the ensemble nature of the collaboration.
- Public discussions of a scene help establish an egalitarian environment, which has a positive effect on the cast as a whole.

- Open critiques make better use of the time.
- Everyone may learn something from group evaluations, whereas during private discussions, the remainder of the cast is excluded and must simply wait their turn.

Public Cast Notes

If you elect to give notes to the whole cast, there are several considerations that can help make public assessments more beneficial than risky.

Public appraisals demonstrate that all members of the cast are equally important to the success of the ensemble and that individual attention is available to all. They prevent suspicion that the director has a favorite, who gets special treatment over the others.

If you *do* have a favorite, make clear why her work should be an example to the others. It's important to establish meritorious standards of admiration. Others in the cast may share your view and actually welcome the opportunity to learn from an exemplary model.

In open discussions, the entire cast can see how you treat each actor, not just any favorites, with courtesy, respect, and admiration—even love. They can hear the encouraging tone in your voice and see the patient concern with which you listen to excuses from an actor who's been criticized.

Everyone will understand the need for deference to a star, but in a sense, everyone deserves "star treatment." You can accomplish this if you try to have at least one note for every actor, regardless of the size of her part, and even if the note is only praise for continuing to do a good job.

Sometimes a problem that seems to be about one person actually lies in the interplay with another player. By discussing the issue openly, you encourage the actors to recognize communal problems and reduce private grumbling. The criticism of one actor often relates to others in the cast as well. For example, if an actor has been sitting on her impulses, you can draw everyone's attention to this common acting problem, which is relevant to their own work; others in the cast may learn from her need to improve. If you offer observations in a constructive manner, actors understand the criticism is not personal; in fact, they are *counting* on the director to help them.

During public notes, it's important to engage each actor in a personal, two-way exchange as you discuss a problem. Criticism is of no value if it's ignored, resented, or not understood. You should cultivate the trust of each actor, so she'll welcome your contribution to her work.

To Be Avoided

Positive communication skills are required to cultivate the best collaboration with your cast. Several traps should studiously be avoided.

Never use sarcasm when there's another way to communicate. Although it's possible to use a sense of humor in criticism, you should never embarrass an actor in front of fellow artists. Public humiliation of an actor is an abuse of a director's power. Few actors will want to work again with a sadist.

It's also counterproductive to weigh one actor's work against another. Don't compare achievements. When I was a child, nothing grated on my nerves more than having my behavior compared to someone else's: "Why can't you act nice, like Jimmie?" In rehearsal, you shouldn't contrast Jimmie's skill or talent with anyone else's. It's useless criticism because each actor's gift is unique.

Some directors use the power of fear to intimidate a cast, but I believe that one can "catch more flies with honey than with vinegar," as my grand-mother used to tell me.

There are, however, actors who seem to need a director to project the strong "father image" of a stern disciplinarian. They won't respond well to praise, but they crave criticism.

Nevertheless, you should offer praise when it's earned, and be sure your criticisms are fair. Other cast members will appreciate watching how you handle the particular needs of each actor, and they'll understand that the severe criticism you may employ with one who needs it won't spill over into your relationships with them.

Above all, resist the temptation to shout. That may sometimes be very difficult to do, but yelling at actors rarely accomplishes anything but alarm. Patience is more productive.

The most perceptive insight I learned from Lee Strasberg at the Actors Studio was this treasure:

> Always remember that if an actor isn't giving you what you want, it's almost never because they don't *want* to please you, but that they don't know *how* to give you the result you're asking for.

If you keep that in mind, you'll discover that you have a reservoir of patience you never knew you had. Patience is one of the most important traits a director can develop. If you focus on helping an actor, you're working *together* to solve the problem; it's easier to be patient with a partner.

Even though you've established an atmosphere of congeniality, never let actors give each other notes. Usually, one director per production is a sufficient number, and if anyone has a suggestion about another actor's work, he should bring it up to the director in private. What you do with this opinion is up to you, but if you pass it on, don't identify your source. Once you decide to give a direction, it's your idea.

You will also need to work out a procedure for receiving an author's notes as well as a producer's and for finding an appropriate time and manner to pass them on. Remember that playwrights and producers are seldom fluent in acting lingo, so your job will be to translate the notes from the writer into actors' terms.

Of course, public critiques can get you into real trouble. At the final dress rehearsal of *Foxfire* at the Guthrie Theater in Minneapolis, frustrated by all the details that are endemic to this stage of work, I was finishing up my notes to the cast. The issue involved making an audience believe that the actor portraying a musician (Richard Cox) was actually playing a guitar. After he tuned up with a few strums on a live electric guitar, a recording took over when he performed the number, miming the fingering. We were having some technical trouble finding a smooth transition from the live guitar to the recording.

As sometimes happens when a problem is publicly discussed, several people began to express their opinions about how to solve it. Hume Cronyn suggested that we just cut the opening strums. I felt it would undermine the illusion that the guitar was actually being played. Mr. Cronyn asked why it wouldn't work his way, and I snapped, "Because I'm the director, and that's the way I want it!"

Well, Mr. Cronyn did not speak to me ever again. I had bruised his considerable ego, and this was a terrible thing to do in front of everyone. It seemed to show a lack of respect for his long and distinguished career. What made it really awful was that he was not only the star of the show, he was the cowriter, the producer, and married to his costar, the incomparable Jessica Tandy. A month of our good work together evaporated in the instant of my ill-considered remark. Fortunately, Ms. Tandy was able to persuade Mr. Cronyn to accept my apology, at least enough to get him to a line-through before the first performance. But he never forgave me my arrogance, so I withdrew as director before the production went on to Broadway.

Despite this example of a critique gone wrong, I try to create an atmosphere of trust in rehearsals and develop relationships based on respect for each individual.

Be Specific

The supreme rule in giving a cast notes, whether public or private, is to be as specific as possible. General ideas or vague concepts cannot be acted. If you want to correct a performance, pinpoint exactly what would make it better. Stay away from talking about attitudes or emotions, and always try to find active verbs that the actor can employ to improve her work.

I cringe whenever I hear a director say, "Show us how sweet your character is." Or, "I'm not getting that you're angry. Give me more anger." If an actor is working properly, her attention shouldn't be on "showing" an audience anything. She should be trying to experience the character's needs within her circumstances; so to remind the player of the external effect she should have is to invite phony indications. A director would be wiser to investigate with the actor the internal causes that bring about the heightened results he's seeking. Help actors personalize to raise the stakes.

One of my least favorite things as an actor was when my director tried to explain what the scene should be, he sometimes described exactly what I *thought* I was doing. A director must see what the actors are doing, and if it doesn't express the result you want, help them find how to *change* what they're doing.

Of course, every director has moments when he just doesn't know what to say. There was a funny example in a rehearsal for *Balm in Gilead* at Circle Rep, when the director John Malkovich said to Burke Pearson, "Oh, yes, and Burke. . . ." He paused, struggling to put his objection into words. Finally, with self-mocking irony, he begged, "Burke, could you, please, just *act* that better?" Everyone had the good sense to laugh.

Demonstrating

It is sometimes very tempting to find shortcuts to communicate what you want an actor to do. *Showing* an actor what you want her to do or demonstrating how you want her to deliver a line should be resisted.

I *never* give an actor a line reading. This is sometimes hard to avoid when an actor's emphasis on a word renders the meaning of a line obscure or even opposite of what's intended. It's a situation akin to a singer not being able to hear that she's slightly sharp on a high C.

In such an event, I simply point out the specific word that's being hit and say that if a different word were emphasized, it would convey the meaning better. If this criticism puzzles an actor, quite a comic routine may develop. I struggle to explain what's wrong with the delivery, without actually speaking the line myself.

Sometimes an actor just says, "Oh, come on. Just give me a line reading. I can take it." But I try to resist the temptation.

In *Redwood Curtain*, Debra Monk and I had an ongoing struggle with one of her lines. Referring to her dead brother's reaction to a clue in the mystery of his adopted daughter's parentage, Debra had to say, "Laird just laughed." For some reason, she emphasized *Laird* and threw the rest away. This sounded very strange, because it's important to know Laird's reaction to a significant plot point. It seemed to me the word *laughed* conveyed the meaning and should be the word emphasized, but Debra just couldn't hear it. "What did Laird do?" I'd ask. Because I adamantly refused to give her a reading, our struggle with the line became a running joke and the bane of Debra's life in the role. After each performance, her first anxious question was: "Did I say it right?" Never mind; it didn't keep her from winning the Tony Award for her performance.

The reason I steer clear of line readings is because I believe speaking the lines is the actor's job and that when a director asks an actor to mimic a delivery, he has usurped the actor's creative territory. This is probably a reaction to my days as an actor in college, when I hated more than anything being given a line reading by a director. I felt all my creativity evaporate with each instruction. Any subtlety or depth I perceived was sacrificed to the expediency of delivering the obvious.

William Hurt and John Malkovich are actors who often have an unusual, not to say eccentric, delivery, but a play is usually the beneficiary of their contributions. They endow a line with an individuality and freshness that makes it sound as if it springs from the impulses of the moment.

Sometimes, a peculiar emphasis may give a line greater depth and shades of meaning than is apparent on the page. That's why a living performance of a talented actor conveys a great deal more than reading the play in your library. So unless the meaning is being completely obscured, allow the actor freedom and flexibility in her interpretation.

I mentioned earlier that when I suggest a movement to an actor, I sometimes try the move myself. It's not my intention to demonstrate, but to *experience* the move I'm suggesting. Often, my muscles will tell me intuitively something is wrong. A move may seem like a good idea, but when you do it, it feels strange, forced, or unnatural. You can discover for yourself why a move is awkward without making an actor go through it.

Most actors don't object to my trying out a move to see if it works before I ask them to do it. During rehearsals for *Childe Byron*, I often found myself limping as I blocked William Hurt's movement as the clubfooted Lord Byron.

If you do attempt the moves you're assigning, keep in mind that your stride may be different from the actor's. If you're six feet tall, as I am, you might cross the stage in three strides, whereas your actress, who's only five feet tall, will need many more steps to cover the same ground.

I think it's imperative that a director should *never* demonstrate an emotion or attitude to an actor. I have no doubt that as I attempt to communicate with an actor while discussing a moment, emotions or attitudes may sometimes unconsciously color my direction. But it's wise to keep in mind that many directors make poor actors, and you don't want your actor to mimic your bad performance.

Taking Notes for Notes

I have been blessed with a good memory for details, so I rarely write down my notes for the cast. Especially in the early rehearsals, we are working so collaboratively and in such small beats that my concentration is on identifying with the actors' experience. At this point, I'm not yet an objective observer from *outside* the creative process.

Naturally, as we begin to cover larger segments in review, I have to keep my reactions in mind until the scene is finished. One reason I don't take notes is that I believe some directors take far too many, weighing their actors down with trivial concerns. I feel that if I can't *remember* a note I want to give at the end of a scene, it probably wasn't important anyway.

By the time the rehearsals reach the stage of run-throughs, it becomes necessary to commit to writing the corrections you want to make. In order to keep your attention at all times on the stage, use an assistant director to take notes. I sometimes whisper just one word or phrase to my assistant (like "faster" or "put on her gloves"), and hope that he'll record at what point in the dialogue I gave him the note. If I know *where* I saw a problem, I usually remember fully what the improvement was I had in mind. It's not important for an assistant to *understand* the criticism, as long as he accurately records *when* it occurred.

With your assistants, you'll need to work out a process of documentation that maximizes their help to you in giving notes. Because I don't actually write the comment, when it comes time to give notes, my assistant is at the center of the action. He reads the word or short phrase I've whispered to him and identifies where in the scene I asked him to write the note. With any luck, I then can wax eloquent about my insight.

As I've noted previously, each director must develop a way of working that is suited to his particular personality. If you can't match the prowess of my memory, you'll need to find your own way to take notes. But the principles of communicating with actors through criticism should hold true, no matter *how* you accomplish the mechanics of note taking.

In any case, don't get bogged down with petty, picky details. There are times near the end of the rehearsal period when notes will naturally devolve to smaller and smaller details, in which you seek to perfect what is already good. But early on, keep your eye focused on the creative elements that will construct a solid basis for the organic realization of the scene. You can quibble later, but first get the important things right.

For many directors, giving notes to a cast is their only hope of getting the performances they want. In the chapter that follows, I will discuss other tactics to help actors achieve their best work to make the play clear and effective.

Chapter Ten

Improving the Work

W hen you begin to rehearse longer segments, like an entire act, you and the cast have an opportunity to discover the through-lines that impel the action forward. If your work up to this stage has been organic, the whole act will be alive and rich in detail, but slow and somewhat private, still focused inward.

Rather than continue to give notes that address individual actors and particular moments, a director can utilize several exercises to help focus the whole cast on getting its inner work to rise to the surface and flourish.

Our work at this point needs to go through a transition, from being based in personal or observed experiences, which have an internal focus, to exploring the abundant creativity that can be found playing together in the present moment.

Looked at another way, it's like a transition from Stanislavski to Meisner, both of whose perspectives we've used in our exploration. Up to this point, we've encouraged the actors to be selfish about their needs and to focus on the truth of their inner lives. Now we want to encourage them to look for inspiration in the behavior of their fellow players.

The Stumble-Through

Once again, though, we must be cautious not to go too fast and jump over obstacles in our path. We still have a lot to learn from obstacles.

The first time we go through a whole act, the goal is to stumble through, with all the rough edges showing, playing through slowly, without interruption. By calling it a *stumble-through,* you relieve the actors of concerns about being perfect at this point. The important thing for everyone to ascertain from the first stumble-through is whether the whole act feels true and the physical life is deep-rooted.

To an outside observer, the act may seem interminable with all the labor still visible. Except for the lighting designer, outsiders shouldn't be admitted to the rehearsal process at this juncture.

It's a good time for the lighting designer to take notes in the script on all the movement, but it's too early for the sound designer or composer to get correct timings. And it's too early for a producer to assess your progress; they'd likely panic. Any external judgments should be kept at abeyance.

Our first stumble-through for *Long Day's Journey into Night* at the Arizona Theater Company illustrates how unfinished a stumble-through can be. You have to understand that this production marked an artistic apex in my career. The reviews unanimously blithered with praise, and the audiences provided standing ovations at every performance. It took on a legendary aura, and in Arizona, people still reminisce in hushed, reverential tones about their experience of this production, to this very day.

This is not meant to boast, but to make clear that the end result of our work was not bad, so this anecdote can be appreciated in that context.

Our rehearsal period had been fantastic. The actors, the stage managers, the assistants, and I felt privileged to be part of such an extraordinary ensemble. Our improvisations had been exemplary, our discovery process, miraculous. We approached our first stumble-through with excitement because we were going to share our work for the first time. One of our designers had flown in just in time to see us put the whole play together. He was thrilled to be there and eager to see what we'd accomplished.

So we began our slow, painstaking excursion through the play, with all the richness of our discoveries on display. Just before the end of the second act, we were startled out of our artistic reverie by a loud sawing sound that shattered the hush of the rehearsal room. Sitting in his straight-backed chair, our blessed designer had fallen deeply asleep! We looked at each other, and laughed. Apparently we weren't quite yet overwhelming. We let our exhausted collaborator snore on while we finished the act.

Of course, he was embarrassed when he woke up as the overhead lights were turned on and apologized profusely. We assured him we weren't at all insulted. But nobody let on just how thunderous his snores had been and how grateful we all were, really, to be taken down to earth, to recognize that we had a long journey to go before any of us would sleep so peacefully.

Work-Throughs

After a stumble-through establishes that you can play honestly through an entire act, it's time to begin the process of work-throughs, in which you hope to improve the growth of the whole cast. As the name implies, these are still not performances, but an extension of the working process.

Rather than simply replicating the procedure of the stumble-through, try using a different exercise with each repetition. Each of the exercises that follow (to be tried in separate rehearsals) helps the cast improve by posing new challenges. Using these exercises, which an audience clearly isn't meant to see, also helps to prevent the cast from letting its work become entrenched at the current level or from prematurely thinking about the audience.

One good exercise is to ask the cast to sing the entire act, as if it were an opera or operetta. This helps the actors to find external expression (a melody or tone) for their inner work, using the dialogue as a libretto. It also unites the cast in a communal, difficult task.

Tell the actors that it doesn't matter whether they can sing or not but to make the effort. They won't be judged by how good they sound; the exercise is to help them discover how to share their inner work in a more public manner.

The actors should improvise melodies that are an expression of what they're doing and saying. The tone of the improvised music will vary greatly, from dramatic arias to comic recitatives. In addition to the melodies, the actors will become more aware of the rhythms of a scene, because rhythm is a key ingredient of all music. It also helps them to connect to what has just preceded their line, because music flows from one part to another.

Initially, for a variety of reasons, the cast may be dismayed by your request. Some actors are self-conscious about how poorly they sing; to others, it may seem a silly reversal of the serious work they've been doing. Everyone will recognize immediately how hard it's going to be.

It takes an enormous amount of energy to sing an entire act, and the cast members will feel their energy jacked up to meet the demands. Summoning the vigor needed to sing is a step in finding the energy level they'll need in order to fill a theater with their intimate work. Without asking them to be any louder, it starts them working toward projection, a necessary element of all stage work.

Sometimes, the actors will discover how moved they become by singing the words. Singing is a wonderful manifestation of emotion. When a feeling becomes very full, one *needs* to sing to give it articulation. Think of the emotional expression in a song like "On the Street Where You Live" from *My Fair Lady*. That same joyous passion must be felt and expressed, even when an actor is playing Freddy in Shaw's *Pygmalion,* on which the musical is based.

The entire cast will get involved in performing this operetta, and everyone will want to see and hear the results. As soon as they exit, they'll turn to watch and listen to their fellow players. It's a good way of rousing the support of all in the company for each other.

On occasion, when you have a good musician or two in the cast, the improvised melodic "adaptation" may suggest how good a musical version of the play actually could be. With several glorious Broadway singers in the cast, our sing-through of *Book of Days: The Opera* should've been booked for the Met.

The camaraderie of the company forms a safety net for taking risks, especially for those who don't sing well. The sing-through rehearsal will produce a buoyant, ebullient atmosphere, and many a laugh will be shared.

Singing through the play will bring more improvement than a prosaic work-through with notes could hope to achieve.

Depending on the play, the next work-through might focus on playing in the gibberish of a foreign language. If it's a comedy, you might suggest the cast deliver every line with a "bad" Italian accent, accompanied by exaggerated gestures, or a thick Southern drawl. Choose your accent according to the direction you feel your cast needs to work. If they're a little too tight, loosen them up with Russian accents that will encourage openhearted emotions to flow. If they're a bit over-the-top, an English accent will tend to bury all signs of emotion beneath a stiff upper lip and help take everything down a notch.

By purposefully distorting the lines, the cast must listen carefully to each other, and it puts their focus again on how to express the words they're using. It frees them from complacent deliveries.

If the actors' dialogue seems too obvious or too casual, you might ask them to code each word in *pig-Latin*. So, Hamlet would say to Ophelia, "Ere-whay is-hay our-yay ather-fay?" Ophelia must reply, "At-hay ome-hay, y-may ord-lay." Hamlet then would cry, "Et-lay e-thay oors-day e-bay ut-shay upon-hay im-hay, at-thay e-hay a-may a-play e-thay ool-fay in-hay is-hay own-hay ouse-hay!"

By speaking in pig-Latin, the actors can discover that the actual words of the scene are also a kind of code for what the characters really *want* to say. The words always carry more meaning than the obvious.

This worked especially well in my production at A.S.U. of Archibald Macleish's *J.B.*, in which the author recounts the biblical tale of Job, setting his trials in a tattered circus. The character of The Messenger, who appears in several different guises, must tell J.B. and Sarah that another of their children has been killed. Each time, he repeats, "I only am escaped alone to tell thee." Pig-Latin helped my student actor find an inarticulate urgency that endowed the lines with the inscrutability of a sibyl.

I have discovered that this exercise is easier for some actors than others. Particularly, the younger members of the company may never have encountered pig-Latin, which was in vogue briefly in the middle of the twentieth century, when teenagers devised a secret language, so they could communicate with each other and the square adults wouldn't comprehend. So, this exercise will probably be more limited in its usage than the singing exercise.

But it does have a lesson to teach actors: there is more to meaning than reciting words. We send secret signals with every line we speak.

Finally, for the third work-through, try asking the cast to whisper the entire act. They should whisper loud enough to be heard by each other, but soft enough to be secretive. This exercise is especially helpful in tuning in to the necessity of listening carefully. It can also act as an antidote to poisonous habitual deliveries. It refreshes the need to communicate. It creates and intensifies intimacy between people, as if they're sharing secrets.

In the twentieth anniversary revival of *Talley's Folly* at the Repertory Theater of St. Louis, the whisper-through bestowed an urgency to the illicit rendezvous between Matt and Sally: the dangerous potential of being discovered by Sally's family. This circumstance is central to the play, but it can easily get lost in pursuit of the different aspects of their complicated relationship. After our whisper-through, the actors always remembered to curb their volume when anger made them raise their voices, and loudness was translated into intensity.

Interestingly, a whisper-through requires almost as much energy as a sing-through. But the discoveries are worth the energy expended.

I learned another useful tool in a work-through from Hume Cronyn and Jessica Tandy, who in turn were taught the technique by the director Alan Schneider. (This is the way many techniques in the theater are acquired, passed on from one generation to the next.)

It might be called a dream-through.

First, everyone must do a thorough warm-up, culminating in a group relaxation exercise. When everyone is completely relaxed, they should all lie down on the floor (mats are desirable), maintaining their total relaxation. Breathing deeply, and with their eyes closed, they begin to speak the dialogue of the play, reaching out to communicate with each other with only their voices.

This quiet rendition of the play will have a sleepy, dreamlike quality, and people may find that their emotions rise unbidden to the surface as in dreams. Relaxation is closely related to breathing, which is very responsive to emotions. Think about how you gasp for breath when sobbing, or how you hold your breath in fear, or hyperventilate in excitement. The deep breathing of total relaxation connects to the feelings that tension restricts and releases them from the prison of the body.

This dream-through should teach us just how effortlessly the inner life of the play can emerge. Complete relaxation is the key to this simplicity, and the cast members should recognize the need to attain a similar degree of relaxation, even when they're up, moving around, and doing business.

You might want to introduce this exercise earlier than work-through rehearsals, or alternatively, it's a wonderful exercise to do the afternoon before the first performance. You probably won't have time for more than three work-throughs after your initial stumble-through, but each exercise should have advanced the endeavors of the cast.

Run-Throughs

Now it becomes time to learn what we can from run-throughs. But before discussing what you can hope to gain from them, let's first consider what a cast who's rehearsed in a conventional way is doing at this point.

In a typical rehearsal process, the director has used run-throughs as her principle mode of rehearsal, sometimes alternating them with "scene work," where particular problems have been addressed. The run-throughs began on the third or fourth day of rehearsal, as soon as the play has been mechanically blocked and all the movement assigned. Throughout this process, the actors have been carrying their scripts with them, writing down blocking, and trying to act the play while reading their lines. After the initial staging, the director's only contribution to the work has been in giving notes.

By the time they've arrived at the last days before tech begins, some of the actors are still carrying their scripts. The director has begun nervously to beg everyone to be off-book by the beginning of tech rehearsals. The work is uneven, because some in the company have learned their lines and become impatient with those who haven't.

Few props or costume pieces have been introduced, because the actors can't deal with them while holding their scripts. The burden on the tech rehearsals will be enormous because all physical elements will be introduced at once, and the cast will have to change their performances to accommodate differences they couldn't anticipate while miming their props. The common cry about the set and props is, "Is this the way it's going to be?"

See what a different process we've used? Before learning their lines, our actors have spent several days researching and improvising their circumstances and relationships. They've made choices about movement only after they've learned the lines for the beat they were exploring.

They've participated in the creation of all the movement, so it's as much theirs as the director's.

They've worked with props and rehearsal costumes from the beginning, and they've spent the whole rehearsal period engaging their fellow cast members with eye contact. They've developed a sense of camaraderie, so they'll sink or swim together, unlike the conventional approach in which the actors often feel at this point that it's every man for himself.

The price we pay for our organic approach is that we've used up most of the time exploring, so we'll have time for only two or three run-throughs before we go into tech rehearsals. But having taken the time to investigate fully every particle of the play, three run-throughs are sufficient to grasp what they can teach us.

With a run-through of an act or the entire play, we are finally at the point in our process where we hope to accomplish the "editing" that will begin the final shaping of the work into a performance. Some directors call this *polishing*.

The most evident goal will be to find the speed at which the play should be played to achieve its maximum effect.

Until now, we have explored the truthful behavior of the characters at a leisurely pace. Now, turning our attention from inside to outside, we must focus on confirming that truthful behavior with verbal exchanges. Technically, this means picking up the cues.

The responses of the actors to each other must be embedded in the dialogue, rather than in pauses; not acting *between* the lines, but *using* the lines to react. The instant response of a character to what has just been said must become instinctual. At this point, the cast must trust that the inner truth they've mined so carefully will be alive in their spontaneous responses.

Good acting is Pavlovian in essence. During the rehearsal period, we train ourselves to respond to the stimulus of the action in the play. It's ingrained by now, so when a cue is given, all the emotional inner life we've rehearsed will spontaneously spill forth.

A speed-through is the best exercise to help a cast realize how little they really need the pauses they've become accustomed to.

I call this exercise "an Italian run-through" because in the days of traveling *commedia dell'arte* troupes, when a company would arrive in a new town to perform on an unfamiliar stage, they would quickly run through everything in the play to be sure they had everything they needed and that everything worked.

This they did at a breakneck pace that left nothing out, but which was accomplished as quickly as possible.

You should instruct the cast to play the entire act or play as fast as they can possibly do it, performing all the moves at breakneck speed, using all the props, leaving out nothing except the pauses. There should be no pauses at all in a speed-through. The actors will learn what plays better at a faster pace, and conversely, where a quick pace cannot be sustained because of emotional weight.

I set a goal of playing an hour's worth of text in twenty minutes. That's going at triple speed, about as fast as people can talk. In a speed-through, every character sounds like Gilbert and Sullivan's "modern major general."

When I got to this stage in my first production of Chekhov's *Three Sisters*, after a rehearsal period that stretched over months, it seemed impossible to imagine playing rapidly. But when the actors tried it, there were many places in which the play sprang back to life, without the ponderous labor of our creative process.

Some of the play will be unintentionally funny at this speed; a genuine, heartfelt moment will suddenly seem like off-the-cuff callous indifference.

But don't worry. When the play resumes its natural pace, the subtlety, grace, and delicacy of the piece will return, unharmed, and will be emphasized by the light quickness that's been discovered to surround it. In order for the profound moments of the play to have their desired effect, the trivial things cannot take the same time or be given equal weight. A speed-through will teach the cast which is which.

After a speed-through, the play will never slow back down to its earlier slogging tempo because the actors will feel fine now about going fast through the areas that can be tossed off, without fear of being superficial. So in our second run-through, the pace will return to a more normal tempo, which should be lighter and quicker than before. Now that we've approached speed from a purely technical angle, we must consider the innate artistic elements that can be explored in our second run-through.

Chief among these is the through-line of action. Stanislavski calls these through-lines the *superobjectives,* which are the impelling forces that unite individual intentions into an arc of action that carries us through the play.

The second run-through should be focused on preparing with these superobjectives in mind, and then letting them propel us through our journey.

At this point, a director should also be giving notes that tie up loose ends, perfecting bits of business and timing, polishing the details of the *mise-en-scene,* and solving any remaining problems.

Perhaps the most illuminating run-through I've experienced happened in *Book of Days,* when we were transferring the production from St. Louis to the Hartford Stage. In the earlier run, we had used pared-down props and a half-dozen benches to suggest different times and places on John Lee Beatty's minimal set. But the benches were heavy to move, and the whole cast had to be employed to shift them between scenes. The action of this play needs to flow with as little interruption as possible, seeking an epic style rather than episodic.

The play had been well received in St. Louis, but because we were afforded a week of fresh rehearsal to remount it in Hartford, I wanted to experiment to see if we could make the play flow even faster. It occurred to me that Shakespeare's plays use little in the way of scenery or props and that frequently only the King gets to sit down.

So I asked the company to do a run-through in the rehearsal room totally without props, and without sitting, as if it were a Shakespearean play. The cast was very excited by the idea. I knew they hated having to move those heavy benches, being responsible for placing the tablecloths, and plugging in the lamps; these chores interfered with their acting.

Well, the Shakespearean run-through was a revelation. The play increased in power exponentially. As with a speed-through, we discovered which scenes needed nothing but the acting and the words to score and which scenes were strained by standing throughout and would really benefit from having something to sit on. But it helped us reduce the number of benches from six to two, which could always be moved by someone who wasn't in the scene preceding or following their placement. Thus, the actors could concentrate fully on playing the scenes, and the quickness of the pace fueled the power of the piece. It's fascinating to discover from your own experience that less actually *can* be more.

In your final run-through in the rehearsal room, the cast will probably feel a little nostalgic about the room that has sheltered their creativity for the past several weeks. A rehearsal room grows to feel like home. The stage managers have storage crates standing by to transport all the props from the rehearsal room to the stage as soon as you're finished.

Remind the company that this run-through will be the last chance to put all the acting work together, before the distractions of tech and dress rehearsals tear them apart.

It's a time to savor the living fabric of the play. If possible the tech crew, the dressers, and the designers should see this run-through. It's the culmination of the actors' creative process, spinning magic without the accoutrements of scenery or lights, defining what Peter Brook meant by an "empty stage."

A director's notes after the final run-through should be as positive and affirming as possible. Don't weigh the actors down with trivial details. Instead, address the truly important aspects: the life and meaning of the play. Remind them how good their work has been and how important the realization of the play will be.

It should be a joyous, sad time.

Chapter Eleven

Transferring the Work to the Stage

Many theater folk dread tech rehearsals as if they were the plague. Without sugarcoating the reality, the transferal of your work from a sheltered rehearsal room to the stage is a necessary venture that offers as much opportunity as it does peril.

This crucial phase addresses the transformation of private work in an artistic cocoon to its public destiny of public viewing. Like the life of a butterfly, our work is evanescent, fluttering for "our hour upon the stage," before fading into memory, and very rarely, history.

It's time to remember our purpose in coming together for this enterprise: to communicate with an audience and illuminate our times.

The vast new space that opens before us may seem intimidating, but instinctively we also begin to tingle with purposeful excitement. Costumes, makeup, lights, and scenery never fail to stir the heart with hope. Now if we can just calm our nerves, our goals are in sight.

The first consideration in this transformation is to make sure that all the movement we designed in the rehearsal space continues to serve the actors, the play, and the audience. Now it becomes vital to consider the sightlines, so that the life of the play can be seen by everyone who attends.

Before the set is quite finished, the lights focused, and the costumes trimmed, a director needs a little time with the cast in the theater devoted exclusively to restaging. These work-throughs are centered on adjusting the physical life of the production to the limitations of reality and solving problems posed by the requirements of the theater.

About three hours per act is needed to adjust the staging to the actuality of platforms and doors, to clean up the timing of entrances and exits, and to check the visibility from the extreme sides of the auditorium.

These activities are even more critical on a thrust stage, where players standing between the audience and other actors may obstruct much of the action from view. Unless you've continuously changed your position while watching in the rehearsal room, the side seats will present the unpleasant surprise of seeing far too much of behinds.

It's usually possible to schedule this essential time in the theater during the final week of rehearsals before techs begin. The building crews typically will work during the day, leaving the theater available for an evening rehearsal with the actors.

Most of what we've designed should work, but some changes will be warranted because of conditions that we couldn't anticipate in the closeness of the rehearsal room.

One of these will be the need to project our voices to cover the distance to the theater's back walls. To achieve this end, there is an excellent exercise that quickly helps actors shift to the energy level they'll need to project.

Distribute the cast throughout the extremes of the theater. Put one actor in the front row and her scene partner in the last row of the orchestra or in the rear of the balcony. Ask them to play their most intimate scene. The actors will feel the energy it takes to communicate; they'll discover the volume they'll need to maintain to reach the furthest member of the audience while playing with their partner only inches away from them onstage. Make sure every member of the cast has a chance to experience this adjustment.

The acoustics of one theater can vary greatly from another. If there are particular problems your auditorium poses, be sure to address them. For example, some theaters swallow up sound when it's directed upstage. This requires the cast to be aware of the need to aim their voices over their heads whenever they turn away from the audience.

On a thrust stage, some of the audience is always *behind* the actors when they're playing in the furthest downstage positions. Those patrons will hear the dialogue as it bounces off the wall in front of the actors and returns to them. Each actor must get a sense of reaching everyone with her vocal energy.

The best time to do this vocal exercise is probably just before you take to the stage to begin a tech rehearsal, while the crew is sweeping up. The stage managers and the lighting and sound designers will need to *hear* the cues to do their work. With this exercise, the company can take possession of the space, which must become their home for the duration of the production.

During dress rehearsals, it's important for a director to watch the entire production from the worst seat in the house, at least once. If it's a thrust stage or an arena, keep shifting your position to assess what every section of the audience will see (and hear).

Sometimes, actors will be a bit resistant to these changes, as essential as they are. When I was directing David Storey's *The Farm* at the Academy Festival Theater in Lake Forest, Illinois, I sat in the last row of the cavernous auditorium to monitor the volume at the first dress rehearsal. Before the run, I told the cast that I'd be letting them know when I couldn't hear them. A young Richard Gere had a very intimate scene near the end of the first act with his sister, played by Debra Mooney, in the hushed hours after midnight, when the rest of the house is asleep. The scene was played before a fireplace, and the glow of the hearth in the moonlight cast a spell of intimacy.

The scene was beautifully acted in the rehearsal room in front of a little space heater, with the lights dimmed. Only a few feet from the actors, I felt embraced by the warmth of the ambiance. But from the back row of the theater, I couldn't hear a word. I called out, "I can't hear you." The actors continued to play the scene at the same volume, as they had rehearsed it. A few moments later, I called again, "I can't hear you." Again there was no adjustment in volume as I watched the muffled scene progress. Frustrated, I yelled out, "I can't HEAR you!" Dropping the intimacy, Richard shouted back, "Fuck you!" I instantly replied, "*That*, I heard."

Darkness makes an audience sense they can't hear as well as when the stage is brightly lighted. In dark or intimate scenes, the actors must find a way to adjust their energy to maintain the illusion, while sharing the substance.

Tech Rehearsals

At least a week before tech rehearsals are scheduled to begin, sit down with the stage manager, the lighting designer, and the sound designer to go through the script and describe what's wanted from each cue. This is a *paper tech* that coordinates where every cue should be marked in the script and the effects you want the cues to accomplish.

Next, spend some time in the theater with your designers and board operators, writing the cues that will transform your descriptions from the paper tech into the actual execution of the lights and sound. At this *dry tech* rehearsal, without actors, you have the chance to set the intensity and timing of the light cues with your lighting designer and the volume and location of each sound cue with your sound designer.

In the dry tech, go from cue to cue, as you've placed them in the script at the paper tech. To see the effect of the light on the stage, you'll need to employ a model. This is usually a stagehand or an assistant to the director or lighting designer, who moves to wherever the director asks him to be at each moment, following the progression of the scene. The model should dress in a neutral color; black is too dark and white is too light to measure the brightness of the lights. As the lighting designer sees the effect of the light on the face of the model, she'll make adjustments that assure visibility for each cue.

The sound cues should be played sequentially to determine volume, tone, and location. The cues should be heard while the lights onstage are at the settings they will be; lightness/darkness affects the perception of the volume and the tone of the sound.

Normally, your sound designer will offer a variety of speakers to choose where you want each sound to come from. There are usually house speakers at each side of the proscenium and sometimes at the back of the auditorium or in the balcony, principally used for music. There also should be onstage speakers: upstage and downstage on each side and upstage center to use for sound effects. Sometimes there are speakers overhead as well. Check the positions of the speakers in relation to the scenery. There's no point in setting volume levels that will have to be changed if a piece of scenery suddenly appears in front of a speaker.

On arena stages or thrust stages, the speaker locations will differ according to the size and shape of the auditorium. Speakers that boost the volume of the actors' voices are distinct from those used for the sound cues and music.

During tech rehearsals, with all the disparate elements coming together, communication can become tricky. For the most part, communicate your instructions to your stage manager, so she can distribute the notes to the appropriate recipients, centralizing all communication through her.

Actors in the Tech Rehearsals

Next comes the incorporation of the actors into the technical plan you've developed. Like a giant, living jigsaw puzzle, all the elements of production must be coordinated into a unified whole.

Usually tech rehearsals are scheduled for ten-out-of-twelve hours. This divides a long day into two five-hour segments, with a two-hour dinner break. The number of these extended rehearsals that Equity will permit varies according to the type of contract. Typically, the larger regional theaters, touring productions, and Broadway contracts allow more days than Off-Broadway and low-end LORT contracts. Amateur productions often have no more than two days for tech rehearsals. On the other hand, some university productions may schedule a week or more of tech to accommodate inexperienced operators, who are learning how to do their jobs.

As suggested in the previous chapter, if possible the technical crew should be invited to see the final run-through in the rehearsal room. In any case, it's a good idea to begin a tech rehearsal by taking a few minutes to integrate the technical staff with the cast.

Make a little speech to welcome the technical crew to your collaboration. Define for everyone the purpose of tech rehearsals and the procedures you'll follow to accomplish those goals.

First, stress how important the technical staff is to the success of the production, and express the gratitude of the actors for their help. Ask each crew member to identify herself and the job she will perform.

Remind everyone that it's going to be a long day and that everyone should take the opportunity to *rest* whenever possible. Suggest that when you stop the action to adjust a cue, the actors should sit down and wait quietly while the lighting designer communicates changes to his board operator. Ask them to keep personal conversations to a minimum, so the technical staff can hear each other over their headphones. Clowning around is forbidden.

Emphasize that tech rehearsals are for the actors as much as the crew. Each actor should make sure that everything she needs is either provided or noted on a list. Appoint one assistant stage manager or assistant director to receive all prop notes. Underline that no missing prop should be taken for granted; it must be noted.

Call attention to safety issues that the cast must be alert to: loose nails, splinters, sharp edges that have yet to be sanded.

Release the actors from the need for deep performances. It's important that they play loudly and clearly, but they shouldn't waste energy on being creative. The stopping and starting and waiting will take too big a toll for them to attempt to sustain belief.

However, I think it's vital to go through the entire script, omitting nothing. Many directors jump from cue-to-cue in tech rehearsals, but I recommend you never do that. The time it takes the stage manager to notify everyone in the cast and crew exactly *where* in the script you are skipping to and the time it takes everyone to remember where they're supposed to be and to get there for the next cue will be greater than the time it would take to *play through* the scene.

Of course, there are exceptions when there are very few cues and lots of dialogue in between. But if you don't take the time at this point to make sure every moment in the play has the technical support it needs, there will be unpleasant surprises to deal with later. Especially for the actors, the technical rehearsals include the introduction of the actual props they'll be using, so nothing should be skipped.

Before you begin the tech work-through, the stage manager should walk the whole cast through a fundamental orientation to the set and backstage. Safety issues should be clearly addressed. An introduction to the traffic avenues backstage may include the particular eccentricities of a theater: where the voms are, how to get to the dressing rooms, even how to get from stage left to stage right backstage. Is there a crossover behind a cyc? Where will the prop tables and quick-change booths be located? Where will the assistant stage manager be stationed?

When everyone is clear about the nuts and bolts of backstage life and all are aware of temporary hazards, give everyone a ten-minute break before the tech begins.

Probably, it will take the longest time to get the opening cues executed exactly as you want them. The beginning of the play involves so many elements to synchronize that it may take an hour or more before you even get to the first line of dialogue. Productions often begin with an opening music cue, and then you must find the exact time (best measured by a stopwatch) when you want the house lights to go to half. Then, find the point in the music that the house lights and curtain warmers go to black, the curtain rises, and the first light cue illuminates the opening image. Finally, the timing and execution of the fade of the music (and sometimes the introduction of a sound effect, like crickets or birds) must be set.

Be as exacting as necessary to get the opening just the way you want it. Not all the cues will take as long, but harmonizing the opening sequence that will introduce the audience to the play is a major hurdle for the first tech rehearsal.

Generally, it will take at least five hours to tech the first act; often it requires as much as ten. If slides or multimedia elements are employed, it can take even longer.

Your goal should be to accomplish as much as you can, while getting the technical effects you want as precisely as possible. In other words, it takes as long as it takes. This is why patience—from the cast, the crew, the designers, and most of all, the director—is essential.

Try to avoid losing your temper at any point in the tech rehearsals. As people tire during the long day, nerves fray, and patience is strained. Everyone will be looking to you as the steadfast captain of the ship to inspire their best work by charting an efficient, safe, and smooth crossing.

Returning to Creativity: Repetition with a Text

Following tech rehearsals, it's important for the cast to refocus its attention on the acting process and the play. The afternoon before the first dress is probably the most productive time to introduce an exercise that will put everyone's concentration back on creativity.

I discovered that Meisner's technique of repetition can be applied profitably to the text to explore the creativity within the present, spontaneous moment. As with repetition, the goal is to bypass the intellect and connect with instinctive impulses in response to an acting partner's behavior. Only now we have *lines* with which to respond.

The process is to repeat what has just been said to you, take it personally, and respond with your line.

So for example, Medvedenko asks Masha at the opening moment of *The Seagull:*

"Why do you always wear black?"

Without pausing to think, the actor playing Masha should repeat the question two or three times, exploring her reaction to Medvedenko's behavior, and then connect what she's feeling to her reply, like this:

"Why do I always wear black? Why do I always wear black?? Why do I always wear black??? I'm in mourning for my life. I'm unhappy."

Now Medvedenko will repeat:

"You're in *mourning* for your life? You're unhappy? You're unhappy?? *Why*? I don't understand. You're in good health. Even though your father isn't rich, he's not bad off. My life is much harder than yours. I only get twenty-three rubles a month, and from that, they deduct for my pension, but I don't wear mourning."

Masha will now repeat:

"You only get twenty-three rubles a month? You only get twenty-three rubles a month, but you don't wear mourning? You don't wear mourning? It isn't money that matters. A poor man can be happy."

And Medvedenko will reply:

"A poor man can be happy? A poor man can be happy? A poor man can be happy? Theoretically, yes. But in reality it's like this. I have my two sisters and my mother and my little brother, and I only make twenty-three rubles a month. We have to eat and drink, don't we? A person has to have tea and sugar. A person has to have tobacco. It's a tight fit."

And Masha will change the subject after taking this in:

"It's a tight fit? A tight fit? It's a tight fit. The play will begin soon."

As you can see, the actor's attention must be on her partner and what his behavior reveals about what he's saying. If the actor takes her remark personally, she will discover her instinctual response—not from exploring within herself, but from connecting to her partner.

This exercise will help the actors to rediscover their impulses in the interplay of the present moment. The energy of scenes that have begun to be eroded by technical concerns will suddenly spring back to life with fresh impulses that illuminate the text by discovering how the dialogue can be spontaneously motivated.

After the distractions of tech rehearsal, the cast will be delighted to return to artistic exploration, and the actors will be ready to put on the clothes of their characters and begin to live in the world of the play.

As mentioned in Chapter 8, this exercise may be used alternatively as a tool of exploration. If it's used in early rehearsals, it probably can't be used again effectively at this juncture. So a director must choose whether to use repetition of the text for exploration, which is a more intellectual application, or at this later point, when it can jump-start the life of the play by stimulating instincts.

Dress Rehearsals

After a couple of days spent perfecting the lights, sound, and props, it's time to add the costumes.

Sometimes a costume designer has the costumes ready early enough that they could be used from the first tech. It seems to me it's better to wait, because there's so much actors need to think about in tech rehearsals that adding costumes overburdens their concentration.

Besides, costumes are so important that they deserve the full attention of a rehearsal dedicated solely to their introduction.

Costumes are of paramount concern to an actor. I've yet to meet an actor who does not relish the opportunity to dress up as someone else. It gets at the very heart of acting, a sophisticated culmination of our childhood games of make-believe. Every actor wants to look her best—or at least, have an image that best expresses her character, which could be very bad indeed. The relationship of an actor to her costumes is very intimate; they're the clothes she'll wear for two hours or more under the heat and exposure of theatrical lights for the run of the show.

Costumes are basic to an actor's craft. The final touches of characterization that pull together all the creative strands an actor has been developing are innately realized in her costumes. It's impossible to exaggerate their importance.

Many things about costumes are vital to an actor, but one of the primary specifications is fit. Ill-fitted clothes are never acceptable. Ideally, the costume designer has had a number of fittings with each actor, and by dress rehearsal, the fit should be perfect.

Often, a designer has a perspective on how a character could look that both excites and terrifies an actor. At the dress rehearsals, the actor will discover how the costume affects her movement, her behavior, indeed her whole characterization. It's how an audience will perceive who she is.

A director can be most helpful by being supportive of the designer's vision, which he's already approved, and at the same time, sensitive to the actors' anxiety. It's not too late to make minor changes to accommodate an actor's needs.

When time and schedule permit, a couple of days before the first dress is scheduled, it's nice to have the actors first try their costumes in an old-fashioned "dress parade." This could take place at any point in the tech rehearsals, whenever you can afford the time and attention to incorporate one.

A dress parade gives each actor a chance to try out her costume onstage, under the lights, while the director and costume designer confer about any last minute changes that might be desirable before the dress rehearsal. It also gives the designer an opportunity to show a director a variety of possibilities, and provides a good time to make a choice. After the luxury of a dress parade, an actor will feel much more confident about her costume when it comes to acting in it at a dress rehearsal. Dress parades are almost extinct in the professional theater, and that's a pity. Maybe you could reintroduce a discarded but valuable tool.

At a first dress, there are almost always some costume elements that haven't been completed. It's endemic to theatrical production. Safety pins and mock-ups may have to serve until garments can be hemmed or the real articles provided. By the second dress, one would hope everything is more or less finished: feathers in the hats, laces in the shoes, jewelry on necks, wrists, or fingers, watch fobs in vest pockets.

Of course, some items require an actor to become well-accustomed to them, like shoes, hats, or capes, and should be made available early. For period plays, most designers will make sword holsters, rehearsal skirts, corsets, and period shoes available weeks before the first dress. It's especially desirable for an actor to have her shoes as early as possible, because they're critical to her movement and must be considered during her exploration.

William Hurt requested a shoe that was rigged to turn his foot, so he wouldn't have to think consciously about Lord Byron's clubfoot; it would have been a limitation he'd always lived with. The designer Michael Warren Powell saw to it that we had the custom-made shoe the first week of rehearsal.

The first dress rehearsal is usually a distracted affair because so much of the actors' attention is on how their costumes work. This is natural. Chalk it up to marking time directorially, but by the second dress, a director might reasonably request that the actors return their attention to their acting, accepting the costumes as their clothes, deserving no more notice than what we normally wear.

Quick-changes are one aspect that's never completely achieved at a first dress. From the front, a director may ponder whether a change will ever be quick enough, but a wise director stays away from the change booth and lets the actor work out with her dresser a faster way to accomplish what, at first, may seem impossible. Each dress rehearsal should bring improvement in the timing, but if it's a difficult change, you may need to arrange special rehearsal time, repeating the change until the desired timing is achieved. A play that's based on quick changes, like *The Mystery of Irma Vep,* should never wait for dress rehearsals to address these problems but should incorporate the quick changes as an essential part of the rehearsal process.

During dress rehearsals, a director will have limited opportunities to make adjustments to the performances or the staging. At the conclusion of a dress, the technical staff usually gathers to get their notes from the director first, while the cast is changing out of their costumes.

Your notes to the cast must be given clearly and succinctly. As suggested earlier, this is the best time to utilize an assistant to record your notes, using a flashlight in the darkened auditorium, while your attention remains focused on the stage.

I often tell my casts not to be depressed when I give them a lot of notes during dress rehearsals because that's a sign that things are going so well that I've got the luxury of pointing out picky details I want perfected. The worse a rehearsal is going, the fewer notes I take, because the things that are wrong are major elements, not quibbling minutiae.

After the days and endless hours of the tech rehearsals, your first goal is to get the actors refocused on their acting. Relaxation, concentration, and engaging their imaginations return as essential ingredients to good work. Once they're past fussing over their costumes, redirect their attention to their circumstances, their objectives, and all the elements that made the play come to life in the rehearsal room.

The danger always present at this point is that the actors are a bit exhausted and may find it difficult to get back to the level of creativity they achieved before. But sometimes actors play well when they're too tired to think too much; they can discover that if they just concentrate on believing, their instincts will lead them back to life.

Final Dress Rehearsal

When you've had enough dress rehearsals to smooth out the finishing touches, give the actors a chance to invite friends to see a final dress rehearsal before they have to perform in front of a paying public.

The first experience of hearing responses from an audience is a watershed in the creative process. Even though it's likely the viewers will be only a small number, any audience will facilitate the essential transition from rehearsal to performance.

I make a brief speech—no more than five minutes—at the last dress rehearsal (or the first preview, if that's the first audience) to mark the importance of this transition.

I introduce myself as the director of the production they're about to see and tell them what a significant moment the occasion is. I explain that for weeks we've been inspired by the play, working in private to explore deeply and personally its every aspect. Now, we've arrived at the final stage of our process, and the most important element of a production must be added: the audience. It's been the goal of our work to share what we've created, and now for the first time, we have that opportunity. I thank them for being our guinea pigs and encourage them to be generous with their responses:

> If you think something's funny, laugh; if you're moved by what you see, feel free to sob. It's your honest response, whatever it is, that will teach us what we need to know.

In a way, it's a warm-up for the audience, to help them understand the nature of what they're seeing. Never apologize for the production or hint that the audience should expect anything except a good time. But do remind them that it's still a rehearsal and that if you need to stop for any reason, you'll do so.

Audiences always respond to this introduction with warmth and applause, and I've instructed the stage manager to begin the play the minute I've finished. As soon as the audience applauds, call the first cue.

Your last notes session with the company after the final dress should be supportive, optimistic, and encouraging. This is no time for recriminations or doubt. You've spent weeks preparing for this moment, and for better or for worse, you've got what you've got.

Blocking Curtain Calls

I postpone blocking a curtain call until the final dress, because until we've arrived at the moment, I don't want the actors thinking ahead of performances or audience reactions. When the curtain falls and our invited audience applauds, I come back down front, stop the applause, and thank them for their response. Then, I explain, "We're now going to block the curtain call," and I invite them to stay and participate if they'd like.

You should have prepared a preliminary order for the actors to appear and take their bows. It's wise to make the bows in groups of three or four (or more) if it's a large cast.

Traditionally, the smaller parts are acknowledged first, the supporting parts next, with each stage of the bows building up to the leading parts, but there are times it's okay to fly in the face of tradition. In the case of *Fifth of*

July on Broadway, I gave an unknown actor named Jeff Daniels the final bow after our star, Christopher Reeve, because I felt the quiet part of Jed was the heart of the play, and I wanted to recognize the ensemble nature of the cast.

If egos are sensitive or if the ensemble has been the "star" of the show, it's good to begin the calls with a company bow, and then go on to individual bows, ending with another bow of the entire company.

Curtain calls are an important component of the audience's experience. Applause is their opportunity to participate in the live event, and their role is to congratulate the players on their accomplishment.

I've seen productions of indifferent quality that, with an ingenious curtain call, convinced an audience they've had a splendid time. The charming bows of Ellis Rabb's ATA come to mind, often choreographed to memorable music. The curtain call for their ultimate production was accompanied by the song, "For all we know, we may never meet again." It was delightfully moving.

Be cautious, however, about being too cute when designing a curtain call. It should be about the actors and the admiration of the audience, not the cleverness of the director. Don't upstage the actors; this is their moment.

In particular, avoid the temptation to repeat tableaux of memorable moments of your staging.

Nevertheless, the style and manner in which the bows are taken are important to the overall direction of the piece, and you should make sure your staging of the curtain call does justice to the whole production, which, of course, includes your contribution as well.

I tell my actors that the best way to take a bow is to move as quickly as possible from offstage to down center and then graciously to luxuriate in the acknowledgment of the audience's praise. Hurry up to get on, then TAKE YOUR TIME in the bow, and then get out of the way for the next bows.

At the end of the individual bows, take a full company bow that shares the audience's approval with everyone. At Circle Rep, our traditional bow ended with all the actors holding hands, and after the last bow, raising their joined hands over their heads, in a group gesture of triumph.

Blocking the curtain call in front of your invited audience enlists their participation and makes them feel part of the process. Of course, as you block the bows, you have to give your instructions quickly so the audience will stay to respond. Having real applause to practice a curtain call makes it fun. It also can give you an indication of when a curtain call has gone on long enough; never strain an audience's goodwill. Leave them wanting more.

After you've blocked the individual parts of the call, start again from the last moment of the play, and run the whole call with lights, sound, curtain, applause, and all.

Interestingly, actors learn very quickly what to do in a curtain call. But if it seems at all ragged, drill it until it's impeccable.

Production Photo Calls

For me, the most odious chore in the entire production process is the necessity of taking production photographs.

Early in rehearsals, a photographer will be scheduled to take publicity shots, used to promote the show prior to the opening. These are a few *set-up* shots the photographer will compose because she knows what the newspapers want. The director's advice may be sought, or not.

With these pictures, encourage the photographers to use as many actors as feasible, and don't let the pictures give away too much about the play. The purpose is to intrigue an audience (or at least an editor) with the anticipation of a new production.

Production photographs, on the other hand, are the ultimate record of the play, with full costumes, makeup, props, sets, and lights. A director will want the acting to be representative of what an audience will see when they come to the theater, not an exaggeration or distortion. It's a necessary part of a director's job because you can't afford to trust anyone else to characterize the visual representation of the production (although I frequently ask my assistant Rand Mitchell to help), and it's very difficult for still pictures to capture action, which is the essence of the experience.

If she can, the photographer should see a complete dress rehearsal the night before she's going to shoot it. This rarely happens, but it provides the optimum conditions for assuring good photographs. If she's seen the production, she'll remember the exciting points of the action that she'll want to capture and anticipate them as they arise. If she doesn't, she'll probably miss the perfect moment and get the letdown.

It would be best to take the production photographs during a dress rehearsal before an audience is invited to see the final dress, but it's unlikely. You may have to live with the distraction of a photographer in the front row, running up and down in front of the stage, snapping away, while the actors are trying to connect with their first audience. It's not the best of circumstances, but necessity can be a cruel taskmaster.

Draw up a list of ten or so moments in each act that capture the action, mood, and character of the play for set-up shots. Prepare the list in advance so taking the photographs will go as quickly and painlessly as feasible.

After the dress, the ten or so set-ups you've chosen for each act should be staged and photographed quickly and efficiently. Start with the last scene, and work your way in reverse chronological order to the beginning of the play.

This makes use of the costumes and settings that exist at the end of the play, and allows actors in earlier scenes to change costumes and makeup.

Between acts, sets may have to be changed. Always, your stage manager will need to be able to adjust the lights to the needs of the camera, because a dim light that's very effective when seen with the naked eye is almost always too dark to photograph. The changes should be as minimal as possible to maintain the integrity of the lighting design.

Some producers are charitable enough to provide soft drinks and pizza during photo calls, recognizing that they're depriving the cast of going out after the show to have a bite. It's not enough to make me appreciate taking production photos, but it may help keep the company's spirits up. Everyone in the cast will want a picture of her shining moment for a scrapbook. Truth be told, I treasure the memories, too.

Previews

Sometimes it's impossible to arrange for an invited audience to attend the final dress rehearsal, and the first preview will be the first encounter the players have with an audience. In those cases, the speech about the importance of the transition from private to public should be transplanted to the first preview. The speech is more than a shoehorn to ease the actors from rehearsal into performance; the moment of transition is crucial to the creative process.

Of course, in some theaters, there are no previews at all, and your first performance is also your opening night. When that occurs, it's vital to have an invited audience at the final dress, so a director must insist on having one.

On the afternoon of the first preview, get your cast together for a couple of hours for a final warm-up. Ask them to sit comfortably and speak the entire play, listening to the music of the dialogue, the rhythms and cadences of the speeches, the ebb and flow of the sound.

This will help the cast refocus on the play itself, which is the origin of all our work. It's why we've come together. It's what we hope to share. As the actors listen to the beauty of the play, their confidence will be awakened. They'll believe anew that this was an enterprise worth doing; that they're fully prepared and ready to play. Or, as mentioned before, this is the best time for the dream-through exercise.

I have to confess that I hate previews. I understand their importance, the good they can do for the cast and the play, but they can be excruciating for a director.

Many directors do their most important work during previews, but my aim is to finish my work by the final dress rehearsal. By then I've said and done everything I can contribute. The previews stretch beyond my most productive point.

With the arrival of an audience, the importance of a director is diminished. His opinions are superseded by those of the audience.

Until now, the director has been the actors' only audience, and his reactions are assumed to be the ones the cast can expect. But with the arrival of the first preview, the director yields his place to the real audience, and the cast begins to learn directly from its reactions.

It's revealing to see how an audience changes a production. What seemed hilarious to the director in rehearsals is sometimes met with no more than smiles from an audience. On the other hand, it laughs in places you never anticipated, seeing humor that's a surprise to director and cast alike.

So during a first performance, a director's attention is divided between assessing whether the production is unfolding onstage as he's envisioned it and learning from the audience's reactions.

The energy level of the cast members is unusually high at the first performance. In subsequent performances, they'll master their nerves and exert more command over the effect they're having. But the first time, they're very vulnerable to the slightest response they sense from the audience.

By the time they reach the curtain call, the audience's apparent approval exhilarates the company, who can breathe a huge collective sigh of relief.

When a director meets with the cast backstage, he must be sensitive to the mood of the cast, which may be euphoric, or conversely, depressed if the reception has been cooler than expected. Then, he must shore up the actors' belief in themselves and try to inspire confidence that continued playing will bring the reception they desire.

It's safe to say that the reaction of the first audience cannot be taken as the final word on the nature of the experience. Audiences who attend a first performance are usually more adventurous and supportive; they like taking part in the risk and are generous with their responses.

A director must make sure that the cast is not misled by the reactions of the first crowd. It would be a mistake to count on any reaction to be echoed by future audiences. Remind the company that each audience is different, and warn them about the dangers of trying to repeat what was effective "last night."

At the same time, because of the euphoria the cast may feel to finally hear audience responses, a director must be cautious not to be too critical; he's now just one voice, albeit a trusted one, among a chorus of responses the actors will listen to.

I made an awful mistake following the first preview of *Book of Days* in St. Louis. The audience response had been very strong, and I was concerned that they'd been overly generous. In my attempt to keep the actors focused on what we still needed to accomplish, I managed to turn a joyous occasion into a sullen, glum, resentful mood. I was out of step with everyone, and my notes were counterproductive. The audience had spoken, and I should have listened.

With the arrival of an audience, a director's influence has been downgraded, so from this point on, he must be humble and careful in trying to push a cast to higher goals. It's wiser to offer congratulations, accentuating the accomplishments that have been confirmed by audience response and to save any criticism for a rehearsal the following afternoon, prior to the next performance.

Equity strictly limits the number of hours you can rehearse after previews begin, but normally you can call the actors for a few hours in the afternoon before a preview, if you don't give notes afterwards.

After previews begin, friends, agents, spouses, and fans will flood the performers with an onslaught of well-intentioned advice. If you've done your job well, the cast has explored the play so thoroughly they'll be able to sift the useful from the inane.

One opinion that will register with all the company is the reaction of the writer. The play has inspired their work throughout, so any cast will hope the author is pleased and recognizes the life they've brought to her script. They'll listen to any criticisms or praise from him with a special regard. A director shouldn't be jealous of the author's influence. You've had your turn throughout the rehearsal period to make your views known. Now the choices you made are subjected to the proof of their effectiveness. So let the writer have her say.

With a new play, previews offer you and the author the opportunity to fine-tune the play. The living performance of the actors and the audience responses may shed light on problems that previously have been obscure. In particular, the author may perceive that the clarity of the performances has rendered some of the dialogue extraneous, and she may see wisdom in cutting the excess.

A director must balance his dramaturgical responsibilities to the playwright with his protection of the actors' creative process. Sometimes cuts can be painful, unless the cast understands the reasons for the deletions and how they will improve the play. Sometimes an individual actor will be asked to sacrifice a treasured line for the good of the play, and that's never easy.

Be sensitive to the loss a performer may feel, and bolster her confidence by praising her sacrifice. Reassure her that the cut isn't her fault, and that you and the author are to blame for not recognizing the need for a cut earlier.

If cuts are made during previews, be sure they are executed early enough that the actors have at least one complete performance with no changes prior to opening. Cuts require healing, so no scars are visible in the performance.

At Circle Rep, we used comment cards to get specific feedback from audiences. These were especially useful during previews, when I sometimes shared them with the cast, reading them aloud. It's obvious that not every comment will shed light, and some may be so far off the mark they're hilarious. Still, it helps to investigate the thoughts behind the laughter and applause. It's possible to laugh all the way through a production and still have a miserable time. Conversely, an audience that's been very quiet may have had the best of experiences.

By the time you reach the last preview, a director has given what he can contribute. Your final notes after the last preview should acknowledge the help you've had throughout the journey and include a generous assessment of everyone's contribution.

Then, turn responsibility for the production over to the stage manager and remind the cast that from now on, they'll need to rely on the stage manager to sustain their performances.

If you've attained the camaraderie that produces the best work, the company will be reluctant to let you go, but like a grown-up child leaving home, it'll be grateful for what you've given it and eager to be on its own.

Chapter Twelve

Enduring the Opening

A director attending the opening night performance is more than a little like Tom Sawyer witnessing his own funeral. Her creative life with the play has ended, yet her presence at the ritual is mandatory. There's nothing more she can do, except passively watch others assess the effects of her existence.

Program Information

Actually, a director's most important contribution to the success of opening night is the information she's provided for the program. It is imperative that the audience knows *when* and *where* the action of the play takes place. The other vital piece of information is whether and when the intermission(s) will occur.

It's rank negligence when a director fails to provide this information, or to check to see that it's been printed correctly.

It's true that Shakespeare often indicates both time and place within his dialogue, because Elizabethan performances took place on an open stage, with little or no scenery to suggest a place, and in the middle of the afternoon, without benefit of theatrical lighting to suggest a time.

Absent Shakespeare's internal clues, it's a director's job to make sure an audience knows two essential circumstances that the actors need them to accept before the play begins: *Time* and *Place*.

When I go to the theater and discover that no time or place is noted in the program and that there's no indication whether or not there will be an intermission, or how many scenes the play contains, I am dismayed by the carelessness these omissions display.

Don't neglect this obligation; it's about the only thing you have to contribute to the opening night performance.

Observing the Audience

During the previews, a director gradually shifts her attention from the stage to observing the audience members. Are they listening attentively? When are they bored or distracted? Are they following and appreciating the action as it unfolds?

At the opening night performance, it's wiser for a director to focus more attention on the audience's reactions than on the stage.

One of my most treasured opening night experiences was at the Circle Rep premiere of *The HOT L BALTIMORE.* In the early days, we were located in a second floor loft above a Thom McCann shoe store on the Upper West Side of Manhattan. In addition to Mel Gussow, the critic from the *New York Times,* our opening night audience included the legendary Harold Clurman, founder of the Group Theater, an eminent director and distinguished critic from *The Nation.*

Lanford Wilson and I found a secure spot backstage where we could spy on the audience, without seeing the actors or being seen by the audience. Mr. Clurman was visible in the front row of our intimate arena stage, and his reaction to the play was like the wonder of a child sitting at the foot of a Christmas tree, watching the ribbons fly off the gifts. He was enchanted. I think his sheer delight meant more to the author and me than all the play's subsequent accolades.

I've discovered that after a production has reached a level that's reasonably close to what I've wanted it to be, it's increasingly difficult to watch it with any objectivity. It becomes excruciating to scrutinize my own work, knowing what's coming next and just how it should be done. After a couple of performances, it's no longer fun even to watch the audience react.

Instead, I've found it's instructive to lie down somewhere (in the balcony, the sound booth, or on a stairway at the back of the house) and listen. From just hearing the rhythm of the actors' delivery and the audible responses of the audience, I can tell how well the show is going. If I try to watch, I get obsessively wrapped up in assessing how well the actors are executing what I've asked them to do; but by just listening, I can sense how the play is playing, as if for the first time. It's like listening to music, and it can calm opening night jitters. Drop out of sight, and tune in.

The Program Note

One odious chore frequently requested of a director in regional theater is to write a program note that addresses her concept of the play and the approach of the production. Since commercial productions often deal with new material, Broadway and Off-Broadway directors rarely need to write such a note. But with classics or revivals, producers probably will want audiences to understand why this production is different from productions of the play they may have seen previously.

When you're asked to write a program note, don't give away surprises you've planned for the audience, but try to prepare them for a new experience by cutting through foregone assumptions. Don't apologize for your approach, and don't boast. Just cultivate a perspective you'd like the audience to have in mind as they take in your fresh viewpoint.

My least favorite thing about these essays is that the critics tend to review the program note, rather than what they experience in the production.

In Appendix I, I've provided my program note for the Ford's Theater production of *The Member of the Wedding* as an example.

The Performance

An opening night performance is almost never typical. The energy of the cast will be highly charged and that can result in either an inspired performance or one paralyzed with tension.

It's amazing how different actors respond to the pressure of an opening night. To some, the opening provides a release for all the creativity they've been rehearsing over the past month. Before an audience, their work blossoms, surpassing any indication they've given during rehearsals of heights they might be capable of reaching. During rehearsals, my friend Helen Stenborg used to refer to the promised transformation as "On the Night."

For other actors, the imposition of the pressure of critics and judgment is an annoying interference with their work process. These actors really work for themselves, like a golf pro who competes really only against himself.

Because of the innate variation of responses, make it an ironclad rule *never* to reveal to the cast publicly who's in the audience at any particular performance.

Critics

For the last generation or so, many critics have taken to coming to review a late preview performance, rather than the opening. Their reasons for doing so are: (1) to see a typical performance, rather than one hyped up by the singularity of an opening night; (2) to avoid the cronyism of opening night, when the audience is made up almost entirely of backers of the show and supporters, family, and friends of the cast; and (3) to give them time to evaluate the virtues and problems of the show thoughtfully and to write without the pressure of an immediate after-the-show deadline. The old days of critics phoning in their reviews to a copy editor minutes after the final curtain are gone, and that's probably a good thing.

However, once producers began to allow critics to come to previews, they've occasionally abused the privilege, sometimes coming well before the previews have achieved their purpose, which is to allow the performances to settle in, to give the actors an opportunity to gauge their effect, and to adjust their work as they learn from audience responses.

One play in particular that suffered from an early critical appraisal was my Broadway production of Peter Nichols's complex and beautiful play *Passion* (or *Passion Play*, as it was known in England). Sometimes, reviews let slip more drama than is being evaluated onstage.

In this case, the *New York Times* was incensed that our producer, Richmond Crinkley (who was also the Producing Director for Lincoln Center), had shut down the Vivian Beaumont Theater for an entire year. When he privately produced *Passion* on Broadway while the Beaumont was kept dark, the *Times* relished the opportunity our opening afforded to express their scorn for Mr. Crinkley.

The *Times* critic, Frank Rich, came to an early preview of *Passion*, more than a week before the official opening. We'd had difficulty during the technical and dress rehearsals coordinating a complicated set, lights, and music, so we staggered into previews shaken by lingering problems. When Mr. Rich saw the show, it was still a bit ragged around the edges, and he duly noted in his review that the play seemed "underrehearsed." While this observation was perfectly true at the early preview he attended, it was by no means the case a week later at the opening, when our achievements were supposed to be judged.

To make matters worse, in his relentless campaign against Mr. Crinkley's tenure at Lincoln Center, Mr. Rich somehow worked into Sunday pieces for the next three weeks his allegation that the show looked underrehearsed. Whatever validity the criticism had a week before opening, the production was certainly no longer "underrehearsed" three weeks into the run, a full month after Mr. Rich had seen it; yet, the out-of-date criticism was repeated weekly in the *Sunday Times*.

Passion was surely one of the five best plays presented on Broadway that season, and yet it was not nominated for a Tony; nor was Frank Langella, who was giving the best performance of his career. We had only one nomination, for Roxanne Hart as Best Supporting Actress. The professional theater is not always fair; some shows of questionable quality are lauded in a lean year, while others are overlooked that have considerable merit. One must keep in mind that neither *A Streetcar Named Desire* nor Marlon Brando received Tony Awards. (They lost to *Mister Roberts* and Henry Fonda.)

As a five-time Tony nominee, I've always maintain that the honor is in the nomination, not who wins. Of course, I'm a five-time loser, so my opinion is none too surprising.

In any case, since the advent of spreading critics out over several previews, a cast never can be sure exactly when they're being judged. Because of the potential negative effect it can have on their concentration, many actors beg not to be told who is going to be in the house at any given performance.

As a result, I always announce before we go into previews that this information will not be made public. The entire cast, crew, and staff of the theater are strictly forbidden to discuss "who is in the house."

I tell the cast:

> If you *want* to know, the stage manager will always have a list of special guests at each performance, including what critics are in attendance, and even where they're seated. If you wish to know, simply ask the stage manager and you'll be told. However, for the protection of everyone else, most of whom do *not* want to know, you must keep this information to yourself.

Every cast I've ever worked with has applauded this policy. I strongly recommend that you adopt it as part of your work process.

The Reviews

Another urgent admonition for the cast is *Don't read the notices!* Once an actor reads in the newspaper about the particular effects of his performance, it becomes very difficult to keep the intuitive nature of the performance from becoming conscious.

Oddly enough, it's perhaps more damaging to read praise for a moment than it is to read negative criticism. When the critic gushes about how the leading lady's lips trembled or the flash in the hero's eyes when he speaks a certain line, the actor will never again approach the moment without thinking: "Oh, here's where my lips tremble" or "Now my eyes have to flash."

Also, reviews trickle in with no particular order. The first review that's available may be devastatingly critical, while the next day another review will offer extravagant praise. There's a huge divergence in critical opinion, and if a cast reads the reviews as they come in, they can't help but be buffeted by the rude shifts of critical winds and allow the latest review to affect their performances. Actors owe it to their audiences not to let a reviewer's opinion alter the performance they're giving.

With a comedy especially, criticism can have a demoralizing effect. My friend Mark Ramont sought my advice about how to cheer up the cast of *The Matchmaker* at Ford's Theatre in Washington, D.C., after they had read a dismissive review in the *Washington Post*. As I told him, it's extremely difficult to get the bubble back into the champagne once it's gone flat.

With the necessity of extracting quotes from reviews to display prominently in front of the theater to attract ticket sales, a cast can't help but get a sense of how the show has been received; but it's best for the press office of the production to save copies of all the reviews to be shared with the cast in a packet at the closing performance, when they can be appreciated in their entirety.

Many actors (or their mothers at least) will want to keep a scrapbook of memorable notices, but the time to collect them is at the end of the run.

When I played Malvolio in *Twelfth Night*, I did not read the press until the show closed; so I was spared the knowledge that the great actor Brian Bedford had scored a triumph in the role the previous summer, so any comparison was bound to be at my expense. I was also spared John Simon's characterization of my performance as: "like a fussy antiques dealer," an image that would have thrown me for a loop while I was acting from a very different perspective.

It's bad enough that audiences read reviews and allow them to affect their enjoyment of a show. One of the first plays I produced in New York was Shaw's *Arms and the Man*. Throughout previews, audiences roared with laughter, and each curtain call received hearty acclaim. Once a negative review appeared in the *Times*, overnight the responses of the audience changed dramatically. They'd been told the production was faulty, and they clammed up.

Equally strange was the reaction to the rave notices for *The HOT L BALTIMORE* when it was awarded the New York Drama Critics' Circle Award for Best American Play of 1972–73. The seriousness of the same award that had been won by plays like *Death of a Salesman* put audiences in a seriously expectant frame of mind. They came to see a "Great Play," not a hilarious comedy. Eventually in it's long run (of three years), this effect wore off, and once again audiences showered the actors with delighted laughter.

Although I urge my casts not to read reviews, as a director I think it's important to read and reflect on them all. Keep in mind that each review is no more than the opinion of one member of your audience. Just as comment cards can display an enormous variety of views, so too can notices in the press. Sometimes, their opinions are diametrically opposed. Which is the one to believe? Read them all so that you can get over the perception that any opinion is any more valid than another simply because it appears in print.

This was never clearer than in the reviews for my Broadway production of *The Seagull*. Our production was perceived as a failure. Critics' evaluations varied widely. Few were on the fence.

To begin with, every critic thinks he has special insight for just how Chekhov, or Shakespeare for that matter, *should* be done. They bring these prejudices with them. Work is judged not by what's been achieved, but by whether the approach fits into the critics' preconceptions.

Here are a few examples from the reviews of *The Seagull*:

Mason takes Chekhov at his word, stressing the humor in what this master humanist always insisted was a comedy.

Linda Winer, New York Newsday

The play is not a comedy, despite Chekhov's remark.

William Sarmento, The Sun

In the inept staging of director Marshall Mason, there is no nuance, no drama, no comedy, no tragedy.

Rosanna Scotto, WNYC-TV

This *Seagull* is all wet. The audience laughed through it, and it's not a comedy.

Pia Lindstrom, WNBC-TV

Under Marshall Mason's far too reverential direction, this *Seagull* is forever earthbound.

Dennis Cunningham, WCBS-TV

At this point, one might suspect the production didn't work for everyone, but exactly what was wrong might be hard to divine.

Among the ten positive reviews, here's a sampling:

Would this *Seagull* have saved Chekhov's life? The answer is complicated: No, if he read the reviews and stayed home. But a resounding Yes!—if he had come to the theater to see for himself. Thanks to Marshall Mason's acute direction, this *Seagull* is filled with discoveries and life lived onstage.

Dan Isaac, Chelsea, Clinton News

Two audience members said it all for me: One was a woman whose face, at the end, was tear-streaked, while her shining eyes told me she'd had a great time. The other was a man who told his friend he liked the performance a lot. "Did you think it was Russian?" he was asked. "No," he answered. "But I liked it a lot."

Leida Snow, WNEW

With Mr. Mason, the National Actors Theater has secured one of the best directors at blending actors into an ensemble.

Edwin Wilson, Wall Street Journal

Mason's staging emphasized summer heat and autumnal storms. Chekhov tells us, and Mason reminds us, of the comforting—and mildly funny—assurance of the continuity of agony. They call it life.

Clive Barnes, *New York Post*

The following Saturday, the incensed Mr. Barnes took his fellow critics to task:

Critics attend performances burdened down with prejudices. Now I am loath to pull rank, but I have little doubt that I have seen substantially more productions of classic theater than any (perhaps two or three) of my critical colleagues across the country. And this *Seagull* isn't bad.

Perhaps "not bad" is faint praise, but Mr. Barnes's defense shows that I wasn't the only one puzzled by the range of opinion.

Early in my career, my professional debut Off-Broadway was greeted with two reviews that sound like they could not have been written about the same production. The play was *Little Eyolf*, a late play by the father of realism and one of the greatest writers of all time, Henrik Ibsen.

Howard Taubman, the chief critic of the *New York Times*, assayed my work with this extravagant comparison:

Ibsen is dealing with incendiary relationships, and to communicate them within a range commensurate with the playwright's style is to take on a challenging chore. The drama's remorseless search for the truth of its character's feelings and motives makes a profound impact. Chief credit for this accomplishment must go to Marshall W. Mason, the director. It is obvious that Northwestern University is training talented people, and Mr. Mason, whose imprint is on this production, must be regarded as one of the ablest.

Meanwhile, his colleague at the rival *Herald Tribune*, Walter Kerr, dismissed that accomplishment with the worst evaluation of my work I would receive for many years:

Mr. Mason's staging does a great deal to emphasize what is stiffest and most solemn in the writing. The principals quickly become lost in their own living room, striding to no purpose, sometimes behaving like so many stuffed bears who have been taught to intone prose.

When one is faced with opinions of one's debut that offer such opposing views, one is less inclined to take any review as definitive.

I've included a letter in Appendix J that we received after *The Seagull* opened. I treasure it more than what any of our critics had to say; that it was written by the brother of one of the actors doesn't render it any less perceptive.

Included with that letter was a clipping of comments by Theodore Roosevelt on critics, which says it all.

It is not the critic who counts; not the man who points out where the strong man stumbled, or where the doers of deeds could have done better. The credit belongs to the man who is actually in the arena, whose face is marred by dust and sweat and blood; who strives valiantly; who errs and comes short again and again; who knows the great enthusiasms, the great devotions; who spends himself in a worthy cause; who at the best, knows in the end the triumph of high achievement, and who in the worst, if he fails, at least fails while daring greatly, so that his place shall never be with those timid souls who knew neither victory or defeat.

About two years after my trouncing by the critics on *The Seagull*, I became the theater critic for the *New Times*, a weekly alternative newspaper in Phoenix, Arizona. When I learned the position was available, I reasoned that if my mentor Harold Clurman had gone from directing to criticism, perhaps I could learn something, too.

And learn I did! I learned the difficulty of writing week after week about productions that are less than inspiring to write about. I learned how tempting it is to be ruthless, because it makes such good copy. I learned that even though more than 75 percent of my reviews were favorable, the perception was that I was terribly mean, even vicious.

Nobody really loves a critic. It's a hard job, but not as hard as creating a work of art. So there need not be too much sympathy for the devils; nobody forced them to be critics.

I did come to appreciate writers more than ever. It's hard to express eloquence with brevity, but editors demand it. I was pleased to win an award for my critical writing in the performing arts category from the Arizona Press Club. Then, I retired as a critic and returned to the arena, hungry again to "dare greatly."

Paying a Visit

It's always been fascinating to me that most directors never return to see a show after the opening night. It's true that a director's job is officially finished at that point, and although royalties continue regardless, no further compensation is offered for attending a performance or monitoring its progress.

I, however, can never resist seeing a show I've directed as often as I can, perhaps because of the close relationships with the actors and the playwright cultivated in rehearsals. In a long run, I attend at least once a week for the first six months and after that at least once a month.

One of the reasons I find it irresistible to return is the growth of the performances. If I've done a good job, it never fails that the work continues to grow, gets deeper and more subtly eloquent. As soon as the cast is free from the pressures of pleasing a director, if they've been started down a road of honesty and creativity, their work will get richer with each performance. The most profound difference is in the fine-tuning of the ensemble, where all individual achievements coalesce into a unified whole.

I think the most delightful experience of returning to a show was in 1973 when Lanford Wilson and I revisited our original production of *The HOT L BALTIMORE*. Lanford had written the play for the members of our company, none of whom were well known. Although we recognized we'd done well in creating an ensemble, it wasn't until we came back from our California production at the Mark Taper Forum that we saw just how extraordinary the original production was.

Of course, we'd created the show off-off-Broadway at the early Circle Rep. I designed and executed the lighting myself. The setting really consisted of "found objects" that we used in rehearsal, and a wonderful faux-marble paint job on the floor was by a designer with no previous experience, Ronald Radice. Lanford and I had built and painted the black risers on which the audience was seated. This was do-it-yourself theater in its purest, most primitive form, but that completely refuted allegations about sows' ears and silk purses.

When the legendary producer Kermit Bloomgarden (*Death of a Salesman, The Music Man, Equus*) moved our production intact to a professional Off-Broadway run at the Circle in the Square downtown in Greenwich Village, many of our company were required to join Equity for the first time. We knew the company was immensely talented, but except for Judd Hirsch and Helen Stenborg, few in the cast had any professional credits on their résumés. The entire budget of the original production probably didn't reach $2,000.

When Gordon Davidson invited us to mount the play at the Mark Taper Forum in Los Angeles, the resources of a major regional theater were put at our disposal. Famous designers, like Noël Taylor (whose clothes for Bette Davis in the Broadway premiere of *The Night of the Iguana* had caused a sensation) were hired to create a new look for the faded hotel and its denizens. Mr. Taylor designed and had the costume shop build from scratch the blue jeans worn by the young Paul Grainger. I think those jeans cost more than the entire Circle Rep budget.

The talent agents and casting directors opened their files for the top talent in Hollywood. Christopher Lloyd and Jennifer Salt headed a cast that included veteran award-winning actors like Margaret Linn, Barbara Colton, and Andrea de Shields. Suddenly, we had the chance for a first-rate professional production. We were in rehearsal for a full four weeks, and the entire process was lovely. The support of the Taper staff made work on the play a joy. And the results were well received by the critics. We had a huge hit now on both coasts.

When we returned to New York, fresh from our first-class professional production, Lanford and I simply sneaked into a performance because we didn't want our friends to realize we were there. We wanted to see the show an average audience was seeing.

Well, the play started, and our little amateur company wandered into the hotel lobby, and began to live. Judd Hirsch and Trish Hawkins were talking over each other's lines in conversational tones that were amazingly real. Then, Conchata Ferrell as April came down the stairs in her bathrobe, complaining about the lack of hot water. She lugged her considerable figure over to a chair and plopped down, as if she couldn't move another foot. I was amazed. This was not blocking. This was a person who sat because she was exhausted from her previous night's work.

It was impossible to realize that Lanford had anything to do with what they were spontaneously saying or that I had anything to do with where and how they moved. It wasn't like a stage; it was like being in the lobby of a sleazy hotel.

It appeared our little amateur company had achieved something almost historic: a complex ensemble and realistic depth that had not been seen since the days of the Group Theater, thirty or forty years before. It was thrilling and humbling to watch. Whatever contributions Lanford and I had made to the production had taken on a life of their own.

This experience probably formed my habit of coming back to see shows with regularity after they'd opened. There's rarely any need for additional notes. A director is just another audience member after opening, no longer a part of the creative process; but who doesn't appreciate seeing his child first walk, then run?

This lesson came crashing into my consciousness when I had been away from *HOT L* for a couple of months. I noticed that Jane Cronin, who had replaced Conchata Ferrell as April, was doing a little piece of business that I had never blocked and was not part of the original performance. When I mentioned it to her backstage and suggested I thought it gilded the lily a bit, she looked at me with eyes round with surprise, and said, "That's the way I've been doing it for months!" The business got an appreciative chuckle from the audience; it was their opinion of the new bit that had developed over the course of playing that was important, not the director's.

Visiting a play you've directed is like seeing an old friend and taking in how well he looks.

Closing Night

My most thrilling closing night performance came at the end of our four-year run of *The HOT L BALTIMORE*. All the actors who'd played the roles over the years came back for the final performance and sat in the front row. At prearranged points in the play, the actors onstage would tag a player in the audience and sit down while his successor carried on the scene. It was a tag-team performance, a relay race. It was one of the most memorable events I have ever witnessed, and a joy to behold.

Years later, when *A Chorus Line* closed after its record run on Broadway, that company adopted this idea and rotated all the chorus members who'd filled those parts over their ten-year run. I'm sure it was equally glorious.

In Conclusion

We've covered everything a director might contribute to a production from the birth of an idea to a closing performance.

As promised, you can see what a multifaceted job a director performs.

What I've tried to do is to document as clearly as possible exactly how I work, and whenever possible, why I've chosen the approaches I've described.

Of course, an artistic triumph can't be guaranteed. In artistic pursuits, there's no formula for success. Each director must find her own way. But I hope I've suggested the nature of the terrain, and how you might avoid the worst pitfalls.

As a director, your personality will find expression in ways that are distinct from mine. I hope that whatever you can take from this examination of our art will be useful as you strive to fulfill the goals of your own work.

I hope you'll try some of my solutions to the problems of directing, because I've seen some of these approaches bear fruit for directors who've adapted them.

One of Harold Clurman's directing students asked him what happens if he has followed all of the advice, done all the work, and the production still fails.

Clurman's priceless answer: "Then I forgive myself."

It's my hope that the principles of directing outlined here will guide you to fewer occasions when you feel the need to forgive yourself.

Appendix A

More Conceptual Resources

Tillhere are several additional resources a director may consider in coming up with a concept. To begin with, a variety of technical implements may inspire you. There is also the inspiration that can be born from working with outstanding colleagues, whose ideas may contribute a concept you might not think of on your own.

Theatrical Tools

Apart from the basic resources of motivation, imagery, space, and style, a director's concept may be influenced by a variety of theatrical tools at his disposal. Some of these scenic devices have been around for ages, but raked stages, turntables, wagons, trapdoors, and the like can seem fresh, even startling, when a creative mind uses them effectively.

I get a tantalizing thrill whenever I contemplate using a raked stage for a production. There's something about a stage tilting toward the audience, giving literal meaning to the terms *upstage* and *downstage*, that excites me. Perhaps it's because as a student, I played a small role in a production of *A Legend of Lovers,* Jean Anouilh's modern French version of Orpheus and Euridice. The director, Jim Gousseff, staged this romantic tragedy on a severe rake: one inch of declination per foot, pretty steep unless you're a mountain goat! But I could feel the power that the angle of the stage lent to our performance.

Raked stages usually rise at an angle of no more than one-fourth-inch per foot. A rake seems to throw the action into the laps of the audience in a way that heightens its empathy. Playing on a raked stage bumps up the actors' energy. It liberates the play from literal reality and elevates the action with dramatic power. Obviously, a raked stage is not appropriate for every play and probably should be used selectively; still, I use a rake whenever I can get away with it. I love the way it alters the experience of a space and the unconscious adjustments it causes in the movement. One word of caution: raked stages are seldom popular with actors. They require a great deal of physical energy to negotiate movement and can be very tiring.

Turntables and wagons are other scenic devices that can influence a production concept. They provide solutions to the problem of multiple scene changes. A turntable allows furniture to float onstage in a graceful arc, without the risk of clumsy stagehands spoiling the mood. Unfortunately, an audience soon guesses how your stage magic is being performed; but the use of two turntables that can revolve in either direction or a *donut*—a revolving ring around, but separate from, a turntable—can keep it guessing.

In my production of Lyle Kessler's satiric parable of American ethics called *Robbers*, we used a turntable that could rotate one way, while the donut that surrounded it moved in the opposite direction. When a scene depicts a couple walking down a street, a turntable can be very effective. As the actors walk against the rotation, the action progresses while they remain down center.

Unfortunately, some of the magic of turntables has faded from overuse. Complex problems that might have inspired innovative solutions too often have been solved by an unimaginative reliance on the tired old turntable.

Wagons and pallets are low, portable platforms that can glide onstage carrying scenic elements. The smaller ones, called *pallets*, usually carry only furniture pieces; the larger ones that deliver whole scenic units are called *wagons*. Both devices allow you to change scenic elements offstage so that the action of episodic plays can flow. Their operation may require a track in the stage floor and some form of wireless control. The limitation of these devices is their predictability, often alternating from stage left to stage right ad nauseum. You can try to vary the timing to make changes less predictable, but once an audience has seen how they work, the only hope is that they'll go faster. Pallets are stylistically conventional in musicals, but their use in dramatic productions may make them seem overproduced. I thought that was the case with the Broadway production of the first part of *Angels in America* but not the second. When he staged *Perestroika*, George C. Wolfe utilized more subtle scene changes.

In some technologically advanced theaters, a director may have the option of using hydraulic elevators or traps. The availability of such devices may stimulate novel uses in unexpected ways, like Hal Prince's inspired concept for *The Phantom of the Opera*, which employed hydraulic elevators in a brilliant evocation of the subterranean depths of Paris. The use of hydraulic elevators remains fresh mainly because their cost keeps them beyond the means of many production budgets.

On the other hand, simple trapdoors have been around forever. They were used by Shakespeare to great effect; it's almost impossible to do the gravedigger's scene in *Hamlet* without one. Many contemporary stages, overlaying a construction of concrete, cannot offer today's director what was a common device in Elizabethan times.

Another time-tested device is the fly loft, which can change the background of a scene by using painted drops or any piece of scenery that can be lowered from above. It's too bad that in their enthusiasm for thrust stages, many contemporary architects have neglected the need for a full fly loft.

Some theaters have limited or unequal wing space, which may inspire a concept that overcomes the limitations. The idiosyncratic architectural configurations at Circle Rep demanded innovative solutions, so we devised a flexible approach to the black box that amazed our audiences. Architectural oddities are endemic to most backstage spaces. Sometimes, as at the Cincinnati Playhouse, they're downright bizarre.

But if wonderful flies and wing space are available, a director can utilize these elements in fresh ways that can surprise and delight even the most jaded theatergoer. Drop and wing sets were a staple of eighteenth century theaters, and still can inspire innovative concepts. Sometimes the simplest elements can fuel the most avant-garde ideas, as Robert Wilson's surreal wing-and-drop creations prove.

On the other hand, the latest technology can impel exploration of uncharted worlds. Technological resources include everything from projections to holography.

Lanford Wilson's *The Mound Builders* dramatizes the painful journey of an archeologist who is reviewing photographic slides that document the tragic events of the previous summer. He is trying to construct meaning from these shards of photographic evidence. In order to share that journey, the audience also needs to see the slides. In the first production at Circle Rep, with the help of my assistant, Peter Schneider (who later rose to fame by renovating and reviving excellence at Disney Animation), I assembled hundreds of slides with four projectors that were coordinated to fill a cyclorama with the same images Dr. Howe was seeing on his monitor. The live action sequences of the previous summer seemed to emerge from the slides, as if the still images became living memories in his mind.

Years later, as technology improved, I employed sixteen projectors in Lawrence and Lee's *A Whisper in the Mind* at A.S.U. to illuminate eight curved sections of a translucent dome with continually changing imagery of the carnage of the French revolution. The advent of complex computer programs that can manage such multiple images makes almost anything you can imagine possible.

Slides can be particularly effective when they can be rear-projected onto a screen covered in front by a scrim so the images are not confined to a screen but can appear to float in an abstract space. Another memorable use of slides was in the 1999 Los Angeles production of William M. Hoffman's *Riga*, where images of the holocaust intermingled with the anti-Semitism, racism, and homophobia of today.

Anna Devere Smith and her resourceful director George C. Wolfe integrated the use of rear-projected slides to brilliant effect in the Broadway production of her one-woman show *Twilight Los Angeles, 1992*.

If the budget is big enough, video and film projections that interact with live actors can expand our conceptions of the nature of theater. Joe Mantello's stunning production of Craig Lucas' *God's Heart* at Lincoln Center was a landmark in the use of live video with live stage action. The budget for this production, which played to only 300 people per night, was rumored to be in seven figures. The playwright John Guare, who saw the same performance I did, shook his head in disbelief. He asked whether I thought stage actors could ever compete with the huge images of projections. I think they'll have to. Once we're past the novelty, perhaps it will be less a matter of competition between technology and live action than a complementary sharing of the stage.

And of course, already slides, film, and video have become old hat. Tomorrow's directors will utilize new, as yet unimagined technology in innovative concepts that will seem so organic and inevitable that we'll wonder how theater was ever done without them.

We'll see productions of *Hamlet* in which the Ghost is a three-dimensional hologram, sending shivers up spines, putting the audience right in Hamlet's shoes.

Already the old use of follow spots has yielded to the miraculous subtlety of Vari-lights, which smoothly follow the action of a play, as they are programmed to do by a computer. A director's concept can emerge from the technology he has available. With enough imagination, amazing concepts can arise from something as simple as the availability of a follow spot.

The use of sound technology can also inspire a director. Circle Rep's Chuck London was an early innovator in the field of sound design; he was the first sound designer who earned equal credit with set, costume, and lighting designers. I've described how integral sound and music have been to my production concepts (like *The HOT L BALTIMORE*). But technological innovations in sound invite new concepts that are only waiting to be imagined.

Sound systems have evolved from heavy old reel-to-reel tape recorders, which I had to lug from rehearsal to rehearsal in my early days of Off-Off-Broadway, to rerecordable compact discs that assure a perfect digital cue every time. To an inventive mind, the possibilities promised by technology are limitless.

Several universities (led by research at the University of Kansas) are experimenting with computer-generated effects onstage. In a modest way, the availability of computer-generated set designs helped me formulate a concept for an in-your-face collection of new plays written by students at Arizona State, which we produced as *Five AZ Pieces*.

I've heard reports of virtual-reality sets that predict the use onstage of the kind of electronic technology we've become accustomed to on television, where news anchors admit that they aren't *really* on the convention floor, but in front of an electronic image superimposed on a blue screen. Electronic overlays were an exciting innovation in the 2000 Olympic Games in Australia, superimposing national flags in the lanes of the swimming competition. Naturally, the 2004 games in Athens went even further with the use of technology to make the viewer feel like she was there.

The astonishing film technology of *morphing* was a landmark in *Terminator II*, but in only a couple of years, it had become so commonplace the technique was available to local pizza ads on television. The groundbreaking technology of a film like *The Matrix* can be utilized by a visionary filmmaker like Peter Jackson to make a work of art that will stand the test of time, like *The Lord of the Rings: The Return of the King*.

But no matter how dazzling these technological advances in film, they remain prerecorded replays. A courageous theater director of the twenty-first century will integrate innovative technology to complement live performances and assure the survival of a vibrant art form by constantly reinventing it.

Hiring Good Colleagues

In addition to casting the roles of the play with the best and most appropriate actors available, a director must select a creative staff to assist in the full realization of a living play.

The set designer, costume designer, lighting designer, and sound designer are essential artistic collaborators.

A composer, a fight director, a choreographer, and a musical director may also be needed.

A stage manager and assistants, an assistant director, and even a dramaturge are helpful.

In each area, it's important to engage people who are supportive of your artistic process, sympathetic to your vision, experts in their fields, honestly critical when they disagree, collaborative in spirit, and if possible, fun to be around.

Of course, it may not be possible to find a staff who can live up to all these fine standards, but that doesn't mean you shouldn't try. It has taken me years of trial and error to establish the relationships I need as a director, but now that I have such a backstage ensemble, I'm very reluctant to work without them because when these collaborations really click, the experience is very close to telepathy.

When someone hires me as a director, it seems to me they should want the whole team. My designers constitute the core of my directorial accomplishments. John Lee Beatty was my principal scenic designer after 1975, when we came together for a production of *Come Back, Little Sheba* at the Queens Playhouse. He took my vague feelings about what I wanted to achieve and gave them dimension, color, and space that created a world for the play to inhabit. Since then, his design for *Talley's Folly* won him a Tony Award, and his transcendent redwood forest for *Redwood Curtain* brought him another nomination, in what has become a plethora of Tony nominations for his work.

Like many designers, John Lee is not a particularly verbal person, but somehow he's discovered how to read my mind. When we were producing Lanford Wilson's *The Mound Builders*, I had a brief preliminary discussion with him about my vague instincts for imagery: a shipwreck of their lives.

A week later, my ideas had begun to take definite shape; at a production meeting, I excitedly described specific details I wanted in the set, before I noticed that John Lee had brought a large black portfolio that probably contained a sketch. To my amazement, when he unveiled his drawing, he had employed the very details I'd been describing. He knew what I'd want before I did.

He understands my every directorial idiosyncrasy. He knows I'll need storage room onstage for the endless number of props I introduce into the action of a play. He knows that if he designs a cubbyhole on the stage, I'll surely use it. If there's a pole, I'll direct actors to swing around on it. If there's a table, my actors will sit on it, stand on it, lie on it. He has learned to anticipate my every need.

I've been blessed with a second scenic designer who's worked with me even longer. David Potts designed *The Sea Horse* in 1974, and has been giving me brilliant designs ever since. In 2005, he won an Emmy for his art direction of Home Box Office's *Deadwood*, just as he was designing my latest production of *Cat on a Hot Tin Roof.* Between these two great scenic artists, I can't go wrong.

Dennis Parichy has been lighting plays for me since 1959. I call him "my genius." We studied at Northwestern with the same lighting teacher, Theodore Fuchs, who established the system of numbering colored gelatin. With Dennis, I can talk in technical jargon if I have to, but I rarely do. Dennis comes to rehearsals, and he lights what he sees there. A lighting designer is the cinematographer of the stage, and a director depends on lighting to focus attention on the action and the picture he wants.

Because Dennis wasn't always available in my later career, I discovered Phil Monat, a gifted lighting designer who has contributed illumination and inspiration for some of my best work.

Costumes are my weak point as a director. I generally take the view that if the designer is happy and the actor is happy, then it's likely that I'll be happy, too. In practice, this is not always the case, so it's important for me to have a designer who understands that I may want to *try* different things before a final decision is made. Thanks to Laura Crow's warm and gentle personality, as well as her strength and resilience, we usually arrive at clothes that are beautiful, appropriate, and that fit the actors perfectly.

Alternatively, I've worked for even more years with Jennifer von Mayrhauser, whose exquisite sense of color has matched my goals for subtlety with graceful shades in countless productions.

Chuck London and Stewart Warner are my sound design team, and they pioneered in this field. Before *The HOT L BALTIMORE* (1973), all theater sounds were lifted from records, and cues were played indiscriminately through speakers on either side of the proscenium. There was no design involved. By the time we had mounted Jules Feiffer's *Knock Knock* (1976), which involved creating twenty or thirty small speakers embedded all over the set to serve as The Voices for Joan of Arc, sound design had begun to earn title page credit, equal to sets, costumes, and lighting. Chuck and Stewart are such perfectionists that they sometimes drove me crazy by constantly tweaking details, but I've never complained about the results.

Over the years, I've developed good creative relationships with a number of composers, especially Peter Kater (twice nominated for Grammy awards), whose CD *Two Hearts* became the soundtrack for *Burn This*. For the past twenty years, he has composed all the original scores for my productions on Broadway and in the regional theaters. Before I met Peter, I worked for years with Norman L. Berman, whose scores stretched from *Battle of Angels* to *Angels Fall*.

I've had the great fortune to work with brilliant fight choreographers like B. H. Barry and Nels Hennum, who identified the kind of struggle I wanted, then worked in collaboration with the actors to come up with safe fights that seemed breathtakingly dangerous. My experience with musicals is limited, but I greatly enjoyed working with Lynn Taylor-Corbet, who turned my clumsy ideas into graceful moves in Richard Adler and Bill C. Davis's *Off Key*.

Of course, most important for the atmosphere of the rehearsal room is the choice of stage managers and assistants. My best advice is to engage people who are problem solvers, not problem makers.

Choose someone like Fred Reinglas, my right hand for many years. Fred was always ready with a joke to lighten tension, always willing to train inexperienced helpers to anticipate every rehearsal need, and always the actors' best friend, which is what the job demands.

Fortunately for contemporary theater, Fred trained Denise Yaney, who sometimes seems to surpass even Fred. (His nickname for her was Eve Harrington.) A stage manager also must know and enforce the rules of Actors Equity, and do so in a manner that's helpful to everyone.

When I use an assistant director, I always get someone who wants to participate and contribute, but who also knows when to keep quiet. I don't hire go-fers. For the past twenty years, Rand Mitchell has been my permanent assistant, and his help, especially with costumes, has been immeasurable.

It may be a good idea to engage a dramaturge, especially if you're working on a new play. Sometimes an objective eye can be helpful in getting the writer and the director over a hump of self-absorption. She might suggest cuts or structural amendments that don't occur to them. Naturally, it's good to find someone who understands dramatic structure, but who's not too "academic" to appreciate the dynamic interplay of collaborative partners in rehearsal.

If you are directing a period play, a dramaturge's help with research is invaluable to you and the cast. No one does this better than Susan Gregg of the Repertory Theater of St. Louis.

Having extraordinary collaborators has made my creative life both joyful and rewarding. When I accepted an Obie Award for my work on *Battle of Angels,* I explained the secret of my success:

> If you have a great play by Tennessee Williams, great designers like John Lee Beatty, Dennis Parichy, and Jennifer von Mayrhauser, and a great ensemble of actors, it's easy to look like a good director.

Appendix B

A Flawed Concept

Richard II

In Chapter 8, I mentioned that when we did *Hamlet,* William Hurt found it difficult to fit spontaneous, truthful behavior within the schematic speech of blank verse. He could speak it beautifully, but as soon as he started to act, verse yielded to impulse.

True artist that he is, William came to me a couple of years later, determined to solve this dilemma. He asked me to direct him as one of Shakespeare's most ornately poetic characters, King Richard II.

Unfortunately, the play in which the character appears has always left me cold. I loved the poetry and knew half a dozen speeches by heart. They're among the most beautiful Shakespeare ever wrote. But the plot of the play mystified me.

It seemed to me that there is virtually no action in the play: beautiful words, fascinating characters, but the only action occurs in the first act, when Bolingbroke duels with Norfolk to settle a quarrel. Richard stops the duel and banishes them both. Bolingbroke sneaks back to England with an army, and Richard, certain that Bolingbroke's intention is to dethrone him, surrenders his crown without a struggle, allowing Bolingbroke to become King Henry IV. Henry has Richard imprisoned, where he contemplates his own downfall. Thinking to please Henry, Exton kills Richard, and is banished for his pains.

There's very little action in this story: it's all talk.

I understood William's desire to tackle the character and the poetry of Richard, but I couldn't find anything in the play that excited me as a director. William let me know he was determined to play the part, and since he was now a film actor of some stature, he could easily convince the Shakespeare Festival to do the play with him, if Circle Rep decided not to do it. Well, I didn't want to lose one of my first homegrown stars to Joseph Papp, so I reluctantly agreed to schedule *Richard II* for the next season.

I then began a struggle to find *something* in the play to spark my directorial imagination. I began to think about the one interesting aspect of the play that seems totally inexplicable: Richard surrenders his crown without a struggle. When has that happened historically?

I came up with two parallels, both of them intriguing examples. The first that came to mind was how Montezuma surrendered to Cortez when the conquistador appeared in Mexico, fulfilling a prophecy of a fair-haired god who would arrive from the East. The Aztec empire was essentially handed over because of this religious belief.

The second historical parallel was when the Celtic King Vercingeterix surrendered to the Romans because they brought an advanced civilization to Britain. *Richard II* is filled with references to an Italian influence on the king, which upset the British aristocracy and brought about the disgruntled atmosphere of the play. So what if the Druids resented a Romanized monarch and found a true Celtic hero to challenge him?

> "What does it matter in the end, to win what your enemy would lose, or to lose what your enemy would win?" the King said.
> "Where will it lead you?" the Queen asked.
> "As far as my energy allows. So the great wheel of destiny will follow its course, eternally moved by love, as far as necessity demands."
> —Conversation between King Vercingeterix of Gaul and his queen on the eve of their defeat by the legions of Julius Caesar in the year 86 B.C., from the movie *Druids*.

I decided a deconstructed approach to the play might stir my creativity, so off my imagination ran: a Celtic *Richard II*!

I decided to begin the play with Richard alone onstage in rags, sitting on the floor of his cell. The first words of the play would be from Act V, Scene v:

> I have been studying how I may compare
> This prison where I live unto the world:
> And for because the world is populous
> And here is not a creature but myself,
> I cannot do it; yet I'll hammer it out.
> My brain I'll prove the female to my soul,
> My soul the father; and these two beget
> A generation of still-breeding thoughts,

And these same thoughts people this little world,
In humours like the people of this world,
For no thought is contented. The better sort,
As thoughts of things divine, are intermix'd
With scruples and do set the word itself
Against the word:
Thoughts tending to ambition, they do plot
Unlikely wonders; how these vain weak nails
May tear a passage through the flinty ribs
Of this hard world, my ragged prison walls,
And, for they cannot, die in their own pride.
Thoughts tending to content flatter themselves
That they are not the first of fortune's slaves,
Nor shall not be the last; like silly beggars
Who sitting in the stocks refuge their shame,
That many have and others must sit there;
And in this thought they find a kind of ease,
Bearing their own misfortunes on the back
Of such as have before endured the like.
Thus play I in one person many people,
And none contented: sometimes am I king;
Then treasons make me wish myself a beggar,
And so I am: then crushing penury
Persuades me I was better when a king;
Then am I king'd again: and by and by
Think that I am unking'd by Bolingbroke,
And straight am nothing: but whate'er I be,
Nor I nor any man that but man is
With nothing shall be pleased, till he be eased
With being nothing. Music do I hear?
(*Music*)
Ha, ha! keep time: how sour sweet music is,
When time is broke and no proportion kept!
So is it in the music of men's lives.
And here have I the daintiness of ear
To cheque time broke in a disorder'd string;
But for the concord of my state and time
Had not an ear to hear my true time broke.
I wasted time, and now doth time waste me;
For now hath time made me his numbering clock:
My thoughts are minutes; and with sighs they jar

Their watches on unto mine eyes, the outward watch,
Whereto my finger, like a dial's point,
Is pointing still, in cleansing them from tears.
Now sir, the sound that tells what hour it is
Are clamorous groans, which strike upon my heart,
Which is the bell: so sighs and tears and groans
Show minutes, times, and hours: but my time
Runs posting on in Bolingbroke's proud joy,
While I stand fooling here, his Jack o' the clock.
      This music mads me; let it sound no more;
For though it have holp madmen to their wits,
In me it seems it will make wise men mad.
Yet blessing on his heart that gives it me!
For 'tis a sign of love; and love to Richard
Is a strange brooch in this all-hating world.

The music is a haunting pipe that signals the entrance of the Duchess of York, climbing to an altar high above Richard. She carries live snakes as a Druid priestess and offers a sacrifice before a live flame. She conjures up her husband, John of Gaunt, the chief Druid priest, who says:

Methinks I am a prophet new inspired
And thus expiring do foretell of him:
His rash fierce blaze of riot cannot last,
For violent fires soon burn out themselves;
Small showers last long, but sudden storms are short;
He tires betimes that spurs too fast betimes;
With eager feeding food doth choke the feeder:
Light vanity, insatiate cormorant,
Consuming means, soon preys upon itself."

Richard enters resplendent as the King in a golden crown and white robes, and we begin Shakespeare's opening scene:

KING RICHARD II
Old John of Gaunt, time-honour'd Lancaster,
Hast thou, according to thy oath and band,
Brought hither Henry Hereford thy bold son,
Here to make good the boisterous late appeal,
Which then our leisure would not let us hear,
Against the Duke of Norfolk, Thomas Mowbray?
JOHN OF GAUNT
I have, my liege.

KING RICHARD II
Tell me, moreover, hast thou sounded him,
If he appeal the duke on ancient malice;
Or worthily, as a good subject should,
On some known ground of treachery in him?

JOHN OF GAUNT
As near as I could sift him on that argument,
On some apparent danger seen in him
Aim'd at your highness, no inveterate malice.

KING RICHARD II
Then call them to our presence; face to face,
And frowning brow to brow, ourselves will hear
The accuser and the accused freely speak:
High-stomach'd are they both, and full of ire,
In rage deaf as the sea, hasty as fire.

(*Enter HENRY BOLINGBROKE and THOMAS MOWBRAY*)

Bolingbroke and Mowbray strip naked, painted blue in the tradition of the early Britons, and they proceed to fight a duel with huge medieval broadswords. Richard interrupts the fight when it's clear that his favorite Mowbray is about to be defeated. He banishes the two men, and we're underway with Shakespeare's story.

By now we've established that the action is unfolding in ancient Celtic times. Richard is dressed in a Roman tunic with a crown that's a wreath of gold, in the style of Julius Caesar, his recent conqueror. He's surrounded by Roman advisers Bushy, Green, and Wiltshire, dressed in Roman tunics and togas, a marked contrast to the long-haired, wild Celtic population who gather to see the duel.

Analyzing how a director comes up with a concept, this Celtic vision of a deconstructed *Richard II* emerged from a problem: how to frame the play with visual contrasts that would heighten the conflict between an "Italianized" king and his primitive Druid subjects. My motive for doing the play comes not from a passion, but from a fortuitous casting opportunity, continuing my work with William Hurt after our promising start with *Hamlet*. But at the heart of the concept is the bare fact that as a director, I'm not moved by the play. By shifting the time of the production, I'm trying to explore imagery that provides me with an excitement I don't find in the text itself.

Both the motivation and the imagery were aspects that inflamed my imagination to come up with a startlingly original concept. When I've described this concept to other directors (especially in the academic world), they've been excited by the concept. They've all wanted to see it.

My downfall was ordained by the last two elements of a production concept: scale and style.

The stage on which we were to perform *Richard II* was a large old barn of a theater with a proscenium stage, seating more than a thousand people, with a cavernous orchestra and a huge balcony. It was an old vaudeville house, with the features and dimensions of a Broadway theater.

My unconventional approach to the play was framed by the most conventional form of theaters. Had we performed in an unconventional space like a gymnasium, with an audience of 100 seated around on the floor, intimately close to the actors, and forcefully involved in the action by their proximity, this wild eccentric concept might have worked.

But with the audience seeing the play from the safety of a dark gigantic auditorium, they were not complicit in the creation, and so their point of view was more objective. They were outside the action, viewing it from afar, in a theater that invited a justifiable expectation of more conventional fare.

The style of the production (transplanting the time of the play to the early Celtic era, when the Druids were Romanized by Julius Caesar in 86 B.C.) became a bizarre spectacle, rather than a galvanizing magnet.

The company was fully committed to the concept, and they gave their all in trying to bring it to life. Their imaginations were kindled to accept the naked duel between two blue-painted Britons, the long-haired wigs of the Celtic warriors, the refined Roman sensibilities of royalty, and the primitive rituals of snakes and fire that conjured up a Druid ceremony. They played all this to the hilt.

Unfortunately, as we began previews, watching from out front with an audience, I became aware that in the context of a proscenium, the production looked ridiculous rather than innovative. With the sinking feeling of failure looming ahead, I called the company together and told them I had decided not to invite the critics. I felt sure that it was wrong to subject my fine company of actors, particularly William Hurt, to the scorn I anticipated they might receive at the hands of the critics. I couldn't let them be punished for my directorial mistake. I was sure that the damage the critical response might do to the careers of my brave company was not worth the risk.

The company was very disappointed. They had committed fully to the concept, and from their subjective vantage point, they felt betrayed by my sudden retreat at the end of our artistic journey. Nevertheless, I feel sure that we would have gained nothing from allowing the critics to evaluate (and savage) what I could see was a flawed production concept.

My only consolation was that of the two historic precedents, I had chosen the Celtic *Richard II,* so we were spared all the messy body makeup that would have been required by an even more absurd Aztec Richard.

As I was preparing this Appendix for publication, I came across a letter that contradicted my assertion that the concept just didn't work. Here's a second opinion:

Dear Mr. Mason:

I, and my class in Shakespeare, saw your production of *Richard II* last week. I taught my usual lesson on imagery in *Richard* before we went to the Entermedia, but your staging was so exciting, so engrossing that my little imagery lesson flew out of my students' heads as they watched, captivated by your brilliant blocking, your 50 A.D. concept, and your original touches. For them and for me, it was a night to remember.

I write this to thank you for bringing such life, such energy, such electricity to this, the most poetic of his plays. I write this out of gratitude for showing my class how Shakespeare plus a creative director can communicate the most wonderful magic.

I took this same class to see (James Earl) Jones in *Othello*. The production was very good, but your *Richard*—overall—was superior. You must be used to people who gush, so I'll stop here by simply saying that I loved it and cannot stop thinking about it.

Professor Richard Evers
English Department
Bergen Community College

Now, if I could just get Professor Evers a job at the *New York Times*!

Appendix C

Essential Tools for Rehearsals

In order to help the actors concentrate on the changes in the action, it's important to divide the play into small units. These beats focus attention on a discrete unit of action that can be explored fully, before moving on to the next beat. The character/beat breakdown chart is a visual map of the units of action the director has created by dividing the play into beats.

The chart is also very useful in helping to construct a rehearsal schedule to divide the available time into rehearsal calls, providing a careful plan to build an accumulation of work into the finished product of a whole play. Here is practical advice on the details of creating these two essential tools for your use.

Making a Character/Beat Breakdown Chart

Microsoft's Excel program offers the quickest and most effective way to make a character/beat breakdown chart. It also can be accomplished the old-fashioned way, using a ruler, a sheet of paper, and a pencil.

Along the top of the page, create a row of cells to indicate the BEAT numbers (Beats 1, 2, 3, 4, 5, etc. or Beats A, B, C, D, E, F, etc.). Along the left-hand margin, make a column of cells to list the CHARACTER names in the play.

The intersection of columns with rows will create a chart of cells that represent each beat for each character. If a character appears and speaks (or is vital to the action) within the beat indicated by each cell, place an X there. If the character is onstage but silent or somehow unnecessary to the action because they're unconscious, dead, or simply background to the main action (as in a crowd scene), put an O. If the character is offstage, but can be heard as an offstage Voice, you might mark it with an A or Y. If the character is not in the beat, leave the cell empty.

The pattern that emerges from observing the X's on the chart depicts a visual graph of the action of the play. You can see at a glance which beats involve which characters, which are intimate beats with only one or two characters, and which are crowd scenes. The rhythm of the stage traffic will be visibly evident.

Your rehearsal schedule should be based on the knowledge you gain from this chart. Only characters with an X in a beat need to be scheduled to work the first time the beat is explored. The characters with O in the scene can be added the next time the beat is scheduled, so you can weave them into the action you've discovered. Those principally involved in the action will have the freedom to explore the beat without imposing on the actors who are less involved. This approach to scheduling recognizes that different levels of involvement produce different levels of creative energy, and allocates time to those who need it most.

Along the bottom of the columns, indicate the page numbers and descriptive names for each beat, so everyone can find the beat in the script quickly and identify the essence of the action.

For clarity, the beats in Act I can by designated as Beats 1, 2, 3, 4, 5, 6, etc. and those in Act II as Beats A, B, C, D, E, F, etc. If there are three acts, you can number the beats in Act II as Beats 21, 22, 23, 24, etc. and Act III as Beats 31, 32, 33, 34, etc. In this way, a glance at the schedule quickly determines whether any beats called for rehearsals are in Act I, Act II, or Act III. Of course, if you have more than 10 beats in an act, you'll need to find a creative solution to numbering them. All participants in the rehearsal process will welcome this kind of clarity.

Making the Rehearsal Schedule

When drafting a schedule, start with several worksheets, so you can change your mind as often as you need to. Again, using Microsoft's Excel program is the most efficient way to accomplish the mechanics.

First, down the left-hand side of the page make a column to list each day of the calendar, from the first rehearsal through the opening night.

Next to the left-hand column with the DAY of the week listed, make a column for the DATE from the calendar. The next column is for the TIMES of the call, and then a wider column to list the actual beats to be rehearsed at the EARLY CALL. In the vertical middle of the page, another column should list the TIMES for the second part of the day, followed by the scenes for the LATE CALL.

Now your worksheet is all prepared and waiting to be filled in.

On the following pages, I've included the character/beat chart and the six-week rehearsal schedule for my Broadway production of *The Seagull*. I've also included the chart and schedule for *Private Lives* to show a more typical rehearsal schedule of four weeks.

THE SEAGULL

Character / Beat — Onstage scene chart

Act	Beat	Page	to	Name	Medvedenko	Masha	Sorin	Treplev	Yakov	Nina	Polina	Dorn	Shamrayev	Arkadina	Trigorin	Cook	Maid
ACT ONE	1	11	13	Half Hour	X	X	X	X	X								
	2	13	16	New Forms			X	X									
	3	16	19	Courting		X	X	X	X		X						
	4	19	22	The Audience		O	O	X	O	X	X	X		O	O		
	5	22	24	The Play		O	O	X	X	O	X	O	X	O	O		
	6	24	28	The Critics		X	X	O	O	O	X	X	X	O	O		
	7	28	30	Nina's Reception		O	X	O	O	X	O	X	X	X			
	8	30	33	Masha's Confession		X		X	O			X					
ACT TWO	21	35	37	Summer Reading		O	X			X	X	X		X			
	22	37	39	Medical Advice		X	X			X	X	X		X			
	23	39	40	Country Life		O	X					X	X	X			
	24	40	41	No Horses		O	X			O	O		X	X	O		
	25	41	42	A Plea to Stay		O		X		X	X						
	26	42	43	The Flowers						X	X	X					
	27	43	45	A Dead Seagull				X		X							
	28	45	49	Rich and Famous						X					X		
	29	49	50	A Short Story						X				A	X		
ACT THREE	31	51	52	Vodka		X				O				X	X		
	32	52	53	A Memento						X				X			
	33	53	54	Packing				O	X					X	X		
	34	54	56	Money and Love			X	X						X			
	35	56	57	Sorin is Sick		X	X	X						X			
	36	57	60	The Bandage				X						X	X		
	37	60	63	Infatuation										X	X		
	38	63	66	Departure		X	X	X			X		X	X		X	O
ACT FOUR	41	67	69	Married Life	X	X			O		X						
	42	69	70	Unrequited Love	X	X			O		X						
	43	70	73	Story of a Councillor	X	X		X				X					
	44	73	76	Nina's Story	X	X	O	X		X	X	X		X			
	45	76	78	A Poor Welcome	X	X	O	X		X	X	O	X	X	X		
	46	78	83	The Card Game	X	O	X			X	X	X	X		O		
	47	83	86	Orphans in the Storm				X		X	X						
	48	86	88	The Cranes Are Crying				X		X				A	A		
	49	88	89	The Shot		O	O		O		X	X	X	X	X		O

X = Onstage, Speaking, needed for ALL calls
O = Onstage, silent & not needed for 1st call
A = Speaks offstage

THE SEAGULL * REHEARSAL SCHEDULE

Day	Date	Time	Call	Time	Call
Tues	Oct. 6	11-3:30PM	Discuss Play & Approach		
Wed	Oct. 7	11AM-2PM	Improv: ARK,TRE,SOR	3-6PM	Improv: CON,NIN,YAK
Thur	Oct. 8	11AM-2PM	Improv: DOR,MED,SOR	3-6PM	Improv: SHA,POL,MED, COOK,MAI,YAK
Fri	Oct. 9	11AM-2PM	Improv: POL,DOR,MAS,MED	3-6PM	Beat 1
Sat	Oct. 10	10AM-1PM	Beat 2	2-5PM	Improv: ARK,TRI
Sun	Oct. 11	10AM-1PM	Review Beats 1-2 Add Beat 3	2-5PM	Improv: SOR,DOR, SHA,MED,POL,NIN
Mon	Oct. 12	***** *DAY OFF* *****			
Tues	Oct. 13	11AM-2PM	Beat 4	3-6PM	Beat 5 (Kostya's Play only)
Wed	Oct. 14	11AM-2PM	Review Beats 1-2-3	3-6PM	Review Beats 4-5 (w/o Play) Add Beat 6
Thur	Oct. 15	11AM-2PM	Beat 7	3-6PM	Beat 8
Fri	Oct. 16	11AM-2PM	Review Beats 1-2-3-4-5	3-6PM	Review Beats 6-7-8
Sat	Oct. 17	10AM-1PM	Work thru **ACT ONE**	2-5PM	Beat 21
Sun	Oct. 18	10AM-1PM	Review Beat 21 Add Beat 22	2-5PM	Beats 23-24
Mon	Oct. 19	***** *DAY OFF* *****			
Tues	Oct. 20	11AM-2PM	Beats 25-26	3-6PM	Beat 27
Wed	Oct. 21	11AM-2PM	Beat 28	3-6PM	Review Beat 28 Add Beat 29
Thur	Oct. 22	11AM-2PM	Work thru **ACT ONE**	3-6PM	Beats 33-34
Fri	Oct. 23	11AM-2PM	Work thru **ACT TWO**	3-6PM	Beat 35
Sat	Oct. 24	11AM-2PM	Beats 31-32	3-6PM	Review Beat 33 w/o SOR
Sun	Oct. 25	11AM-2PM	Beat 36	3-6PM	Beat 36
Mon	Oct. 26	***** *DAY OFF* *****			
Tues	Oct. 27	11AM-2PM	Review Beat 36	3-6PM	Beat 37
Wed	Oct. 28	11AM-2PM	Review Beat 37	3-6PM	Beat 38
Thur	Oct. 29	11AM-2PM	Run thru **ACT ONE**	3-6PM	Beats 41-42
Fri	Oct. 30	11AM-2PM	Run Thru **ACT TWO**	3-6PM	Beat 43
Sat	Oct. 31	11AM-2PM	Work thru **ACT THREE**	3-6PM	Beat 44
Sun	Nov. 1	11AM-2PM	Beview Beats 41-42-43-44	3-6PM	Beat 47
Mon	Nov. 2	***** *DAY OFF* *****			
Tues	Nov. 3	11AM-2PM	Review Beat 47	3-6PM	Beat 48
Wed	Nov. 4	11AM-2PM	Review Beats 47-48	3-6PM	Beats 45-46
Thur	Nov. 5	11AM-2PM	Review Beats 45-46	3-6PM	Beat 49
Fri	Nov. 6	10AM-1PM	Run Thru **ACTS ONE & TWO**	2-5PM	Work Thru **ACT THREE**
Sat	Nov. 7	11AM-2PM	Run Thru **ACT THREE**	3-6PM	Run Thru **ACTS TWO & THREE**
Sun	Nov. 8	11AM-2PM	Run Thru **ACTS ONE & TWO**	3-6PM	Run Thru **ACTS THREE & FOUR**
Mon	Nov. 9	***** *DAY OFF* *****			
Tues	Nov. 10	11AM-2PM	Run Thru **ENTIRE PLAY**	3-6PM	Run Thru **ENTIRE PLAY**
Wed	Nov. 11	2PM-6PM	In Costume on set **ACTS I & II**	7:30-10:30PM	On Set: **ACTS III & IV**
Thur	Nov. 12	2PM-6PM	**TECH ACT ONE**	7:30-10:30PM	**Continue TECH**
Fri	Nov. 13	12:30-5:30PM	**TECH**	7PM-12Midnt	**TECH**
Sat	Nov. 14	12:30-5:30PM	**DRESS**	7PM-12Midnt	**DRESS with PHOTOS**
Sun	Nov. 15	***** *DAY OFF* *****			
Mon	Nov. 16	1-5:30PM	**DRESS**	7:30-11PM	**Invited DRESS**
Tues	Nov. 17		Rehearsal if needed T.B.A.	7:30PM	1/2 Hour for **First Preview**

NOEL COWARD'S PRIVATE LIVES DIRECTED BY MARSHALL W. MASON

Character / Actor assignments:

Character	Actor
Sibyl	Stephanie
Elyot	Don
Victor	John
Amanda	Mary
Louise	Pam

Beat chart (Beat | Scene | Page | Sibyl | Elyot | Victor | Amanda | Louise):

ACT I

Beat	Scene	Page	Sibyl	Elyot	Victor	Amanda	Louise
1	Happy & Glad	1–5	X	X		X	
2	A Different Sort of Love	5–9	X	X		X	
3	Alone Together Married	10–14			X	X	
4	Wilder & More Strained	14–19			X	X	
5	On Honeymoon	19–20	O	X		X	
6	Feeling Very Odd	20–24	O	X		X	
7	Behaving Like a Lunatic	25–29			X	X	
7A	Sibyl in Tears	29–30	X	X		O	
8	Cigarettes & Cocktails	30–35	X	X		X	
9	Potent Cheap Music	35–37	X	X		X	
10	Deceptive Moonlight	37–39	X	X		X	
11	Escape	39–43	X	X		X	
12	To Absent Friends	43–44	X		X		

ACT II

Beat	Scene	Page	Sibyl	Elyot	Victor	Amanda	Louise
21	After Dinner Revery	45–48	X	X		X	
22	Those Five Years	48–51	X	X		X	
23	Dancing to Sollocks	51–55	X	X		X	
24	Around the World	55–58		X	X	X	
25	A Crick in the Neck	58–60		X		X	
26	Someday I'll Find You	60–61		X		X	
27	Love & Death	61–65		X	X	X	
28	Diamonds & Brandy	65–69		X	X	X	
29	The End Finally Forever	69–72	O	X	O	X	

ACT III

Beat	Scene	Page	Sibyl	Elyot	Victor	Amanda	Louise
31	Bonjour!	73–75	X		X		X
32	An Insufferable Morning	75–78	X	O	X	X	
33	Unprecedented Etiquette	78–80	X	O	X		
34	Let Them Fight	80–82	X	X	X	X	
35	Hammer & Tongs	82–86		X	X	X	
36	Rapid Changes of Front	86–88	X	O	X	X	
37	Divorce Settlements	88–93			X	X	
38	Not for a Year	93–95	X	X	X	X	X
39	Coffee & Brioche	95–98	X	X	X	X	
40	A Duet for Four	98–101	X	Z	X	Z	

PRIVATE LIVES REHEARSAL SCHEDULE

Day	Date	Time	Call	Time	Call
		10:00 AM	Production Meeting		
Tue	Feb. 12	11AM-2PM	Introduction & Plan	3-6PM	Research Discussion
Wed	Feb. 13	11AM-2PM	Improv Elyot & Amanda	3-6PM	Improv, Amanda & Victor
Thur	Feb. 14	10AM-2PM	Improv Elyot & Amanda	3-6:30PM	Improv, Elyot & Sybil
Fri	Feb. 15	11AM-2PM	Improv Elyot & Amanda	3-6PM	Beats 1-2
Sat	Feb. 16	11AM-2PM	Review Beats 1-2	3-6PM	Beats 3-4
Sun	Feb. 17	10AM-Noon	Review Beats 3-4	1-4PM	Beats 6-7A
Mon	Feb. 18		***** DAY OFF *****		
Tue	Feb. 19	3-6PM	Review Beats 6-7A	7-10PM	Beat 7
		10:00AM	Production Meeting		
Wed	Feb. 20	11AM-2PM	Beats 5-6-7-7A	3-6PM	Beats 8-9
Thur	Feb. 21	11AM-2PM	Review Beats 8-9	3-6PM	Beats 10-11
Fri	Feb. 22	11AM-2PM	Review Beats 1-2-3-4-5-6-7-7A	3-6PM	Review Beats 8-9-10-11-12
Sat	Feb. 23	11AM-2PM	Review Beats 1-2-3-4-5-6	3-6PM	Review Beats 7-7A-8-9-10-11-12
Sun	Feb. 24	10AM-noon	Work ACT I	1-4PM	Beats 21-22
Mon	Feb. 25		***** DAY OFF *****		
Tue	Feb. 26	3-6PM	Beats 21-22-23	7-10PM	Beats 23-24-25
		10:00AM	Production Meeting		
Wed	Feb. 27	11AM-2PM	Beats 21-22-23-24-25-26	3-6PM	Beat 27
Thur	Feb. 28	11AM-2PM	Beats 27-28	3-6PM	Beats 27-28-29
Fri	Mar. 1	11AM-2PM	Work ACT I	3-6PM	Beat 31
Sat	Mar. 2	11AM-2PM	Work ACT II	3-6PM	Beats 31-32-33
Sun	Mar. 3	10AM-noon	Beats 31-32-33-34	12-3PM	Beat 35
Mon	Mar. 4		***** DAY OFF *****		
Tue	Mar. 5	3-6PM	Work ACT I & ACT II	7-10PM	Beats 36-37
		10:00AM	Production Meeting		
Wed	Mar. 6	11AM-2PM	Beats 31 THRU 37	3-6PM	Beats 38-39
Thur	Mar. 7	11AM-2PM	Beats 38-39-40	3-6PM	Work ACT III
Fri	Mar. 8	11AM-2PM	Work Thru Play	3-6PM	Run Thru & Notes
Sat	Mar. 9	11AM-2PM	Run Thru & Notes	3-6PM	Run Thru & Notes
Sun	Mar. 10		***** DAY OFF *****		
Mon	Mar. 11	12PM-5PM	Tech Rehearsal	7PM-12	Tech Continues
Tue	Mar. 12	12PM-5PM	Tech/Dress	7PM-12	Invited Tech/Dress
Wed	Mar. 13	12-5PM	Dress Rehearsal	7:30PM	1/2 Hour for 1st Preview
Thur	Mar. 14	1-6PM	As Called	7:30PM	1/2 Hour for 2nd Preview
Fri	Mar. 15	1-5PM	Cast Warm Up	7:30PM	1/2 Hour for Opening Night

Appendix D

Alternative Casting Considerations

In addition to the casting process described in Chapter 4, there are some special circumstances you may encounter. On one hand, you may need to deal with the phenomenon of your casting choices being limited to a specific company of actors. On the other, you may find yourself dealing with a casting director, who's been hired to assist you in finding the right actors for the parts. You also might find yourself considering well-known actors or film stars who will not audition for a part, because they have a reasonable assumption that you should be acquainted with their work.

These special situations require additional suggestions for finding the best cast you can, which will assure you of an easier journey in bringing a play to life. In almost any situation, you'll need to provide a character breakdown and a list of scenes to be prepared as sides for auditions.

Casting Within a Company

Throughout my eighteen years as Founding Artistic Director of Circle Repertory Company, it was difficult to persuade guest directors that sometimes it was not only possible, but also *preferable* to cast against type by using the superb actors who were members of our company.

Casting from within a company improves the chances for a rare theatrical phenomenon: ensemble playing. The rewards of an ensemble often justify casting against type. Companies who've created a body of work together develop creative shortcuts that allow a director to concentrate on the finer points of a production. The advantage to a director of a well-trained ensemble is comparable to a violinist playing a Stradivarius: your instrument is finely attuned to express every subtle grace note.

Circle Rep was founded on a model that produced history's greatest plays: a resident company of writers and actors. Shakespeare wrote for a company of actors that included Richard Burbage, Will Kemp, and Robert Armin. Molière wrote for a group of actors that included his wife, himself, and a company of *commedia* artists. Chekhov wrote for the Moscow Art Theater, a company that included his eventual wife, Olga Knipper, and the actor/director Constantine Stanislavski.

Circle Rep was founded to offer contemporary American writers an opportunity to write for a specific company of highly trained actors. It was not a new concept, but a long-neglected one. Over the years our writers included Tennessee Williams, Lanford Wilson, David Mamet, Sam Shepard, William M. Hoffman, Terrence McNally, John Patrick Shanley, Craig Lucas, Jon Robin Baitz, Jules Feiffer, William Mastrosimone, Milan Stitt, Herb Gardner, John Bishop, Corinne Jacker, Marsha Norman, Julie Bovasso, Roy London, Berilla Kerr, Edward J. Moore, Timothy Mason, Harvey Fierstein, Romulus Linney, and many others.

Our company of actors, who inspired these writers to write specifically for them, included Kathy Bates, Tanya Berezin, Timothy Busfield, Lindsay Crouse, Jeff Daniels, John Dossett, Brad Dourif, Pamela Dunlap, Lisa Emery, Conchata Ferrell, Neil Flanagan, Stephanie Gordon, Farley Granger, Spaulding Gray, Jonathan Hadary, Trish Hawkins, Michael Higgins, Judd Hirsch, Jonathan Hogan, Ruby Holbrook, Barnard Hughes, William Hurt, Judith Ivey, Cherry Jones, Swoosie Kurtz, Christine Lahti, Zane Lasky, Bobo Lewis, Lou Liberatore, Robert LuPone, Joan MacIntosh, Joe Mantello, Mary MacDonnell, Debra Monk, Deborah Mooney, David Morse, Cynthia Nixon, Mary Louise Parker, Christopher Reeve, Tony Roberts, Edward Seamon, Lois Smith, Nancy Snyder, Helen Stenborg, Danton Stone, Beatrice Straight, Lynn Thigpen, Rob Thirkield, Richard Thomas, Douglass Watson, Fritz Weaver, Peter Weller, Jimmie Ray Weeks, Patricia Wettig, Amy Wright, and others.

It seemed to me that if a director couldn't cast a play from *this* company, he lacked imagination.

Our acting company was fortified with guest artists, who included Danny Aiello, Joan Allen, Kathy Baker, Alec Baldwin, Scott Glenn, Ed Harris, Timothy Hutton, Piper Laurie, Jennifer Jason Leigh, Leueen MacGrath, William H. Macy, John Malkovich, Kevin McCarthy, Laurie Metcalfe, John Cameron Mitchell, Demi Moore, Gary Sinise, Kathleen Turner, Liv Ullmann, and Bruce Willis, among many others.

At Circle Rep, a major consideration in choosing our plays was whether the play had roles suitable for casting the company. For instance, although we'd done a workshop production of Bill C. Davis' *Mass Appeal,* we sent it on to Manhattan Theater Club because we didn't feel we could cast it well within our company. The play went on to great success on Broadway and in film, but it wasn't "right" for us.

In the Circle Rep production of Schiller's *Mary Stuart,* I cast two Jewish actors (Stephanie Gordon and Tanya Berezin) in the roles of Mary Stuart and Queen Elizabeth, icons of the Catholic and Protestant faiths; unconventional casting, to say the least. I seized this opportunity to cast against type for good reason. The imaginations of these two "Queens of Circle Rep" transformed them into Scottish and English monarchs of the Renaissance, because they had a long history of playing together, and their individual and contrasting qualities had equipped them perfectly for the confrontation scene in the third act. Their years of competition at Circle Rep informed their work with a depth that would be hard for two strangers to equal in a brief rehearsal period.

If you are faced with casting within a company, try to appreciate that you're being offered a gift: the possibility of true ensemble work. If you feel you can't cast the play with the variety and skills of the actors available to you, perhaps it would be wise to choose a play better suited to the talents of the company. It's a matter of perspective, and the surprises that a company can bring to a production should be eagerly anticipated, not dreaded.

It's increasingly rare today to find genuine acting companies that might offer this opportunity, but there are several that do. The superb companies at the Milwaukee Rep or the Steppenwolf Theater Company surpass the casting possibilities of more conventional venues.

Once I was asked to find a play for seven women and three men, members of a graduating class at U.C.L.A. Not an easy assignment. How many plays spring to mind? I chose a Tennessee Williams' one-act *Ten Blocks on the Camino Real.* My concept was to imagine that the marooned characters in the play were vintage Hollywood stars trapped on location.

I asked my young actors to play movie legends eternally condemned to play mythic characters. So my young actress played Greta Garbo playing Camille; her young costar played Marcello Mastroianni as Casanova; and Kilroy was modeled on Sylvester Stallone's *Rocky.* The Gypsy's daughter was Sophia Loren, and her mother was Melina Mercouri; Lord Byron was Tennessee Williams himself, in a white suit with a panama hat. Wigs abounded. I switched the sexes of several parts, so the hotel owner Mr. Guzman became Madame Guzman, modeled on Marlene Dietrich. The ominous Street Cleaners (meant to be male) became refugees from other films: Anna Magnani as if playing the Flower Seller from *A Streetcar Named Desire,* in league with Rita Hayworth, enticing Kilroy in Salome's dance of death.

It was a wild concept, suited to this ad hoc company, and it was lots of fun to create. When creativity is fun, it lightens the dreary burdens of success or failure. Casting limitations stimulated this complex, multilayered concept, but I'd love to use it again in a professional production.

Casting Directors

If you're not casting from a company, a casting director can be very helpful. Casting directors stay up-to-date on thousands of actors, from those right out of acting school to featured players you might not have caught on television.

At Circle Rep, I had little need for casting advice, because Circle Rep was a natural magnet for young talent. Every fledgling actor who came to New York wanted to audition for Circle Rep at one of the general auditions we held monthly. We took the best young actors into the Circle Lab, where we got to know their work even better, enlarging our company's talent pool.

Since the demise of Circle Rep, as a freelance director I find a casting director's advice essential because I see only about fifty movies a year, perhaps thirty stage productions, and very little commercial television. It's comforting to work with people you've worked with before or whose work you've seen for yourself; but if you work only with people you know, your casting possibilities are severely limited.

Casting directors keep up with the activities of a much broader network of actors than most of us. It is their area of expertise.

When it's time to set up auditions, a casting director will ask you for a "casting breakdown" in which you describe the characters in the play with specifics as to age, sex, and particular qualities. Here's mine for *The Member of the Wedding:*

Casting Breakdown

for
The Member of the Wedding
Directed by Marshall W. Mason
Ford's Theater, Washington, D.C.

Bernice Sadie Brown. Bernice is a 40–45-year-old African-American woman of great presence. Although uneducated, she possesses a no-nonsense intelligence that endows her with an innate dignity, a warm mothering nature, and a straightforward honesty. She rules the house with authority and ease. She is patient, strong, and sensitive. Her instinct is to be protective of those she loves. She has a rich, mellow voice and an understated sense of humor. Bernice wears an eye patch that sometimes covers an artificial eye.

Frankie Addams. Frankie is a gangly girl of 12 years, tall, thin, and awkward. A bit of a tomboy, she sports a boy's haircut. She is dreamy and restless, with bursts of energy that alternate with periods of intense inner focus on her dreams and fantasies. The actor should be no taller than 5 feet 2 inches and must possess a lyrical voice, easy to listen to.

John Henry West. John Henry is a delicate 7-year-old boy. Sensitive but eager to please, he has a charming ebullience, energetic, and sweet. He wears round gold-rimmed glasses that give him a judicial air, older than his years. The actor should be no taller than 48 inches.

Mr. Addams. Frankie's father Royal is a handsome widower 40–45 years old, even-tempered and well-mannered. He owns a jewelry store and is a bit old-fashioned, dressing conservatively. He has a deep voice and a friendly, masculine authority. He should be six feet tall or more.

Jarvis. Jarvis is Frankie's brother, a good-looking hunk about 21 years old. He is tall and well built, a perfect specimen for the army, which he recently joined. About to be married, he is an ideal catch for his lucky bride. Athletic, good-natured, and easygoing, Jarvis today would be on *The Bachelor.*

Janice. Jarvis' fiancée is a pretty, fresh-looking girl of 18 or 19. She has a natural feminine charm that is a little undermined by her determination to be liked. She should be 5 feet 8 inches or so, the perfect top-of-the-wedding-cake match for Jarvis.

Mrs. West. Nicknamed "Pet," she is John Henry's mother. She is an attractive, vivacious 33-year-old. She should have a good sense of humor and a memorable laugh.

Helen Fletcher. Helen is a self-possessed, feminine young lady of 13 or 14. She's well brought up but a trifle snooty. She has definitely discovered boys, and she knows she is attractive to them. She should be five feet 2 to 4 inches.

Doris. The same age as Helen, but not as attractive. She wears glasses and is maybe a little plump.

Barney MacKean. Barney is an incredibly well-built 13-year-old football player. He should be blond, with the classic all-American looks of a teenage Robert Redford. He should be no taller than 5 feet 8 inches. They call him "a Greek god."

Sis Laura. Sis Laura is an ancient African-American lady, very thin and frail. She's probably nearly 90 years old. She sings and sells vegetables. (Only 2 lines)

T. T. Williams. T. T. is a self-important, somewhat pompous African-American man of about 50. He is a portly figure, dressed like a church deacon, and is both timid and overpolite.

Honey Camden Brown. Honey is a slim, limber African-American man of about 20. He wears colorful, sharp styles. Somewhat brusque in manner, he's a mixture of hostility and playfulness. He's high-strung and volatile. He plays blues on a trumpet. He should also be able to whistle well.

A casting director will ask your suggestions for what scenes to prepare as sides. Be specific in describing the qualities you're looking for and select scenes that give an opportunity to evaluate those qualities. Here are the sides I suggested:

The Member of the Wedding

SIDES

Frankie: pp. 25–28 / pp. 47–49 / pp. 50–52 / pp. 85–88
John Henry: pp. 47–49 / pp. 50–52 / pp. 105–106
Jarvis: pp. 2–5 / p. 100
Janice: pp. 2–5 / pp. 6–7 / p. 100
Mr. Addams: pp. 6–11 / pp. 66–68
Mrs. West: pp. 6–8
Helen: pp. 19–21
Doris: pp. 19–21
Sis Laura: pp. 35–36
T. T. Williams: pp. 63–64 / pp. 67–70
Honey Brown: pp. 43–45 / pp. 68–69 / pp. 108–110
Barney: pp. 115–117

I usually sit down with the *Players' Guide* or the *Academy Players Directory* (available online to casting directors) and look through the pictures to refresh my memory of actors I recognize. I make a list of every conceivable actor for each part, trying not to censor myself, always giving an actor the benefit of imagining an extraordinary range. I then go over this list with the casting director, who can add many names that may not be registered.

Then she can call agents and ascertain each actor's availability. We soon find out which "movie stars" (who are what every producer seems to want) will consider doing a play and under what circumstances we might approach them.

The casting director and her staff will then set up auditions for you and take care of all the details of scheduling and preparing the sides you request. They usually have ongoing relationships with actors because they are conduits for getting jobs. Many actors look upon casting directors as friendly advocates for their talents, and the presence of a casting director may help them relax by minimizing the fear of being judged.

The casting procedure described in Chapter 4 evolved from years of experience with casting directors helping.

Keep in mind that a casting director is a facilitator who smoothes the way for you to meet and see the best actors available. The casting expert's opinion may or may not echo yours, and the degree to which you trust her judgment will depend on your experiences. A casting person's job is to assist you to find what you're looking for, not to influence your vision of the play. But a casting director can sometimes be a powerful ally, helpful in persuading a doubtful playwright or producer that your choice is the right one.

Offers and Meetings

Often, the more famous actors will read a script only if it's "offered" to them right up front. So, before you agree to have a script sent, be sure she's really the actor you want for the part. There's always a chance she'll say, "Yes!" and then you're stuck. Unfortunately, an offer halts the casting process until you get an answer because ethically no other actor can be approached in the meantime.

Some well-known actors will consent to a "meeting" with a director if they're interested in the play or part. A meeting consists of spending a few moments professing mutual admiration, then discussing feelings and insights about the play and character. From such a meeting, you can evaluate how suited an actor's voice, carriage, and personality are for a part. You should get a sense of whether you can communicate well or whether you suspect intuitively that problems will arise. Most importantly, gauge how the actor has been affected by what she's read and whether her connection to the material comes from a personal "river of experience" that will illuminate the character.

A good deal may be learned from a meeting, but *not* what her performance will be like. The instant an actor begins to speak the written lines, one can learn more than a meeting could ever reveal. Only in an audition can you actually witness the imagination of the actor interact with the material. A meeting without hearing an actor say the lines reduces your chance of being sure your casting is the perfect choice.

A pleasant lunch with Meg Ryan (I was trying to woo her onstage for *Bus Stop*) led only to my picking up the check, but an equally pleasant lunch with Christine Lahti led to her remarkable Alma in my *Summer and Smoke* for the Ahmanson Theater in Los Angeles.

Casting meetings with Nicholas Cage and Linda Hamilton over separate lunches led to their commitments to star in a proposed film of *Burn This*. Unfortunately, the domestic and foreign distributors who would have financed the movie couldn't agree as to which star was necessary to their marketing, so *Burn This*, like thousands of other worthwhile film projects, remains unmade.

After reaching a certain level in their careers, many actors resent having to audition for a part. They may feel that their talent should be beyond question if their work is readily available at a video store. They may also harbor a distrust of readings, based on past experiences.

Nevertheless, actors who've achieved considerable fame will consent to read if they want the part badly enough. Brendan Fraser was eager to do a play after finishing the less-than-rewarding *George of the Jungle,* so he readily agreed to read for our off-Broadway production of *Robbers* (even though he didn't wind up getting the part, which I now regret). Do everything you can to engage an actor's trust by making her feel safe in an audition. It will help to reassure her that you're not looking for the results of a performance.

You can't force an actor to read, but if you encourage them to say a few of the lines, you may avoid a costly mistake. I was so delighted by Lorraine Newman's work on *Saturday Night Live* that we cast her to replace Swoosie Kurtz in *The Fifth of July* without an audition. Her lack of experience onstage became clear too late to back out of a commitment.

I try to make clear that an audition isn't about whether an actor is good or not: we wouldn't be interested in them if we didn't know they were good. An audition gives us an opportunity to observe an actor's *process*. If this is clearly understood, many actors will agree to read a short scene for you. After all, they're probably a little curious to evaluate how *you'll* be to work with, as well.

Appendix E

First Rehearsal of Summer and Smoke

*T*o help you see how a first rehearsal might start, following the principles discussed, here's a verbatim transcript of the beginning segment of my first rehearsal for Summer and Smoke *at the Ahmanson Theater in Los* Angeles, 1987. The production featured Christopher Reeve as Dr. John and Christine Lahti as Alma.

Today I'll be doing a lot of talking, but after today, it'll be much more about what you have to explore and discover than anything I'm going to be able to tell you. But today, I'll outline a plan for you to understand the direction our work will take.

We haven't decided whether to read the play or not. There are sometimes good reasons for reading a play, to let everyone hear the music of the dialogue, its progressions, and so forth. But there are also very good reasons for *not* reading a play: because you might expect that you must perform, somewhat prematurely, since it's only the first rehearsal.

The producers are not here today, and will not be around very much, because I insist on keeping the rehearsals among just we artists. From time to time, when there are run-throughs, we'll let them have a peek at what we're doing, but for the most part, we're going to do our work, and to hell with the producers.

Our rehearsals will be everyday Tuesday through Sunday, from 11 A.M. until 6:30 P.M. This allows you a couple of hours of sunshine in the morning, and also allows you to miss the rush-hour traffic at the end of the day. We'll take an hour and a half lunch break, because in L.A., it takes half an hour to get to and from anyplace to eat. Generally, our rehearsal day is for six hours, because I've discovered that I've only got about six hours of brainpower available. So I like to make efficient use of the time available for rehearsal, and not waste it with chitchat. So please be prompt, because 11 A.M. means to START.

Please allow yourselves time for a warm-up before a rehearsal begins, because it's very important for an actor's physical instrument to respond to the uses of the imagination. We have mats available for you here, or you can do your warm-up at home, but be ready to start at 11.

The Ahmanson is a theater in excess of 2,000 seats, but don't be frightened by the size. My previous experience here taught me that we can do very intimate work, quite truthfully, as though for a camera, because the microphones pick up and share your work with the audience. Nothing needs to be exaggerated. It's a much easier theater to play than the Mark Taper Forum, even though it's three times larger, because on the thrust stage at the Taper, there is always someone behind you, and here we have the joy of a proscenium, where everything we do goes directly out to the audience.

We'll need to discuss parking, banking, and so forth before the morning is over. There's been a request from a photographer to document our rehearsal process, and so I've agreed to allow pictures to be taken each Tuesday morning for an hour, to capture on film whatever we happen to be doing, thereby documenting a progression through four weeks, and at the same time preserving the privacy of our rehearsals.

The performance schedule allows us an extended day off, from the end of the Sunday matinee (about 5 P.M.) until Tuesday night at 8. The opening week is a bit different, because we have to squeeze in seven previews.

We'll try to be something of a family here, but our family will be based on mutual respect. "Give everything you've got in the artistic process, and demand everything you need." *Family* doesn't mean we'll always be lovey-dovey, because families sometimes fight, and it will be good for us to fight. But we want to avoid the kinds of fights that emerge when the work is not based on respect for each other's artistic needs. If we have disagreements, we'll try to work them out through communication because if we, the artists, cannot communicate with each other, how can we hope to communicate with an audience?

I want to build an atmosphere of mutual trust and respect here in our rehearsal process, so that we know what we're doing and why we're doing it.

I very much believe that acting is an art, just as playwriting is an art. They are somewhat different, because a writer examines his or her experience, then attempts to describe reality, inventing drama out of the raw material of experience. An actor starts with the playwright's words and intention as a guide, but we still have to go through the same creative process. We must personalize the journey the playwright has outlined, and examine what has happened in our own lives that illustrates and illuminates the area of the playwright's focus. We'll try to relate our life experiences to what we find in the play, and this requires some research.

For example, there are two doctors in the play, and they happen to be father and son. What does that mean: to be a father? Some people will relate to that word with glowing feelings of warmth, while others will remember beatings and mistreatment. Our personal understanding of a word such as *father* is like that of the poet who wrote: "And then, death came, as terrible as prunes."

To personalize to this degree may not make for very good poetry, but it makes for very good acting. No one will know the personal meanings you may ascribe to the words you use, but they'll feel the effect of the personalization. Each actor will have to start with the reexamination of his own father, and what the word means to him.

Why do two such different men become doctors? And beyond the psychological motivation, what *is* a doctor anyway? What did we know about medicine at the time of the play, what were the limitations of treatment? We want the doctors in the audience to recognize the truth and accuracy of our work. We must base our work in reality, and that requires a lot of research.

We're going to set the play in the 1920s rather than at the turn of the century. The reason for moving the time is that *Summer and Smoke* is very much about change, and the years that followed the end of the First World War were rife with change. Long skirts and the repressed Victorian age gave way to short skirts and a more permissive moral era. Cars began to gain speed, and the prohibition of alcohol created speakeasies. These changes echo the kinds of change the play examines on a personal level between Alma and John. And it's a period that reflects the adolescence of Tennessee Williams.

The play is set in the fictional town of Glorious Hills, Mississippi. We must create this town, and we'll have a diction expert to help us with the specific dialect of a Mississippi accent, which will help to unify us as a group.

Acting is the only art in which we create at the very moment that the audience is actually experiencing the creation. Rehearsals are for exploring and discovering, but every time you go onstage, your imagination has to come to life and create freshly, just as if it were the first time. We need to build our work very solidly on actions that flow from the circumstances of the play, so that we know what we're doing, and not be dependent on an elusive element like inspiration. If we base our work on playing the actions we'll discover in rehearsals, you'll have the beautiful experience of going onstage and letting yourself go, and you'll imagine that you are living the part. That's our goal: not to just interpret someone else's work, but to inhabit and illuminate the people you portray.

We use the word *ensemble* to describe the phenomenon of a group of people working together in an extraordinary way. There are two facets of ensemble work that we can aspire to. The first is the kind of teamwork exemplified by a basketball team: on your toes, awake, alive, in the moment, now, together.

But there's a second, much deeper aspect of ensemble that grows out of one simple principle: that we all inhabit the same world, the world of the play. We must be deeply immersed together in creating the physical circumstances of the environment.

For example, the play begins on the Fourth of July, in a public park, where Alma speaks about the Gulf wind. If she's the only one who feels that wind, then it's only an empty line. But if all the people onstage feel and create that wind together, it obtains a reality an audience can experience when the line is spoken, as she fans herself.

The fourth wall in the house does not exist; yet we have to create that wall together, so that we're all looking at the same wall. By creating this world together, you'll discover the experience of true ensemble.

The most important thing about our rehearsal process is our attempt to discover the actions of the play. If we base our work on actions, rather than feelings, the emotions will come. So we'll be looking for the psychological actions: what do I want? Or what do I want to avoid? These desires are sometimes called *objectives* or *intentions,* and they describe the needs of the characters that we'll be attempting to discover in the rehearsal process.

These needs in turn will lead us to physical actions that express or repress those needs within the context of the physical and psychological environment. You and I, working together, will discover the physical life: What do I do? Where do I go? And these choices are based on: What do I want?

Together we'll explore and discover which physical actions provide the best opportunity to express or repress your needs. The *need* to move will come from your work, and the choice of *where* you move is mine.

It's our intention, not to *show* the audience, but to bring them in to our experience.

In order to explore the physical movement, you need your hands free to deal with props, which will be part of our work from the very beginning. You'll also need to have your eyes free, to engage or avoid the eyes of those playing with you.

I also need you to be in a state of creative vulnerability, so that I can see the impulses that are the signs of a need to move.

For these reasons, I need you to memorize your lines for each beat before we attempt to undertake the exploration of our physical reality.

I call my approach "working in movie style," because we learn the lines for a scene before we do it. After we've explored a beat and discovered a physical life, we could bring in the cameras and film it. But we won't have to, so our work will go on growing.

Let's take a break now, and when we come back, we'll divide the script into the units of action that are called *beats* on the rehearsal schedule.

Appendix F

Preproduction Research

L
ike writers, directors' ideas come from a combination of personal experience and observation. Research can sharpen our awareness of both.

In the chapter on research, I outlined how a director can utilize research in the rehearsal process. But before rehearsals begin, a director might benefit from doing some research herself that might stimulate a concept. Field trips are especially rewarding, as well as tax-deductible.

When I was preparing to direct *Tobacco Road* with Barnard Hughes and Barbara Bel Geddes, I took a trip to rural Georgia for research. I saw many images that influenced the concept of my production: abandoned television sets, washing machines, jalopies—the detritus of our mechanized civilization that were strewn about the front yards of the backwoods culture.

A trip to Raburn County, Georgia, similarly influenced my concept for my production of *Foxfire* (with Hume Cronyn and Jessica Tandy) at the Guthrie Theater in Minneapolis. This time the imagery grew from my observations of bluegrass musicians, clog dancing, and a moonshine whiskey called White Lightning.

My visit to the O'Neill house (the Monte Cristo Cottage, as it's known) where *Long Day's Journey into Night* takes place was seminal to my concept of the use of space in my production of that play several years later. Most designs for the play use a living room with huge dimensions; but what struck me was how small and claustrophobic the actual room was. Certainly the scope of the play invites a large scale for a tragic landscape; but I wanted also to depict how the family was confined, right on top of each other. The cramped space illuminates so much about the forces tearing the family apart: there is no privacy.

I asked Ming Cho Lee to design a set that suggested both the scale of the tragedy and the intimacy of that room.

Based on pictures we had taken, we designed a ground plan of the living room that was exactly the spare size of the actual room. The confinement of the main action to this room, crowded forward on the edge of the stage, etched the psychological tensions of the family intensely, while upstage of the scrim walls, a huge empty space depicted an abstract house with the poetic stature of the tragedy.

When I've directed Shakespeare, I've assembled a cast ahead of a rehearsal schedule to do preproduction research on the nature of Elizabethan poetry in iambic pentameter.

When I'm working on a play by Chekhov, I meet with the cast ahead of the rehearsal to suggest areas of research they need to investigate before rehearsals begin. If a production demands it, advanced research needs to be done on the dances, customs, and activities of eras strikingly different from our own.

Of course, preproduction research need not be tedious. Several of my students thoroughly enjoyed a research trip to Puerta Vallarta, Mexico, where they learned how they might incorporate tequila into their performances for *The Night of the Iguana.* "Wasting away again in Margaritaville!"

Appendix G

A Summary of the Meisner Technique

The great teacher Sanford Meisner devised exercises that focus on an area of acting that Stanislavski identified but did not develop: the creativity in the present moment.

Stanislavski refers to this opportunity as "communion" and "adaptation," but his suggestions about how to achieve them are vague and hard to understand. Meisner gives specific guidelines that help actors commune together and adapt to each other's behavior.

Meisner's exercises are based on instant repetition of a partner's observations and "taking your partner's behavior *personally*." Everything you see in your partner's behavior is because of *you*! By simply repeating, we bypass the intellect and release instinctual responses.

When an actor focuses on the behavior of his partner, he experiences spontaneous impulses that are rich sources of creativity. This spontaneous creativity is an invaluable asset when improvising, when there is no written dialogue.

Neither the director nor her cast needs to have studied Meisner's techniques to use them in improvisation. I'll summarize what a director needs to understand about these exercises; how to instruct the actors about the "rules" and how to design improvisations based on them, for spontaneous exploration.

First, there is the *objective*, which Stanislavski identified as the internal origin of action. An objective is a driving desire to accomplish something. Most actors work with some form of this fundamental element of acting, adapted to their own craft. Meisner defines some criteria for objectives that help both actors and directors to achieve strong performances. An objective should be

- expressed as a verb,
- motivated by intensely personal needs,
- specific,
- urgent, with circumstances that require immediate action,
- heightened by a time limit, and
- focused on the acting partner.

The exact nature of the need is probably strongest when it is secret, and the motive is hidden from the partner.

To confound one actor's objective, Meisner invented an exercise called the *independent activity*. This is a strongly motivated physical activity in which an actor can invest his concentration and which he could accomplish best without interruptions from his acting partner. This activity should be

- a real task, requiring actual props,
- physically difficult to accomplish,
- urgently motivated by imaginative circumstances,
- heightened by a time limit, and
- personally justified.

Some examples of independent activities are:

- repairing a broken vase with glue (imagining it to be valuable, and that it's essential to hide the accident from someone you care about, who loves the vase and will never forgive you for breaking it);
- rolling a large pile of quarters into rolls a bank will accept (in order to buy a plane ticket that will take you to your sister's wedding this afternoon);
- restringing beads belonging to your mother (after you've broken them, while wearing them without permission).

When a partner with an urgent objective confronts an actor pursuing an independent activity, conflict will almost certainly result.

As a director, if you can suggest stimulating imaginative circumstances to each actor (preferably kept secret from each other), you can stand back and let the actors explore your invented circumstances and experience unplanned, spontaneous creativity.

Encourage your actors to concentrate on their two conflicting (but secret) urgencies and to repeat whatever has been said as a means to explore what they feel.

This description is a severely simplified outline of Meisner's techniques, but it should be sufficient to help you and your actors find a solid basis for a creative improvisation. For a fuller understanding, read *Sanford Meisner on Acting*.

Appendix H

Checklist for Setting Up an Improvisation

My suggestions about how to set up an improvisation are given in detail in Chapter 6, but the specifics are buried in the text. To check whether you've included all the elements you'll need in an improv, here is an outline you can use as a checklist, for easy reference.

Exercises

- Relationships
- Mirror
- Baby
- Ensemble

  1. Creating the environment together
  2. Group exploration of theme

Alone in My Room

Purpose: To discover an inner life of impulses leading to an external action, like speaking a line

- Sensory creation of physical details
- Involve the imagination to believe you're alone

- Do a simple activity.
- Speak from an impulse.
- Alone in my character's room

Objectives and Independent Activities

- Difficulty of physical task
- Time limit for urgency
- Personalize a justification
- Don't do anything unless an impulse makes you do it
- Take partner's behavior personally
- Repeat what's just been said, until you have an impulse to change it

Improvisations: General Elements

- Choose events that are background to written scenes
- No preordained conclusions
- No time limit
- Discourage invention of dialogue
- Public Circumstances: the event to be explored
- Specify time of day, year, season, etc., and location
- Private Circumstances: secret events or surprises
- Objectives
- Independent activities
- Discussion: What happened? What insights were gained?

Appendix I

Program Notes

The Member of the Wedding

It's been more than fifty years since Carson McCuller's poignant portrait of the ache of adolescence first caught the imagination of an American audience.

First, it was acclaimed as a novel in 1946. The *New York Times* observed: "Rarely has emotional turbulence been so delicately conveyed."

Then in 1950, with the help of her friend Tennessee Williams, Ms. McCullers adapted her novella for the stage, where it ran for 501 performances and won the New York Drama Critics' Circle Award for Best Play. That production starred an impeccable cast of Ethel Waters, Julie Harris, and Brandon de Wilde.

Most memorably, the play was made into a classic movie, capturing forever those three great performances on film, and earning an Academy Award nomination for Julie Harris in 1952.

What, then, can a production in 2005 hope to bring to such a celebrated work? By now, we've seen countless coming-of-age stories, and what was fresh in 1946 is overly familiar today. If a 21st century audience is to experience the power of this masterpiece, we must find a fresh lens to focus on the timeless longing that's so gracefully etched in the play.

So in this production, we've elected to look at this "longing to belong" in broader terms: a white world and a black world that coexist, each unaware of the true nature of the other. The longing to belong is not only Frankie's yearning; it's the unspoken condition of the black people who populate the background. The casual racism embedded in the play is almost shocking to contemporary sensibilities, and yet even today our two worlds continue to glide by each other, unequal in ways that we conveniently ignore.

To me, the drama of Honey Camden Brown's yearning for freedom that unfolds in the shadows of a white world remains intensely timely and powerful. Berenice's losses in the course of the story lead her to a new life, freed from her role as surrogate mother to two white children, whose own journeys inexorably remove them from her care.

By freeing the play from its realistic bonds, it's our hope that you'll see the ideal world that Frankie imagines in her brother's wedding as a metaphor for our own dreams of a perfect world, dreams that are daily undermined by the dark reality of indifference.

Appendix J

A Different View

Disappointed with our critical reception for the National Actors Theater production of *The Seagull*, I was heartened to receive this letter, which we posted backstage for the cast to see.

To *The Seagull* Ensemble:

This is to express my appreciation for your splendid performance, and a memorable evening at the theatre. I love Chekhov, and more so the older I get; I admired your interpretation, which truly reflected the brightness and shading, the coloration, the authenticity, the soul of his work; a monumental subject, well executed.

I understand that the critics have not been unanimously kind. So what! Most critics are not out to do justice to the subject, but to do themselves homage. It was so, even in Chekhov's day. They aim consistently toward the negative, growing arbitrary with power, which they exercise without fear of censure or appeal.

What you are ALL doing is a very fine thing, and in the finest tradition of the New York stage: an ensemble of worthy veterans and talented youngsters, rolling up their collective sleeves to tackle a challenging masterpiece, and succeeding in their lofty aim. The cast may now take a bow.

The result of this worthy exhibition is high achievement: the sets, music, staging—all first rate.

He attached to his letter some favorite words (from T. Roosevelt, see Chapter 12), and then continued:

235

These should be golden days, together in the arena, submerged with tremendous effort and great enthusiasm, sharing inspirations, struggling with minor daily adjustments of the stage artist's palette. You are bringing honor to a worthy craft.

I applaud each of you.   BARRY VOIGHT

Index